DIOGENES

A quarterly publication of

THE INTERNATIONAL COUNCIL
FOR PHILOSOPHY AND HUMANISTIC STUDIES

Berghahn Books
Providence • Oxford

DIOGENES

Director: **Jean d'Ormesson**
Editor: **Paola Costa**

The English language edition of *Diogenes* is published and distributed by
Berghahn Books
165 Taber Avenue, Providence, RI 02906-3329, USA
Tel: (401) 861-9330   Fax (401) 521-0046
E-mail: BerghahnBk@aol.com

3, New Tec Place, Magdalen Road, Oxford, OX4 1RE, UK
Tel: (01865) 250 011   Fax (01865) 250 056
E-mail: BerghahnUK@aol.com

to whom all requests concerning subscriptions and information should be
addressed. Editorial matters will continue to be handled by the Editor's office in
France (*Diogène* – CIPSH, Unesco House, 1 rue Miollis, 75015 Paris).

Each annual volume is published in four issues, including index.
Annual Subscriptions
Institutions: US$120.00 /£80.00; Individuals: US$40.00 /£24.00
Agencies: 5% discount
Individual issues: $15.00/£10.00
For airmail delivery outside the U.S. add US$20.00 /£11.00

To order, by mail: Please send your request to *Berghahn Books* at the above address.

Parallel editions published simultaneously:
Arabic edition: National Centre for Unesco Publications, 1 Talaat Harb Street,
Tahrir Square, Cairo, Egypt;
French Edition: Gallimard, 5 rue Sébastien Bottin, 75007 Paris;
Spanish edition: Universidad Nacional Autónoma de México, 3er circuito de la
Investigación en Humanidades, Dr. Mario de la Cueva, Zona
cultural, C.U., c.p. 04510, Mexico, D.F.

The articles published in *Diogenes* express freely the most diverse opinions, for
which neither the Editors nor the Publishers can in any way be held responsible.

The journal is not responsible for manuscripts sent to the Editorial Office,
nor can it return them unless they are accompanied by
International Reply Coupons. Manuscripts are held for one year in the
Editorial Office at the disposal of their authors.

Printed in the United States by
Western Newspaper Publishing Co., Indianapolis

ISSN: 0392-1921

DIOGENES

Number 176

Contents

Foreword

Paul Ricœur

Tolerance is a tricky subject: too easy or too difficult. It is indeed too easy to deplore intolerance, without putting oneself into question, oneself and the different allegiances with which each person identifies. But it is too difficult to establish a total coherence between the multiple moral, legal, political, spiritual exigencies that claim to ensure it legitimacy: whether it be about truth, about liberty, about justice, about solidarity, about benevolence. More precisely, is a conviction coming from one or another of these above mentioned registers conceivable without the belief in its truth? But then, how escape from the intolerance of truth? And if liberty implies a right to error, how avoid pouring intolerance into indifference, and how prevent indifference from transforming itself into a tolerance towards the wrong done to others, in particular to the most fragile?

In this issue of the journal *Diogenes*, we have wanted, to the extent that it depended on us, to play the difficulty. This is why we have framed the articles devoted to legal aspects and those devoted to the spiritual aspects of tolerance in two series that answer to one another and for which the titles could have been exchanged: *to think tolerance – obstacles and limits to tolerance*. For, how could we think tolerance without evaluating its obstacles and measuring its limits? And how carry out this critical exercise without some premonition about the conceptual hold of the idea of tolerance? Yet tolerance is only thinkable when both the obstacle of intolerance has been conquered, and exposed to the sort of deterioration against which the intolerable protected it.

In this sense, the entire issue consists in a progression against intolerance and the intolerable.

But if tolerance does not reduce itself to a lukewarm compromise but must be taken as a steep road between two abysses, it is first as a virtue, as much public as private, that it gives itself to thinking. This is what we have wanted to signify in placing in a position of bookplate in a sense Norberto Bobbio's praise of the *mitezza*. It is a praise that merited this difficult virtue, at the forefront of the discussion and argumentation. Yet this praise has the price of a little semantic enigma; how translate *mitezza* into other languages besides Italian? This difficulty in translating announces the difficulty in thinking tolerance, its reasons, its obstacles, its limits.

Overture
In Praise of *La Mitezza**

Norberto Bobbio

Among the ancients, ethics was resolved largely through the treatment of virtues. Suffice it to recall Aristotle's *Etica Nicomachea*, which was for many centuries a prescribed text.[1] In our times such a treatment has almost disappeared. Today moral philosophers discuss values and choices, on both analytical and propositional levels, and their major or minor rationality, as well as discussing rules or norms and consequently rights and duties. One of the last significant writings devoted to the classic subject of virtue was the second part of Kant's *Metaphysics of Morals (Die Metaphysik der Sitten)*, titled *The Theory of Virtue (Die Tugendlehre)*, the first part of which discusses the *Theory of Law (Die Rechtlehre)*. However, Kant's ethics is especially one of duty, and more specifically of inward as distinguished from outward duty, with which the theory of law is concerned. In the former, virtue is defined as the necessary willpower to accomplish one's duty, as the moral strength required by man to fight those defects which prevent or become an obstacle to the accomplishment of duty. Kant's theory of virtue is an integral part of the ethics of duty and, as explicitly and repeatedly declared, has nothing to do with Aristotelian ethics.

During the centuries when European philosophy was prominent, the traditional subject of virtues and, correspondingly of defects or vices, became the subject of treatises on the passions *(de affectibus)*. One may think of Descartes's *Les Passions de l'âme*, of Spinoza's *Ethica*, the section titled *De origine et natura affectuum*, or Hobbes's introductory chapters to his political writings, *The Elements of Law Natural and Politic* and *Leviathan*. Instead the theory

* "Meekness"

of ethics found its place in the doctrine of natural law, which it retained for some centuries, where the perspective of the law or of norms (moral, legal, ethical) prevailed in the analysis of the elements of morals, hence the resolution of ethics in the theory of duties and rights respectively. In the classic and more well-known treatise, Pufendorf's *De iure nature et gentium* in the chapter on human will, there is hardly any space devoted to the subject of virtues in the traditional sense.

The analysis of virtues continued to have its natural expression in the writings of moralists, of which no traces remain today. In fact, in an affluent society the moralist is generally regarded a killjoy, someone who will not go along, who can not enjoy life. A moralist has become synonymous with a moaner, with an unheeded and quite ridiculous pedagogue, with someone who preaches to the wind, or criticizes customs – fortunately equally boring and innocuous. If one wishes to silence a protesting citizen, one still capable of becoming indignant, simply call him a moralist, and he is done for. In recent years there have been many occasions to observe that whomever criticizes the general state of corruption, the abuse of power, both economic and political, is forced on the defensive and saying: "I am not doing this as a moralist." In other words, he did not want to have anything to do with that kind, which was generally held in such low esteem.

Alisdair MacIntyre's provocative work *After Virtue – A Study in Moral Theory* was unknown to me at the time.[2] It was translated into Italian in 1988 by Feltrinelli, and it is now well known here. This work is an attempt to reinstate the subject of virtue (which was unjustly and detrimentally abandoned) to its honorable place, and submit it to today's reader in order that it may continue its interrupted journey, starting from Aristotle. MacIntyre's thought proceeds through a continuous polemic, which in my view does not always appear genuine or very original, against emotionalism, the separation between facts and values, against individualism which he terms "bureaucratic," and against all the ills of the modern world for which he considers the Enlightenment principally responsible, through the prevailing of ethical rationalism, with its inevitable convergence into nihilism. This is certainly not the place to dwell on a critical analysis of this book, which interests me here as a confirmation of the neglect into which the theory of virtue had lapsed. In fact the author presents his work as a work against the current, as a return to tradition, as a challenge to "modernity." One of his preferred targets is the ethics of norms. The ethics of virtue is contrasted to the ethics of norms, which has become prevalent in modern and contemporary ethics, and which constitute the ethics of rights and duties.

I have always hesitated to accept such drastic contrasts, because they favor unilateral attitudes with respect to intangible subjects, such as those pertaining to philosophy, where the truth is never peremptorily, definitively and indisputably on either side, and also with respect to a possible interpretation of history, this huge container filled randomly with a thousand things, to the extent that it is almost always dangerous and inconclusive to isolate one among the many.

That traditional ethics was prevalently an ethics of virtues in contrast to an ethics of norms (or rather, of laws) is quite a debatable judgment. One would need to forget the *Nomoi (The Laws)*, one of Plato's great works. In Aristotle's *Etica Nicomachea* itself, an aspect of the virtue of justice consists in the custom of obeying laws. The subjects of virtue and the law are continuously interwoven, even in the ethics of the Ancients. At the roots of our moral tradition and as the foundation of our civic education, there are both the demonstrative nature of virtues as types or models of good actions, and the preaching of the Ten Commandments, in which good actions are not simply pointed out but prescribed. The fact that the Ten Commandments generally forbid immoral rather than command virtuous actions is unimportant. The commandment "Honor your parents" is a call to the virtue of respect.

Instead of stirring artificial conflicts between the two ways of considering morals, that is, between the ethics of virtues and the ethics of duties, it is more useful and sensible to recognize that these two types of morals represent two different but not opposed points of view from which one can judge what is good and what is bad in the behavior of men considered for themselves, and in their mutual relations. Their clear contrast, as if one set of ethics can exclude the other, depends solely on the incorrect perspective of the observer. Both have good action as their object, understood as an action motivated by the search for the fulfillment of Good, which is the goal. With the difference that while the former describes, indicates and proposes the action as an example; the latter prescribes it as a kind of behavior to be adhered to, or as a duty. The various short treatises on virtues and those *de officiis* complement each other, both in the theoretical consideration of morals as well as in moral teaching, in the same way as the catalogue of cardinal virtues and that of charitable deeds, proposed, as we remember well, in the form of precepts, supplement rather than contrast each other in the teaching of morals in school, of which we are from infancy the recipients. The lives of eminent figures, heroes and saints, who promote good deeds by pointing to examples of the virtuous, emerge from the tradition of the ethics of virtue; whereas the kind of catechism which induces one to do good by proposing models of good action emerges from the ethics of norms. Their efficacy is cumulatively not alternatively different. Instead of contrasting virtues with norms, it would be wiser to analyze the relation between them, the different, rather than opposed, practical needs out of which they emerge and which they obey.

Similarly and concurrently with the revival of the subject of virtues, which seemed to have disappeared from philosophical debate, the subject of passions was again taken up, but with a different kind of intellectual vigor, breadth of historical erudition and originality in outcomes, even if with the same intent of anti-rationalist polemic, through Remo Bodei's monumental work *Geometria delle passioni*.[3] Compared with the re-evaluation of virtues, Bodei's work resembles the opposite side of the coin. While the ethics of virtue taught moderation, and therefore discipline of passions ("*pleonexia*, the insatiable longing for possessions, represented the moral sin of classical ethics"),[4] Bodei questions whether one should perhaps revise the "passion-reason" antithesis, and reinstate passions in their deserving place within the reconstruction and understanding of history, in the same way as "desires," that is, those "passions arising from waiting for both goods and satisfactions anticipated in the future,"[5] occupy an increasingly wider space in contemporary society. Among other things, Bodei draws our attention to the distinction, dear to Hume, between on the one hand, calm or calculated passions, and on the other, aroused or burning passions. As will become evident at the moment of defining *mitezza*, I introduce a symmetrical distinction, between strong and weak virtues.

I would also like to add that a further reason – perhaps more than a reason, I should say an opportunity – for my decision to revive this discussion is due to the fact that I was recently forced to reflect on the uncommon use of the category of *mitezza* applied to the "law," the use of which, even as a long-time reader of juridical texts, I had not yet encountered. I am referring to Gustavo Zagrebelsky's *Il diritto mite*[6] which was impossible to review prior to asking: "Why *mite*?"

Those who invited me to express myself knew that I would have no hesitation in choosing "my" virtue: I was only uncertain about which of the two terms to use: *mitezza* ("meekness") or "mildness." Ultimately I chose *mitezza* for two reasons. In the verse of the Beatitudes (Matthew 5: 4), which in Italian reads "Beati i mansueti perchè questi possiederanno la terra," "Blessed are the mild for they shall inherit the earth," the Latin text of the *Vulgata* uses *mites* and not "mild." The reason why this translation was adopted is unknown to me: it is one of the many issues which I leave in suspense and which are cramming my unpretentious discussion. The second reason is that "mild," at least originally, is said to refer to animals rather than to persons, even if figuratively it is also said of persons. (But the same applies to *mite*: meek as a lamb. However, an animal is "mild"because it has been domesticated, whereas the lamb is by nature the symbol of *mitezza*). The decisive argument derives from these respective verbs: *ammansare, ammansire, or mansuefare*, to domesticate, tame or render docile, which refer nearly exclusively to animals: it is said that we "tame a tiger" but only jokingly would we say that we "tame a mother-in-law." In Dante's work it is stated that Orpheus made the wild beasts docile. "To mitigate" however, which is derived from *mite*, refers almost exclusively to human acts, attitudes, actions and passions: in other words, to mitigate is to attenuate the rigor of a law, the severity of a sentence, to appease the physical or moral pain, the anger, the rage, the disdain, the resentment, the zeal of passion. "With time, the hatred between the two nations was mitigated,"one might read in a dictionary, while it would be silly to say that it "became docile."

With regard to the two abstract nouns that designate the respective virtues of "mildness" and of *mitezza*, I would say (but it is more an impression than a conviction, as I am not undertaking a rigorous discussion) that *mitezza* goes deeper, while "mildness" remains closer to the surface. Or rather *mitezza* is active while "mildness" is passive. Or further, "mildness" is more a personal virtue, *mitezza* more a social virtue. Social exactly in the sense in which Aristotle distinguished personal virtues, such as courage and moderation, from justice, the social virtue *par excellence*, which is a positive inclination towards others (while courage and moderation are only good tendencies in respect of oneself). What I mean is that "mildness" is an inward disposition of the individual, which can be appreciated as a virtue independent of the relation with others. A mild person is calm and peaceful, someone who is not offended by minor issues, who lives and allows others to live their life, and who does not overreact to gratuitous malice, not because of weakness but out of a conscious acceptance of everyday ills. Instead *mitezza* is an inward propensity that shines through only in the presence of the other: a *mite* person is someone whom the other person needs in order to overcome the evil within himself.

In the writings of Carlo Mazzantini, a Turinese philosopher of the generation preceding mine and no longer prominent but very dear to me for his deep philosophical vocation, despite the wide gap in our different understanding of the task of philosophers – I discovered a eulogy and a definition of *mitezza* which I found striking. He states that *mitezza* is the only supreme "power" (note the word "power" used to designate a virtue which makes one think of the opposite, that is, powerlessness, although not resigned powerlessness) which consists "in letting the other be himself." Further adding that "A violent person has no power, because he takes away the power of giving to those against whom he uses violence. Power rests instead with whom possesses the will not to yield to violence but to *mitezza*." Therefore: "to let the other be himself" is a social virtue in the true and original meaning of the word.

The following linguistic observation had not occurred to me when selecting the topic. It seems that *mite* and *mitezza* are words that only Italian has inherited from Latin. Although in French there is *mansuétudine*. The French use *doux* (and *douceur)* in nearly all instances in which we use *mite*, for example: *un caractère doux, un hiver doux*. When Montesquieu contrasts the Japanese and their cruel temperament with the Indian people who are of a *doux* (in Italian translated as *mite*) nature, the word appears more precise and less general to us. If we Italians said *dolce* or "sweet" without committing a crime of linguistic lese-majesty, we would still have the feeling of being guilty of a Gallicism, something not altogether familiar, as in the chapter *La dolcezza delle pene* in Beccaria's famous *Dei delitti e delle pene,* which we readily translate by *mitezza.* Beyond these briefly sketched linguistic observations, but sufficient to provide some indication as to the issue before us, I think the fundamental topic to be developed is that of the location of the virtue of *mitezza* within the phenomenology of virtues.

Beyond the classical distinction between personal and social virtues, there are others which I have not taken into consideration. Among these there is a further classical distinction between ethical and dianoethic virtues (*mitezza* is certainly an ethical virtue), and that introduced through Christian ethics between theological and cardinal virtues (*mitezza* is certainly a cardinal virtue). Instead it seems opportune to introduce a distinction, which I am not aware of as having already been made, between strong and weak virtues. Of course in this context "strong" and "weak" do not at all mean that they have a positive and negative connotation respectively. The distinction is analytical not axiological. Instead of a definition, I would rather use examples to convey to you what I mean by "strong virtues" and "weak virtues." On the one hand, there are virtues such as courage, steadfastness, prowess, daring, fearlessness, farsightedness, generosity, liberality, clemency, which are typical of those who are powerful (we could also call them "regal" or "courtly virtues," and perhaps even "aristocratic," no malice intended); that is, of those who have the task of governing, directing, commanding, leading and who have the responsibility of establishing and maintaining states, to the extent that they are likely to manifest themselves above all in political life, and (according to contrasting points of view) in that sublimation or perversion of politics that is war.

On the other hand, there are virtues such as humility, modesty, moderation, bashfulness, demureness, chastity, continence, sobriety, temperance, decency, innocence, naivety, guileless, simplicity, and among these mildness, gentleness and *mitezza*, which concern the private, the insignificant, the inconspicuous person, someone located at the lower end of the social hierarchy, who does not have any power over anyone and sometimes not even over himself. The person who goes unnoticed and does not leave any trace in the archives, where only the experiences of memorable figures and facts are stored. I term these virtues "weak" not because I consider them inferior or less useful or noble, and therefore to be appreciated less, but because they characterize that other part of society where the humble, the hurt and the poor are located. They are those subjects who will never be rulers, those who die without leaving any trace of their passage upon this earth other than a cross in a cemetery with a name and date, those who do not concern historians because they do not make History, but represent a different history, with a small 'h', the submerged history, or rather non-history (although over the last few years there has been some discussion of a micro-history contrasted to macro-history, and it could happen that perhaps in micro-history there may be also a place for them). I am reminded of Hegel's wonderful pages written about those men of universal history, as he terms them, the founders of states, the "heroes": they represent those who can claim as lawful what to the common man is not, even the use of violence. There is no place for the *miti* among them. Woe betide the *miti*, for they will not inherit the earth. I think of some of the most common epitaphs bestowed by fame upon the powerful: magnanimous, great, victorious, bold, reckless, as well as terrible and blood thirsty. But in this gallery of the powerful have you ever seen a *mite* ? Someone has suggested to me Ludwig the Affable. However this title does not allow for much glory.

To make these notes more complete it would be interesting to peruse some of the texts within the literary genre of the *Specula Principis*, in order to compile an exhaustive list of those virtues regarded as the qualities and prerogatives of a good ruler. I am thinking in particular of *L'Educazione del principe cristiano* by Erasmus (the anti-Machiavelli, the other side of the "demonic face of power"). The following are listed as the supreme virtues of the ideal prince: clemency, gentleness, equity, civility, benevolence, and also prudence, integrity, sobriety, temperance, vigilance, charity and honesty. This is extraordinary: nearly all of these virtues are what I termed "weak." The Christian prince is the opposite of Machiavelli's prince or Hegel's hero (a great admirer of Machiavelli). And yet I could not find *mitezza*, other than with reference to those punishments which must be *miti* (which does not include the death penalty on the basis of the old but still new argument that the infected limb must be removed to prevent the healthy part from becoming contaminated). Because each virtue can be more successfully defined if its opposite vice is kept in mind, the opposite of *mitezza*, in the sense that one says of a penalty that it is *mite* or "mild," is severity or rigor; *mitezza* can thus also be rendered to mean "leniency."But it is certainly not this meaning that I have adopted in the present justification.

Other opposites of *mitezza*, as I understand it, are arrogance, haughtiness, despotism [7], which according to different interpretations can be either virtues or vices of politicians. *Mitezza* is not a political virtue, rather it is the most impolitic of virtues. In the prevalent accepted meaning of politics, the Machiavellian or, to be up-to-date, the Schmittian, *mitezza* is exactly the other side of politics. It is in fact for this reason (it may be a professional distortion) that it is of special interest to me. One cannot cultivate political philosophy without trying to understand what is beyond politics - in other words without being deeply involved in the nonpolitical sphere - without establishing the limits between the political and nonpolitical. Politics is not everything. The idea that everything is politics is simply monstrous. I can say that I discovered *mitezza* in this journey of exploration beyond politics. However the *miti* have no part in the political, or even democratic, struggle, and here I mean the struggle for power that does not make recourse to violence. As is well-known, the two animals which symbolize the politician are the lion and the fox (see chapter 18 of *The Prince*). The *mite* lamb is not a political animal: if anything, it is the predestined victim whose sacrifice is used by the powerful to appease the demons of history. A maxim of popular wisdom states that "he who makes himself a sheep shall be eaten by the wolf." Because the wolf is also a political animal: Hobbes's *homo homini lupus* in the state of nature is the starting point for politics, the *princeps principi lupus* in international relations is its continuation.

Before anything else, *mitezza*, "meekness", is the opposite of arrogance, understood as the exaggerated view of one's merits, that justifies the abuse of power. The *mite* person does not hold a high opinion of himself, not because of a lack of self-esteem, but because he is more inclined to think of the impoverishment rather than the loftiness of man, and because he is a man like all others. Even more so, *mitezza* is the opposite of haughtiness, which is ostentatious arrogance. The *mite* person does not show off, not even his *mitezza*. In other words, the ostentation, or display in a gaudy or insolent way, of one's claimed virtues is in and of itself a vice. Thus an ostentatious virtue is transformed into its opposite. Whomever feigns charity lacks charity. And, only someone who is stupid would feign intelligence. And quite rightly *mitezza* is the opposite to despotism. This is because compared to haughtiness despotism is even worse. Despotism is not only a feigned, but an effectively exercised abuse of power. The haughty person shows off his power, the power to subdue others in whatever form, as for instance one would swat a fly, or squash a worm. The despotic person exercises power through all kinds of abuse and misuse, acts of arbitrary and when necessary ruthless domination. Instead, the *mite* person "lets the other be himself," even if this person is arrogant, haughty or despotic. He does not become involved in relations with others with the intention of competing, vexing and ultimately winning. He is not interested in any contest, competition or rivalry, and hence also in victory. In fact, in life's struggle he is the perpetual loser. The image he holds of the world and history, that is, the only world and history he would want to live in, is of a kind where there are neither winners nor losers, and this is because there are no contests for primacy, neither are there struggles for power, nor competitions for wealth. In short, what is missing are the very conditions which allow the separation of men into winners and losers.

Having said all of this, I would not like anyone to confuse *mitezza* with submissiveness. In wanting to delimit and define a concept, both the methods of opposition (for example, peace is the opposite to war), and of analogy (peace is analogous to a truce but is something different from a truce) may be used. I employ the same expedient to arrive at the identification of *mitezza* as a virtue. After having defined it through a contrast, I will now endeavor to refine its definition by analogy to those virtues which are considered akin or similar (but different) to it.

A submissive person is someone who gives up the struggle, owing to weakness, fear or resignation. Not the "meek" person: he refuses the destructive battle of life out of a sense of annoyance or uselessness of its intended goals, of profound disgust in those things that spark greed in most people, of a lack of this passion that, according to Hobbes, was one of the reasons for "the war of all against all," that is, conceit or boastfulness which push men to want to stand out. And finally, it may be due to an overall absence of this stubbornness or obstinacy that perpetuates quarrels even over trifling matters, through a succession of reciprocal spites and reprisals, or the absence of a feuding or vindictive spirit which in the long run inevitably leads either to the death of both, or to one prevailing over the other. This is being neither submissive nor yielding, because yielding is the inclination of someone who has accepted the logic of the contest, the rules of a game where ultimately there is a winner and a loser (according to game theory, it is a zero sum game). The *mite* does not harbor a grudge, he is not vindictive, nor does he hold resentment towards anyone. He does not persist in brooding over past offenses, rekindle hatreds or reopen old wounds. To be at peace with himself, he must first be at peace with others. He is never the one who starts the fire, and when started by others he does not allow himself to be burnt, even when he is unable to extinguish it. He crosses the fire without being harmed, and weathers inward storms without becoming angry, without overstepping his limits, maintaining his composure and his willingness.

The *mite* is a calm person, but, I repeat, he is not submissive, nor is he affable, because affability contains a certain rudeness or coarseness in judging others. The affable person is credulous, or perhaps someone who is not sufficiently alert to suspect the possible malice of others. I have no doubt that *mitezza* is a virtue. Although I doubt that affability is, because an affable person has an asymmetrical relationship with others (for this reason, provided that it is such, it is a passive virtue).

13

Nor is *mitezza* to be confused with humility (humility elevated as a virtue by Christianity). Spinoza defines humility as *tristitia orta ex eo quod homo suam impotentiam sive imbecillitatem contemplatur,* "the sadness arising from the fact that man contemplates his impotence or weakness," and this sadness is in turn defined as *transitio a maiore ad minorem perfectionem,* "the passage of man from a higher to a lower perfection." The difference between *mitezza* and humility resides, in my view, in that "sadness." *Mitezza* is not a form of "sadness," because it is rather its opposite form, *laetitia,* understood exactly as the passage from a lower to a higher perfection. The *mite* is a cheerful person because he is inwardly convinced that his is a better world, and he prefigures it in his everyday life by effectively exercising the virtue of *mitezza,* even if he knows that it does not exist here and now, and that perhaps it will never exist. Furthermore, the opposite of humility is excessive self-satisfaction, simply put, pride. And as already stated, the opposite of *mitezza* is the abuse of power, in the literal sense of the word, oppression. The *mite* can be depicted as the precursor to a better world; whereas the humble person is only a witness of the present world, very noble but without hope.

Neither can *mitezza* be mistaken for modesty. Modesty is characterized by a not always honest, but often even hypocritical, underestimation of oneself. *Mitezza,* "meekness," is neither an underestimation nor overestimation of oneself, because it is not a disposition towards oneself, but as already stated, it is always an attitude with respect to others, and is only justified by the way of "being towards the other." This does not mean that the *mite* person cannot also be humble and modest. But the three aspects do not coincide. We are humble and modest for ourselves, whereas we are *mite* towards others.

As a way of being towards others, *mitezza* borders the region of tolerance and respect for the ideas and lifestyle of others. Yet, the *mite* person is not just tolerant and respectful. Because tolerance is reciprocal: in order for tolerance to exist, there must be at least two persons. A condition of tolerance exists when one tolerates the other. If I tolerate you but you do not tolerate me, there is no state of tolerance, but on the contrary, there is domination. It is not unlike that for respect. According to Kant: "Every man has the

right to expect the respect of his own kind, and he himself is recip-
rocally obliged to respect others." The *mite* does not ask for, nor
expect any reciprocity: *mitezza* is a disposition towards others that
does not need to be reciprocated in order to be fully actualized. As
it is also with benignity, benevolence, generosity, beneficence,
which are both social as well as unilateral virtues (this should not
appear as a contradiction: they are unilateral in the sense that the
direction of one towards the other does not correspond to a similar
direction, be that the same or contrasting, of the latter towards the
former, that is "I will tolerate you if you tolerate me." But instead:
"I safeguard and value my *mitezza*, or generosity, or benevolence,
with regard to you, independent of the fact that you may also be
mite, or generous, or benevolent towards me." Tolerance proceeds
from an agreement and endures as long as the agreement lasts;
while *mitezza* is a donation and has no pre-established limits.

To complete the picture one must bear in mind that beside the
virtues which are akin, there are also those which are complementary, that is, virtues which coexist and thus reinforce each other. In
connection with *mitezza*, two come to mind: simplicity and charity
(or compassion). But with this warning remark that simplicity is
perhaps the necessary precondition for *mitezza*, and *mitezza* is a
possible precondition for compassion. In other words, in order to
be *mite* one must be simple, and only the *mite* can be favorably disposed towards compassion. By "simplicity" I mean to shun useless
abstruseness intellectually, and ambiguous positions practically. If
you wish, you can think of it as being close to lucidity, or clarity or
rejection of simulation. It seems to me that understood in this way,
simplicity is a precondition or rather a predisposition towards
mitezza. A complicated person is seldom disposed towards *mitezza*:
he sees intrigues, plots and ambushes everywhere, and thus he is
as diffident of others as he is insecure of himself.

With regard to the relationship between *mitezza* and compassion, I would consider it not as a necessary but only as a possible
one, in the sense that *mitezza* can (not must) be a predisposition
towards mercy. But as Aldo Capitini would have said,[8] mercy is an
"addition." It is so obviously an addition that among all living
beings only man experiences the virtue of mercy. Mercy is a feature of his preeminence, his dignity, his uniqueness. How many

virtues are there symbolized by an animal! Among the many, some of those evoked here: simple as a dove, *mite* (here, "mild") as a lamb; the noble steed, the gentle gazelle, the courageous and generous lion and the faithful dog. Have you ever tried to imagine mercy in an animal? You can try, but it may be difficult. Vico stated that the civilized world emerged from men's sense of shame, when men terrified by Jupiter's thunder bolt abandoned the fair Venus and took their women into the caves. Even if we accept that the civilized world emerged from a sense of shame, only mercy distinguishes the human world from the animal world, that is from the non-human realm of nature. Sometimes it can happen that "compassion dies" (as stated in a partisan song familiar to those of my generation) even in the human world. In the animal world compassion cannot die because there it is unknown.

I feel obliged to conclude these swift observations by explaining the reasons for which, faced with a rather extensive catalogue of virtues, I specifically chose *mitezza*.

You probably may have thought that I chose *mitezza* because I regard it as particularly congenial to me. I must confess candidly that this is not the case. I would like to have the nature of a *mite* person, but it is not so. I go into a fury too often (I say "fury" and not "heroic fury")[9] to regard myself as such. I love *miti* persons, that is true, because they are the ones who make this "flower bed" more inhabitable, to the extent of making me think that the ideal city may not be that imagined and described in every detail by utopians, where justice is so rigid and severe as to be unbearable, but one where kindly customs have become universal practice (like the China idealized by eighteenth century writers). From the way I have represented it, it is probable that *mitezza* has appeared as a feminine virtue. I have no difficulty in admitting it. I am aware that by saying that *mitezza* has always seemed desirable to me precisely because of its femininity, I am disappointing all of those women in revolt against the age old male domination. I think that it is destined to triumph the day that the city of women is realized (not that of Fellini). For this reason, I have never encountered anything more detestable than the cry of the most adamant feminists: "Tremble and shiver, the witches are hither." I can quite understand the polemic meaning of such an expression, but it is nevertheless dreadful.

Therefore, *mitezza* is not a biographic choice. In and of itself it is a metaphysical choice (in the sense that it is grounded in a conception of the world that I could not justify otherwise). However from the point of view of the circumstances which prompted it, it is an historical choice. In other words, it may be regarded as a reaction to the violent society in which we are forced to live. Not that I am so naive or lack the worldly experience to believe that human history has always been an idyll: it was once defined by Hegel as "a huge slaughterhouse." However, today there are the "megatons," which represent the ultimate development for "the fate of the earth" (to quote Jonathan Shell's book title). Today, as the experts inform us, with all the weapons accumulated in the arsenals of the great powers, it is possible to destroy the earth many times over. That this is possible does not necessarily mean that it must occur. Even if a nuclear war should be unleashed, the experts still say that the earth would not be totally destroyed. But just consider for a moment what a difficult task it would be to start all over again! What terrifies me are these dreaded megatons combined with this will for power that has not diminished: in this century, the century of two World Wars and forty years of latent war between superpowers, it has increased and sublimated. However, it is not only about the will for power of the great entities. There is also the will for power of the smaller ones, that of the lone striker, the small terrorist group, the one who throws a bomb into a crowd where the greatest possible number of innocent people is likely to die – in a bank, a crowded train, a waiting room, a train station. It is the will for power of whomever identifies with this self justification: "I, a humble, insignificant and obscure person, kill someone important, a protagonist of our time, and because of that I am more powerful than he; or I kill with a single blow many insignificant and obscure people like myself, but who are absolutely innocent. In other words, to kill a guilty party is an act of justice, to kill an innocent victim is the extreme manifestation of the will for power."

I trust you have understood me: I identify the *mite* person with the nonviolent, and *mitezza* with the refusal to exercise violence against anyone. Hence, *mitezza* is a nonpolitical virtue. Or even, in a world bloodstained by the hatred of great (and small) powers, *mitezza*, "meekness," is the antithesis of politics.

Notes

1. This article was originally presented on 8 March 1983 in Milan as part of a program of lectures organized by Ernesto Treccani and supported by the Fondazion Corrente. It has been revised and updated by the author. The original idea was to produce a "Short Dictionary of Virtues," to be examined by a number of prominent contemporaries. Having been invited to participate, the author took "meekness" *(la mitezza)* as his theme. This article was first published in English in: *ConVivio. Journal of Ideas in Italian Studies*, Vol. I, No. 1 (April 1995), pp. 21-38. An earlier Italian version appeared in December 1993 in: *Linea d'ombra* and later in a collection of Bobbio's essays, titled *Elogio della mitezza e altri scritti morali*, Milan, 1994.

2. A. MacIntyre, *After Virtue. A Study in Moral Theory*, Notre Dame (Indiana), 1981.

3. R. Bodei, *Geometria delle passioni*, Milan, 1991.

4. Ibid., p. 17.

5. Ibid., p. 20.

6. G. Zagrebelsky, *Il diritto mite*, Turin, 1992.

7. The notion of *prepotenza* derives largely from politics and refers to a "despotic, tyrannical" temperament or character.

8. Aldo Capitini was a professor of education and an anti-Fascist who was repeatedly imprisoned; an organizer of pacifist movements, he is one of the outstanding Italian theoreticians of non-violence.

9. Allusion to Giordano Bruno's famous work *Des fureurs héroïques* (bilingual ed. with annotations by P.-H. Michel), Paris, 1954.

Interlude*
The Anatomy of Hate

Vaclav Havel

When I think of those who have hated me in the past, or of those who still hate me, I can see that they share various characteristics which, when grouped together for the purposes of analysis, suggest a possible general interpretation of the origin of hatred.

Such people are never superficial, hollow, passive, indifferent, or apathetic. Rather, their hatred seems an expression of an unsatisfiable desire, a kind of hopeless ambition. In other words, it is the result of a necessary evil. In a sense, their hatred is stronger than they are. I do not share the belief that hatred is the pure absence of love or humanity, a simple gap in the human spirit. On the contrary, hatred shares many of the characteristics of love, especially its self-transcending aspects: the fixation on another, which turns into dependency and finally the relinquishing of a portion of one's own identity to the other. Just as the lover sighs for the beloved, and can't live without him or her, so does the hater sigh for the object of his hatred. Just like love, hate is essentially an expression of a burning and absolute desire, although here tragically inverted.

Haters, at least the ones I've known, seem to suffer a pain that nothing, absolutely nothing, can assuage: a feeling that, quite naturally, does not correspond to reality. It is as though these haters wanted to be endlessly honored, loved, and respected, as if they constantly suffered from the painful feeling that others were not

---

* The editors have asked prominent personalities from around the world to contribute to the theme of this issue in order to give it a more personal flavor. These contributions appear as Interludes. The following text is taken from a speech delivered by Vaclav Havel, then President of the Czechoslovak Federal Republic, at a conference on "The Anatomy of Hate," held in Oslo, Norway, on 28 August 1990.

sufficiently grateful toward them, were unpardonably unjust because their honor and love was not boundless, which was the way it should have been: indeed it is as though the others are altogether unaware of their merits.

Hatred – like unhappy love – conceals a type of transcendentalism. The hater allows himself to be consumed by his yearning for something unattainable. And it is unattainable because of the unworthy world's fault – the world that prevents him from reaching the object of his desire. Hatred is a demonic attribute of a fallen angel, a state of mind that aspires to replace God, even believing itself to be God, and whose torment lies in the knowledge of not being God and never being able to be Him. It is the trait of a creature who is jealous of God and beats his breast because, as he sees it, he lives in an evil world conspiring against him, blocking his way to his rightful place next to the throne of God.

The hater so overestimates his value that he is constitutionally incapable of seeing himself as the cause of his metaphysical defeat. Instead, as he sees it, it is the surrounding world that deserves the blame. The problem is that the world is too abstract, too vague, too incomprehensible. He needs a personification of his feeling because hatred, this special kind of tumescence of the soul, requires an equally singular object. The hater is thus in search of an offender. Clearly, this offender is but a stand-in: arbitrarily chosen, he is easily exchanged for another. For the hater, as I've said, the hatred is more important than its object. And these objects can be rapidly replaced without prompting any fundamental change in the hater's relationship to them. This is not difficult to understand: the hatred is directed not against a particular person but against what that person represents: so many obstacles on the path to the absolute, the path to absolute acknowledgment, absolute power, to total identification with God, with the Truth and the world's order. Hatred of one's neighbor thus proves to be nothing other than the physiological incarnation of a hatred of the universe, perceived as the cause of one's universal defeat.

We can go farther. The hater does not smile: he puts on airs. Incapable of joking, he knows only bitterness and sniggering. Unacquainted with self-irony, he can never be truly ironic. Only someone who can laugh at oneself can truly laugh. The hater's chief identifying characteristics are: a sad expression, quickness to take offense and make outrageous statements; he's prone to yelling and incapable of the distance from oneself required to take note of one's own irrationality.

These qualities betray something of much significance. The hater is altogether lacking in feelings of belonging and taste, shame and objectivity. He is incapable of doubting or asking questions, and lives without any awareness of his ephemerality and that of all things. The experience of authentic absurdity – the absurdity of one's own existence, the feelings of alienation, awkwardness, and failure, and the sense of self-limitation and guilt – is totally foreign to the hater. Obviously, the common denominator to all this is a quasi-metaphysical absence of any sense of proportion. The hater never grasps the measure of things, nor of his own possibilities or rights; he has never understood the nature of his own existence, nor of the existence of gratitude and of the love for which he might hope. He understands only that the world belongs to him; and he expects from that world an unlimited acknowledgment of this fact. He does not understand that the right to miracle and the acknowledgment of this miracle are things that must be earned by actions. On the contrary, the hater sees only his eternally guaranteed and unlimited rights, which can never be challenged. In short, he thinks that he possesses an unconditional and universal pass, which will even get him into heaven. Anyone who dares to challenge that right becomes an enemy who has wronged him. Understanding his right to existence and acknowledgment in this way, he is always angered by anyone who does not go along with him.

All haters accuse their neighbors – and, through their neighbors, the entire world – of being evil. The source of their rage is the feeling that an evil world and nasty people refuse to yield them what belongs to them by right. In other words, they project their anger onto others. In this sense, haters are like spoiled children, unable to understand that there are times when one must be worthy of receiving what one gets; and even when we don't get everything we think we're entitled to, it is not due to the malice of others.

* * *

Hate is one. There is no difference between individual and collective hate. Anyone who hates an individual is almost always capable of collective hatred, and even capable of spreading it. It can even be said that collective hate – whether religious, ideological, doctrinal, social, national, or any other kind – is like a funnel that ultimately engulfs anyone who is actuated by hate. In other words, the basic resource of all collective hatred is the ability to hate individuals.

There is still more though. The collective hate that people capable of hating share, spread and deepen, exercises a magnetic attraction over a multitude of people who would not otherwise seem inclined to become haters. We are speaking here of small and weak people, egotistic and lazy-minded, who are incapable of thinking for themselves and therefore subject to outside influence.

The attractiveness of collective hatred – a form that is infinitely more dangerous that the hate of one individual for another – is based on several seeming advantages.

Collective hatred eliminates feelings of isolation, weakness, and powerlessness, the impression of being ignored and abandoned. By providing a sense of cohesiveness, collective hatred makes up for the lack of success and recognition. Collective hatred creates a strange brotherhood, based on a form of mutual understanding that demands nothing more from the hater than his hate. It is not difficult to belong to such a group, and there is no fear of being left out. Indeed what could be more simple than sharing a common hatred for a particular object and accepting a common "ideology of prejudice" toward this object? It is so easy, for example, to say that Germans, Arabs, Blacks, Vietnamese, Hungarians, Czechs, Gypsies or Jews are responsible for all the miseries of the world, and especially for the despair that gnaws at the injured soul of the hater! There will always be enough Vietnamese, Hungarians, Gypsies and Jews to stand in as responsible for all the world's ills.

The community of haters offers another advantage to its members. By indulging in exaggerated expressions of hatred toward whatever group of offenders is currently being blamed, and in worshiping symbols and rituals that celebrate the hating group, the members can find unending comfort and reassurance about their own value. Brought together by uniforms, insignias, flags and hymns, the participants both confirm their identity and confirm, increase, and reinforce their value in their own eyes.

While individual aggression is always risky because of the specter of individual responsibility, a society of haters in a sense legitimizes aggression. The collective expression of hatred creates an illusion of legitimacy, or at least a spirit of "common cover." Concealed in a group, crowd, or mob, the potentially violent person is emboldened; each one eggs on the other, and all because of their large number, feel justified.

Finally, by offering an object of hatred that is uncomplicated and therefore immediately recognizable, the principle of collective hatred fundamentally simplifies the haters' lives, incapable as they are of thinking for themselves. It is so much easier to condemn the world's general injustice when the "offender," the group to be hated, is immediately identifiable by the color of its skin, name, language, or area in which they live.

Collective hate offers a final, insidious advantage: the modest circumstances in which it can grow. There are numerous mental states which, although appearing to be innocent and common enough at first glance, in fact prepare the ground for the almost unnoticed growth of hate: a ground that is vast and fertile, and in which the seed of hate sprouts quickly and takes deep root.

* * *

All forms of hate, even the most incipient, must be combated with all our strength: both because as a principle hatred must always be faced, and also because it is in our own self-interest to do so.

Bherunda, a mythical bird of Hindu legend, is depicted as having one body but two necks, two heads, and two distinct consciousnesses. After sharing an eternity together the two heads begin to hate each other and decide to cause harm. Both consume stones and are poisoned. The results are predictable. Bherunda is overcome by spasms and dies in terrible agony. Krishna, in his infinite mercy, brings him back to life in order to teach men once and for all where hatred leads.

23

All of us who live in the young democracies of Eastern Europe should keep this legend constantly in mind. Bherunda's fate will be ours if we succumb to the temptation of hatred of the other.

But with this difference: for us there will be no Krishna to save us from our new misfortune.

To Think Tolerance

Paul Ricœur

Two essays have been placed under this title. The first is written in the spirit of continental European moral and political philosophy. Its emphasis is on the tensions and paradoxes inherent in the idea of tolerance. The first paradox: the possibility of tolerance, far from being based on the renunciation of the *absolute* nature of the conviction, depends on the contrary on the capacity for absolute engagement which itself gives rise to an unconditional right towards respect. Another paradox: while, in the case of scientific truth (rational or empirical), understanding and consent coincide, in the case of belief (moral, religious, or aesthetic), there is a striking divergence between the *contestable* nature of the affirmation and the *risky* nature of the attachment; but such is the cost of the unconditional. An extreme paradox: it is at the very heart of the idea of truth that a split between *possessing* and *sharing* must be operated; and it is then in the realm of dispossession and non-knowledge that the art of *mimicking* an opposed conviction within oneself – ultimate bulwark against the temptation to impose one's own portion of truth on others – can be learned. The spirit of Karl Jaspers permeates this lucid meditation.

It was left to a philosopher of Anglo-American culture to investigate at their crossroads the *arguments* capable of *legitimizing* tolerance. This discussion is based entirely on "liberal theory," in the ethico-political as opposed to economic sense of the term. In order to arrive at the alternative invoked in the title of the article, the author had to go back from the *practices* of tolerance, compatible indeed with diverse, even opposed, motivations, to the *attitudes* about tolerance that are accessible to discussion. But on which grounds argue from, the moral or the political? When acknowledged to those whose opinions and customs I disapprove of, is the right to not be constrained a moral or political judgment? The

conceptions of tolerance itself will differ depending on the answer
to the specific question of the nature of the tie between *disap-*
proval and *abstention* of constraint. Formulated in terms of morality, the "contrast" inherent in the idea of tolerance is justified with
recourse to the idea of moral autonomy: the other's morality, the
argument runs, is in his or her own hands, and it is not the business of others to interfere; political tolerance is then nothing more
than a corollary. But how ensure that the value accorded to autonomy by liberalism not rejoin the other doctrines labeled by it as
sectarism? We are then thrown on the side of a merely political
doctrine of tolerance, based on the idea that it is not the State's
role to impose one way of living as opposed to another, even that
which refers to the idea of autonomy. It is therefore on the legitimation of political authority that the debate is displaced; and then
a variety of moral attitudes, capable of lending support to political *liberalism*, are presented – among which the author is happy to
emphasize the kind of skepticism, or at least the absence of fanatical conviction, that presided in the *practices* of tolerance that arose
in the seventeenth century.

Tolerance:
Between Liberty and Truth*

Jeanne Hersch

Tolerance is not, as is often thought, an attribute of urbanity that can be equated with other similar values, such as politeness. Nor is it – or at least it should not be – considered the oil that facilitates the smooth functioning of the engine of human desires, in spite of their differences of opinion. Rather, true tolerance takes root in the same soil as human rights. And this root is at the same time shared by liberty and truth. It is an untamed, barely diplomatic, root, burrowing deep in the soil of an absolute demand.

It is because the human being is capable of committing himself absolutely – risking life and sometimes more than life – that he is entitled to unconditional rights. It is because his commitment to that considered true can be absolute that a violation of the human dimension as such can take place: it occurs when there is an attempt to impose a different point of view or a requirement that one behave in a manner opposed to his or her belief. The absolute nature of this conviction or moral exigency demands of the other human being not a lessening of his or her own conviction or moral exigency; it requires instead an absolute respect for the other's conviction or different exigency, even when far from sharing it. This is the very foundation of human rights. And it is also the foundation of true tolerance, which in no way renounces the search for truth.

The attempt to impose – by threat or actual violence – a mode of behavior or belief on another is not only a violation of human rights but an essentially meaningless act. This is because any conviction, any voluntary action, is the realization of a thought. But

* The editors wish to express their warm thanks to Professor Hersch and to UNESCO for allowing *Diogenes* to reprint this article which was first published in the UNESCO volume *Tolérance, j'écris ton nom*, Paris, 1995.

all constrained thought is non-sense, that is to say non-thought. Thought exists only when there is a search for true meaning. If this were not the case, it would be possible to conceive of a truth, made coherent and intelligible to the mind, that would nevertheless not require assent. In such a case it would be possible to say, for example, in response to a demonstration of a geometric theorem: "I understand the proof, I just don't agree with it." But because the proof is of a purely rational nature, such a declaration would be meaningless. Either I do not understand the demonstration, which means I do not experience the constraint that it seeks to exercise upon my reason, and as a consequence, my thought remains free in regard to the proof; or else I do understand it, which means I accept its necessity.

On the level of pure reason, as well as on the level of empirical experimentation (although to a somewhat lesser degree), acknowledgment of evidence and free judgment coincide, that is, there is accord between "understanding" and "consenting." But this accord or coincidence ends as soon as the thinker's subjectivity comes into play – as soon as the historical data constituting the subject's "I," in all its inexhaustible concreteness, intervenes.

It is on this level that the problems associated with free choice, and the concomitant temptation of constraint, first appear. It is here too that cultural diversity – the various traditions, philosophies, and religions – comes into play; which seems to go without saying sometimes requires the total stake of life and being, remains forever subject to challenge and never can be evident. And it is here, because their respect is never a given, even though their violation is absurd, that the respect of human rights imposes itself absolutely.

Some believe that the concept of an absolute, in any form, is the irreducible enemy of Human Rights. And these try, in exchange for increased peace and tolerance, to declare the absolute as out of bounds, thereby reducing human existence to a set of rational or empirical certainties provided by the sciences. I believe they are heading in the wrong direction. Indeed, the empirical level itself provides us with an extreme alternative: to live or to die, which humanity experiences differently from all other species, through our historical consciousness. If we were to suppress from human nature the absolute, which bears man's moral nature, we would reduce the human being to its animal nature alone, thereby dooming it to the struggle for life, without either law or faith in anything other than success. This would be the end of human specificity. And there would be no more human rights; intolerance might lose its sting, but tolerance would lose its meaning.

If we want the human factor as such to exist, we must accept everything that comes with this condition, including the risks of the absolute that our moral nature embodies. There can be no cut-rate humanity, simplified and stripped of its inherent difficulties. This is why humans *must have* rights, and absolute rights. And this is also why the maze of these rights is so entangled, so full of contradiction and paradox. It is not only that contradiction excludes the recourse to force; it is also that the respect owed to absolute convictions seems sometimes to require its use.

The fundamental demand of intolerance is that the other make him or herself similar in kind to a supposed majority or to another self. This reductionist demand has four primary fields of application: thought, belief, action, and being. The imperialism of intolerance is based on the exclusive valorization of one's own opinions, in opposition to what others might think, believe, do, or be. At the heart of this attitude lies the identification of the self, and all its personal, ethnic, cultural, religious, and historical characteristics, with human values per se; so much so that this self sees itself as coinciding with the good of humanity as such. Thus at the root of all forms of intolerance is the presumed possession of a privileged model. On the level of thought, it is a matter of possessing the truth, or at least of mastering the methods that guarantee possession of it. On the level of belief, it is about belonging to the tradition whose foundation best corresponds to the historical data, as well as being the most fruitful and creative tradition over the centuries, the one that best satisfies the requirements of human development. On the level of action, it is a matter of laying claim to those historical developments most favorable to the promotion of peace, well-being, and the organization of human societies. On the level of being and becoming, of highlighting those accomplishments most apt to provide – both extensively and intensively – the widest possible array of ideas and thoughts, inspiring human

29

beings to actualize the various aspects of their responsible freedom in their own lives: the ability to invent their earthly presence and to choose the trace they want to leave behind.

However, it is strikingly obvious that such a form of intolerance, while laying claim to these values and to these ends, is in direct contradiction with its own justification because of its very claim to possess the single correct model of humanity. The nature of the human condition is such that it cannot escape its own inner contradictions; moreover, the essentially unresolvable nature of these contradictions must be consciously acknowledged as soon as humanity takes responsibility for itself. In brief, far from being justified in designating a single model of the human condition as valid and then proceeding to impose this model on all others *ad majorm homis gloriam*, mankind's humanity demands instead an act of asceticism, an exploration of non-knowing, of a field of irreducibly contradictory demands, corresponding not to the knowledge of a model but to the discipline of a dispossessed knowing.

An increased indifference to what is true does not – as some have asserted – produce an increase in true tolerance. On the contrary: what must be done is elucidate the values, criteria, and meanings that constitute the various embodiments of human truth, thereby clarifying the nature of the agreement that each kind of truth requires. One does not agree with the verification of a scientific hypothesis in the same way as one does a political principle, a religious faith, an ethnic doctrine, an art form, a musical composition, an aesthetic system, or a scale of moral values.

The nature of intolerance will itself vary according to the kind of agreement in question. However, the first thing that must be established is the value attributed to the various kinds of difference or even divergence. A difference of opinion may provoke hostility or scorn; but it may also produce curiosity and interest. Initially, everything depends on the depth of interest or conviction in the way the evidence is treated – but it also depends on the imaginative favor with which heterodox attitudes are considered from the outset. Some people are open to anything and everything, which however does not prove a true and deep openness to otherness: it may rather be the consequence of a superficial attitude or total lack of commitment to anything. At the same time there are other people, profoundly rooted in a given conviction, who may nevertheless try to understand – to mimic – with equal depth the conviction of another; they will "lend" their own inner being to it; and in so doing they may find an unsuspected creative dimension unleashed from within themselves. Such are the risks, and the opportunities, of true human communication.

A prerequisite to such inner growth is the abandonment of a single form of knowledge. But this is not simply a matter of a "negative dogma." It is a matter of really having experienced the inner unity of being – a unity irreducible to the multiplicity of our approaches, to their discontinuities and complexities, to the contradictions and incoherences of our own mind, or to the inadequacy of the criteria we use in forming judgments. Once having experienced this unity we can then grasp and accept that the human project remains forever rooted in time. And that the other person, whoever he or she is, is rooted in time differently than I am, in his or her own manner; and because for him or her, just as for me, the possible forever outstrips the actual, we both deserve that absolute respect, of which tolerance is but the tormented reflection.

In this sense, rather than being a lukewarm commodity rooted in indifference, tolerance realizes its never-ending and absolute purpose in the historical condition of the human being, forever in search of an unattainable truth.

In other words here again, the error – and the temptation – consists in substituting a presumed "possession," a "holding" of truths and of principles of action, for a deepening of being, a revealing of the self. The alternative is always: will I impose on another my way of thinking, my beliefs and ways of organizing life, my actual conception of "the true" and "the good," and use every means of constraint at my disposal in order to insure that this "true" and this "good" are imposed on the world outside me – OR, will I, by an act of imagination that will permeate every level of my being, try to "mimic" with my own being the other's way of thinking, his beliefs or her ways of organizing life and action, others' versions of "good" and "true," by conceding that my original attitude was full of limitations and errors that could have resulted in mutilations of my potential human condition, of which it is my duty as a free and responsible subject to realize?

This is the alternative for human subjects who are themselves always transcended by the truth of their mission. Obviously, this mission entails an element of non-knowledge, of definitive non-possession – and I mean here, along with Karl Jaspers (and in contradiction with what many others have asserted), that no commitment can be considered truly absolute without a sense of the transcendence of the true.

Other strange reversals have arisen. We are beginning to understand why philosophy, for example, can only be the "friend" but not "owner" of wisdom – why "the love of wisdom" fundamentally precludes the claim to possess it. We are beginning to grasp the role that contradiction can play even within rational thinking, which without it would be unable to say itself – even if somewhat grudgingly – that the absolute respect for human rights is not only something that I owe to each and every human being regardless of the person's stage of development or ethnic group, but that the very possibility for *my* thought to have meaning is conditioned upon a prior acceptance of the principle of the absolute nature of human rights.

On the other hand, any attempt to impose on human beings, whomever they are, a way of thinking, believing, acting or judging, is solely doomed to the non-sense of the force of causality, except that it remains irrevocably a betrayal of the self.

In order to clarify the matter a bit more it might be useful here to try to understand the nature of the impatience, even the irritation, we feel when confronted with the other's refusal to conform to our ways. It will be necessary to distinguish among various levels of the phenomenon and to use examples in which the concrete stakes are as small as possible; this because what we are trying to understand is the nature of divergent judgments themselves, independent of any consequences.

Let us assume that a divergence has cropped up between two persons regarding the authenticity of a document playing a role in a sacred history. This divergence may be a matter of little import to one of them, while to other it strikes at the very heart of his or her faith. For the latter, the result may be a suspension of faith or, in an opposite direction, the document may take on added significance as a result of its having been contested. The contested naked fact therefore takes on, depending on the case, a signification, and from this, a different efficiency. Its assessment depends on something other than its empirical reality. It passes through the constitutive suspension of a non-knowing.

And it is by the awareness of this non-knowledge, and by the search for truth, that each one of us needs to understand – truly understand, that is to say, mime – the effort of knowing, and the partial awareness of truth, which is that of the other.

It follows from the preceding that true tolerance, far from renouncing the search for truth in exchange for peace, stimulates a profound and authentic quest for it. Yet this does not mean that the search itself can be the basis for peace. This is because truth is not the only matter at hand here. Man, Rimbaud wrote, is a body and a soul. And once the body is invoked we are talking about living and dying, and not about the self alone. Yet, as recent developments have shown, all assistance to life ultimately leads to a choice between the use of force and its abandonment. However, a right imposed by force alone is neither a right nor a truth; and yet there are no rights without a police to defend them. Otherworldliness is an inhuman luxury – hence the birth, at the United Nations, of a new risk and a new hope, with the duty of intervention in the affairs of all States.

Toleration,
a Political or Moral Question?

Bernard Williams

There is something obscure about the nature of toleration, at least when it is regarded as an attitude or a personal principle. Indeed, the problem about the nature of toleration is severe enough for us to raise the question whether, in a strict sense, it is possible at all. Perhaps, rather, it contains some contradiction or paradox which means that practices of toleration, when they exist, must rest on something other than the attitude of toleration as that has been classically described by liberal theory.[1]

There are undoubtedly *practices* of toleration. Holland in the seventeenth century pursued different, more tolerant, policies towards religious minorities than Spain in the seventeenth century, and there are many other examples. However, the mere existence of such examples does not tell one all that much about the underlying attitudes. Practices of toleration may, for instance, merely reflect skepticism or indifference. Such attitudes were certainly important for the growth of toleration as a practice at the end of the wars on religion. Some people became skeptical about the distinctive claims of any church, and began to think that there was no truth, or at least no truth discoverable by human beings, about the validity of one church's creed as opposed to another's. Other people began to think that the struggle had helped them to understand God's purposes better: that he did not mind how people worshiped so long as they did so in good faith within certain broad Christian limits. These two lines of thought, though in a certain sense they run in opposite directions, do end up in the same position, with the idea that precise questions of Christian belief did not matter as much as people had supposed. This leads to toleration as a matter of political practice, but, as an attitude it is less than toleration as that has been strictly understood. Toleration "requires us to accept people and permit their practices even when we strongly disapprove of them;"[2] but skepticism and indifference mean that people no longer strongly disapprove of the beliefs in question, and their attitude is not, in a strict sense, that of toleration.

It is true that for even a practice to be called "tolerant" there has to be some history or background of intolerance, or at least a comparison to be drawn with practices elsewhere. If there never has been anything except indifference on a certain matter, then there is no room for the concept of toleration. Indeed, when the norm begins to be indifference or absence of disapproval, references to toleration may seem inappropriate and even offensive: the homosexual couple living in an apartment block would probably be insulted to be told that the other inhabitants of the block "tolerated" their ménage. It is a feature of "toleration," as that term is standardly used, that it represents an asymmetrical relation: the notion is typically invoked when a more powerful group tolerates a less powerful group. This point in itself relates to toleration as a practice rather than to toleration as an attitude. Indeed, it related to a particularly important instance of toleration as a practice, namely the refusal to use the law as an instrument for discouraging a group and its beliefs. The very fact that the question to be considered is the use of the law implies that the decision is being made by a more powerful group, that is to say the group which has the opportunity of so using the law. As we have already seen, this practice in itself can express more than one attitude, only one or a few of which earn the title of "toleration" in a strict sense. All those attitudes, however, whether those of indifference or of genuine toleration, can hold just as well between groups who have roughly equal power, where neither of them would be in a position to enforce a law against the other, even if it wanted to. It is the practice of toleration or intolerance as a *political undertaking* that introduces the asymmetry associated with the concept, and not the underlying attitudes, whatever they may be. A tolerant attitude, and equally a tolerant disposition born of indifference, can obtain just as much between groups who are equal in power.

So what is an attitude of genuine tolerance, as opposed, for instance, to mere indifference? As Scanlon has pointed out,[3] it has to find a place between two opposed possibilities. On the one hand, there are behaviors and attitudes that ought not to be tolerated, to which toleration is inappropriate. Towards murder and child abuse, one is not supposed to hold back one's disapproval, or one's disposition to deploy the law, in the name of toleration. For the liberal these intolerable attitudes will of course include attitudes of tolerance: no liberal feels called upon to tolerate racism or bigotry, and overt expressions of racisms and bigotry are things that he may well think are properly restrained by the law (even though, above all in the United States, liberals have a problem in determining the point at which the proper restraint of racist or bigoted expressions becomes a restraint on free speech, and itself offensive to toleration). The first area, then, in which toleration does not apply is that in which the agent's negative attitude towards other views is not appropriately restrained by an accompanying attitude of toleration. The second kind of case in which toleration is not appropriate is that in which the agent feels that his negative attitude towards other views should not itself exist, and that what he has to learn is not to sustain that attitude, nor to restrain it through toleration, but to cease to have that attitude altogether. This will be so, for instance, in the case of an attitude towards homosexual relations, of the kind that has already been mentioned.

So the sphere of toleration has to be one in which the agent has some very strong view on a certain matter; thinks that people with conflicting views are wrong; and thinks at the same time, that in some sense, those others should be allowed to have and express those views. This formulation certainly captures an outlook which is enough to sustain a practice of toleration; however, it is still not enough to capture the attitude of toleration in a strict sense. An agent might, for instance, feel that others should be allowed to express their views, because he regards the balance of power between his own group and that other group as too sensitive and unstable to be challenged by an attempt to impose what he regards as the correct view. This is not toleration. Toleration implies, rather, that one believes that the other has a right not to be constrained in the matter of the views that he holds and expresses.

What is the nature of this right? At this point, I believe, there are two ways that we may go, and they lead to two different conceptions of toleration. Under one of these conceptions, the right in question can (very roughly) be labeled as moral right, while on the other it may be labeled (equally roughly) a political right. The distinction can be seen if we consider a formulation that Thomas Nagel has written of the relations between toleration and liberalism. Nagel writes "liberalism purports to be a view that justifies religious toleration not only to religious skeptics but to the devout, and sexual toleration not only to libertines but to those who believe extra-marital sex is sinful. It distinguishes between the values a person can appeal to in conducting his own life and those he can appeal to in justifying the exercise of political power."[4] It is this outlook that is supposed to save liberalism from being, in Rawls's memorable formulation, "just a sectarian doctrine." The idea is that the principles of toleration associated with liberalism will occupy a higher ground relative to particular moral outlooks enabling them to co-exist in a framework of mutual toleration and respect forming a stable pluralistic society of the kind that Rawls has described.[5]

In Nagel's formulation, the tension characteristic of the attitude of toleration is expressed by saying that the tolerant agent will, on the one hand, think that a certain conduct or a certain way of life is sinful, but at the same time think that the power of the state should not be used to suppress that conduct. But there are at least two ways of understanding this contrast. On one reading, the agent's thought is this: "This other agent has a sinful and disgusting way of life and engages in sinful and disgusting practices. However, it is nobody's business to make him, force him, induce him, or (perhaps) even persuade him to take another course. It is up to him – his morality is in his own hands." It is as a particular consequence of all this that political power should not be used to constrain him. The contrast in this form expresses what I take to be a moral doctrine, one that has, incidentally, a political conclusion. This moral doctrine expresses an ideal of moral autonomy.

On the second reading of the contrast expressed in Nagel's formulation, the agent's thought is, rather, this: "This person's way of life is sinful and disgusting. Indeed we should do everything we decently can to persuade him to change his ways and to discourage other people from living like him. We may appropriately warn our children not to consort with his children, not to share his social life, and discourage as many people as we can from think well of him so long as he lives in this way. However, it is not appropriate that the power of the state be used in this way." This I take to express a political doctrine, a doctrine expressive of the liberal concept of the state. It may be that the tolerant agent's contrast in this second, political, form itself rests on some moral ideas in particular about the nature of the state; but, in this form, the political conclusion does not follow as a special case from a moral doctrine which is more generally and also intrinsically related to toleration even outside politics – a doctrine such as what might emerge from the first reading of Nagel's formulation as expressing the value of autonomy.

If toleration as a moral attitude is grounded in the value of autonomy, as just suggested, then there are strong arguments for thinking that liberalism's defense of toleration as a practice should not essentially rest on its belief in the value of that attitude. There are several reasons for this. First, it is very difficult both to claim that the value of autonomy is the foundation of the liberal belief in toleration, and at the same time to hold, as Nagel and Rawls and other liberals hold, that liberalism is not just another sectarian doctrine. A belief in autonomy is quite certainly a distinctive moral belief, and one that carries elaborate philosophical considerations along with it.

A second difficulty is that the moral attitude that focuses on autonomy presents, in a peculiarly severe form, the difficulties which, as has already been suggested, are associated with the attitude of toleration. On this account, the agent who disapproves of the other's values should refrain from any untoward pressure on the other to change his outlook. There is, of course, the question of what "untoward" will mean, but it is essential that the account of the liberal outlook, that the idea of such untoward pressure, goes wider than merely the matter of direct political interference. No doubt, on the usual account of autonomy, rational argument will be regarded as appropriate as a means of influencing the other's opinion. But if one takes the ideals of autonomy seriously, there will be a real question about, for instance, the kind of expressions of disapproval that apply social or psychological pressure upon the other. The concept of autonomy is supposed to leave the other free from external, causal, "heteronomous" influences which may cause him to change his opinion for non-moral reasons, such as those of desire for social conformity. But if the agent who disapproves of the other's values and is committed to the attitude of toleration is cut off from all such expressions, it becomes increasingly unclear what room is left for the agent genuinely and strongly to disapprove the other's values. The idea of a strong, moral disapproval which can be expressed only in (something like) a rational argument, and is otherwise required by the demands of toleration to remain private, seems too thin and feeble to satisfy what has been agreed to be the requirement of a tolerant attitude, namely that the agent does in fact strongly disapprove of the practices about which he is being tolerant.

Of course, it is in fact impossible to draw any clear, or perhaps reasonable, line between kinds of influence and persuasion that are supposedly compatible with the ideal of autonomy, and those that are not. This is an inherent weakness in the concept of autonomy, grounded as the ideal is in a Kantian conception of what is and what is not within the province of the rational will. However, the aim of the present argument is not to dismiss the ideal of autonomy altogether, but to ask how far, if it is accepted in some form, it can provide the grounding of a tolerant attitude which in turn can be taken to underlie liberal tolerant practice. The immediate point can be put like this: there is one question of what kinds of influence or social pressure would count as trespassing on the other's autonomy, and there is another question about the forms of expression that will have to be available to agents if they are to count as seriously disapproving of the other's conduct and values to the degree that calls upon the supposed attitude of toleration; and there is simply no reason to believe that the answer to those two questions will necessarily coincide. We could guarantee that they would coincide only if we drew the boundaries round the other's autonomy in the light of what the disapproving agents need to do in order effectively to express their disapproval; but this manifestly is not available under the present construction of the tolerant attitude, since it is precisely the value of the other's autonomy which is supposed to be drawing the limits to what the tolerant but disapproving agent is permitted to do. It is for this reason that the construction of the tolerant attitude in terms of autonomy presents a particular extreme version of the conflict always inherent in toleration, between disapproval and restraint.

A version of this problem can arise with defenses of liberal toleration, even if they are not based on such demanding notions of autonomy. Critics who deny that the liberal state can avoid being just another sectarian doctrine often claim that liberal states indeed enforce on set of attitudes rather than another – attitudes roughly in favor of individual choice (or at least consumer choice), social cooperation, secularism, and business efficiency. The methods by which these values are forced on a liberal society are more subtle than those condemned by liberalism, but the outcome is much the same. Thomas Nagel gives a liberal answer to this criticism by distinguishing sharply between *enforcing* something like individualism, on the one hand, and the practice of liberal toleration, on the other, though he does not in the least deny that liberal educational practices and other social forces in liberal society are not "equal in their effects." It may well be in fact that liberal society tends to erode religious and other traditional values, even though liberal practice is tolerant of them.

I have elsewhere criticized this distinction of Nagel's[6] on the ground that the use that he makes of it is not neutral in its inspiration, but rather begs the question in a liberal direction. I put this by saying "[the use of this distinction] makes a lot out of a difference of procedure, whereas what matters to a non-liberal believer is the difference of outcome." What I meant by this was that the non-liberal believer is not going to be persuaded that this distinction makes all the difference. However, it is perfectly compatible with this that the liberal state could decently use Nagel's distinction to defend, at a political level, what it is doing. What the liberal state cannot do – and this is the immediate point – is to rely on the distinction *and also to ground its tolerant practice in the value of autonomy*, in the way that is presently being considered. For there is surely no substantive sense of autonomy – except one that has been designed precisely to coincide with liberal practice – in which a group of believers could be said to enjoy autonomy in deciding on preserving their religious beliefs when they are overwhelmingly affected by social influences which tend to erode that belief.

It may be that the project of grounding liberal toleration in a moral value of autonomy has been particularly encouraged by the historical and ideological importance of religious toleration. One very important argument in favor of religious toleration has traditionally been found in the idea that the attempt to coerce religious belief is essentially fruitless, because the forces of the state cannot reach a person's center of conviction. The most that the states could secure would be conforming behavior, but for many, at least, the aim of religious persecution was to secure more than this. This argument can be seen as appealing to a certain conception of autonomy, a free exercise of individual's capacities to arrive at religious conviction. However, the appeal to autonomy is this connection is really quite special. The argument between those who supported religious toleration and those who were against it is revolved around ideas of salvation, and correspondingly the ideas of autonomy that may be invoked here appeal to the relations between individuals and God, together with some conception of what God might expect of his creatures with regard to their dispositions to worship him – a conception which, in the hands of those favoring religious toleration, is likely to suggest that God is not particularly interested in conforming behavior delivered by the power of the state. When the question of toleration is generalized beyond the issue of religious toleration, the structure of ideas is not available. In the religious case, the tolerant party could, at the limit, claim that, so far as we can understand God's purposes, the idea of coerced religious belief makes no sense, and that coerced religious practice without belief can make no sense in the eyes of God. But there is no comparable set of considerations that can be used if we are trying to resolve the question, for instance, of tolerating the sale or display of pornographic materials, and an appeal to the value of autonomy is not going to do much to resolve that question.

For all these reasons, it seems to me that the attempt to ground the practice of toleration in a moral attitude directed to the value of autonomy is bound to fail. At this point it will be helpful to

turn our attention to the second interpretation of Nagel's formulation that was distinguished above, the one that leads to a distinc-
tively political conception. Here the idea that the political power is
withheld from enforcing certain outcomes, not because the people
affected have a right under the good of autonomy to choose their
way of life without undue external influence, but because state
power should not be used in that kind of purpose. As I have
already said the political idea itself may well have one or another
kind of moral root, but under the interpretation we are now considering it does not have its root in furthering or expressing an
ideal of autonomy. Prohibition, rather, is simply and solely on the
use of state power to affect the behavior in question. If such a
view is taken about the restriction of state power, then toleration
as a practice will indeed follow. This leaves open the question
whether any distinctive *attitude* of toleration at all will underlie
the tolerant practice. All that has been argued so far is that tolerant practice is not plausibly grounded in a moral attitude affirming the value of autonomy. Autonomy has in fact played a
particularly prominent role in moral conceptualizations of toleration, and this may encourage the idea that the search for a directly
moral defense of the attitude of toleration may be a mistake. However that may be, instead of trying to reach the politics of liberalism from a moral assumption that concerns toleration, we should
rather consider first the politics of liberalism, including its practices of toleration, and then ask what, if any, kinds of moral
assumption are related to that.

There is an essential difference between legitimate government
and unmediated power: one of the few necessary truths about
political right is that it is not merely might. Those who claim political authority over a group must have *something to say* about the
basis of that authority, and about the question of why the authority is being used to constrain in some ways and not others. Moreover, there is a sense in which, at least ideally, they must have
something to say *to each person* whom they constrain. If not, there
will be people whom they are treating merely as enemies in the
midst of their citizens, as the ancient Spartiates, consistently,
treated the helots who they had subjugated. This requirement on a
political authority we may well call the *Basic Legitimation Demand.*

There are many substantial questions about the Basic Legitimation Demand and its consequences, which cannot be considered
here.[7] There are two very general principles which seem reasonable, and which are relevant to the present discussion. First, the
idea that the basic legitimation demand has been met by a certain
state is not the same as the idea that it has been met in a way that
would satisfy us. The distinction between the use of power which
can reasonably claim authority, and the arbitrary use of power,
tyranny or mere terror, applies for instance to historical forma-
tions, such as medieval kingdoms, who's claims and practices
could not be acceptable to us. When those other states exist now,
in our world, of course other questions arise, of our moral and
political relations to illiberal regimes. It may possibly be true that,
in the modern world, only a liberal order can adequately meet the
Basic Legitimation Demand, but, if so, this is because of distinctive features of the modern world, not because legitimate government, necessarily and everywhere, means liberal government.

The second general point is this: when it is said that government must have "something to say" to each person or group over
whom it claims authority – and this means, of course, that it has
something to say which purports to legitimate its use of power in
relation to them – it cannot be implied that this is something that
this person or group will necessarily accept.[8] This cannot be so:
they may be anarchists, or utterly unreasonable, or bandits, or
merely enemies. *Who* has to be satisfied that the Basic Legitimation Demand has been met by a given formation at one given time
is a good question, and it depends on the circumstances. Moreover, it is a political question, which depends on the political circumstances. Obviously, the people to be satisfied should include a
substantial number of the people; beyond that, they may include
other powers, groups, elsewhere sympathetic to the minority,
young people who need to understand what is happening , influ-
ential critics who need to be persuaded, and so forth. (If this position seems alarmingly relativist, it is important, indeed essential to
these questions, to reflect that in the end no theorist has any way
of advancing beyond it. He or she may invoke absolute or universal conditions of legitimacy, which any "reasonable" person
should accept; but in doing this, he or she speaks to an audience

in a given situation, who share these conceptions of reasonable-
ness, or whom the theorist hopes to persuade – by this very text,
among other things – to accept them).

In these terms, the problem of liberal toleration can be understood as follows. With regard to a contested issue of religious or
moral belief, the liberal state addresses a number of different
groups. They include (1) minorities who would like, if they had
the power, to impose their own belief. If they take the liberal state
to be legitimate, and to have some claim of authority over them,
then they must recognize that there are some legitimate demands
of government other than those inspired by their own creed. They
will also recognize, if they have any sense, that in their actual situation these demands will be shaped by other citizens. If they do
see all this, then, if their beliefs and practices do not offend too
grossly against the core beliefs of liberalism (a point we shall
return to), it will be sensible for the liberal state to meet their
acceptance by tolerating them, and so sustaining a situation, so far
as possible, in which this group can accept that the liberal state
makes a claim on them.

Alternatively, such a group may think (or, if the liberal state acts
ineptly, come to think) that there is no legitimate government outside their own creed, and that the liberal state makes no legitimate
demand on them. If they do think this then they are potential
secessionists or rebels, who must make their own political decisions about the extent to which they are prepared to carry their
secession. The liberal state must meet this as any prudent state
which wants to avoid violence meets the possibilities of secession,
or, on the way to that, of disruption. Their methods may sensibly
include, as long as things go moderately well, the continuation of
toleration. But if the point comes at which toleration has to cease,
the liberal state has an entirely reasonable account of why it has
ceased, and the minority group, whatever they say for political
reasons, cannot be surprised at what is happening.

Among the groups that the liberal state addresses, there may be
(2) a majority with the belief which they could impose. If this
majority is powerful and convinced enough, and if this belief is
not itself part of the core liberal outlook, it is perhaps unlikely that
there will be a liberal state: if there is, this will be because the

majority, or enough of it, has reason to think that it should not be imposed. One kind of reason may be that they think that it is not the kind of belief that is worthwhile trying to impose: this is the kind of outlook that has already been recognized in the case of religious toleration. This outlook will be the product of a certain kind of reflection on certain kinds of beliefs. Another, different, reason may be that the people in the majority recognize that the minorities who disagree with them – who may or may not be of the type (1) – will feel coerced if this belief is imposed, and they do not think that in this matter the price is worth paying in terms of the loyalty, cooperation and amicable relations of those peoples.

It is in this areas, of course, that the outlooks of minority groups (or of their co-believers elsewhere) are very often misrepresented. In particular, such groups may be depicted as consisting entirely of intransigent fanatics or disloyal secessionists. (This is a standard move, at the present time, in the demonization of Islam). The attitudes needed here by liberals are, above all, realistic social understanding, a desire for cooperation if possible, and political intelligence.

Last among these examples (but not last among all the political possibilities), the liberal state may be addressing (3) a group, the members of whom may have no desire to impose their beliefs, but whose practices and outlook offend against core liberal beliefs. This may be so, for instance, if the group structurally offends against what the liberal majority sees as a gender equality. But at this point liberal toleration falls away in any case, and we are at a level of substantive disagreement (about gender roles and the nature of sexuality, for instance) where liberalism simply cannot avoid presenting "another sectarian doctrine." At this point, there is no hope of liberalism's gaining indisputably higher ground. The only higher-order considerations it can deploy in thinking about what to do are the resources of political good sense: to consider how things look to the minority (not something, in fact, that liberals have excelled in doing); weighing the cost, already mentioned, of coercion; and reflecting on the precedent effects of coercion in disputed matters of morality, as part liberalism's generally healthy respect for the unintended effects of coercive power. There is no reason why these considerations in a given case should prevail.

They do prevail, however, so that the minority's practices are tolerated rather than seen as intolerable, the attitudes that will have brought this about will be the kind of political attitude and understanding that have been mentioned.

These rough and superficial sketches of various possibilities that may comfort the liberal state support, I believe, the conclusion that if we approach toleration as a political rather than in the first place a moral issue, we shall find hard to discover *any* one attitude that underlies liberal practice. What the sketches suggest is that, given a liberal state and its typical patterns of legitimation, in the cases where toleration is thought appropriate (and we have seen that there are many cases in which it is not), toleration will be supported by a variety of attitudes, and none of them is very specifically directed to a value of toleration as such – still less to the moral belief in toleration based on the value of autonomy which was identified earlier in the discussion. The attitudes which are needed include such social virtues such as the desire to co-operate and to get on peaceably with one's fellow citizens and a capacity for seeing how things look to them. They also include understandings that belong to a more specifically political good sense, of the costs and limitations of using coercive power. Behind these, again, will certainly be needed some of the skepticism, the lack of fanatical conviction on religious issues, in particular, which earlier we saw made an important contribution to the practice of toleration, even though they are inconsistent with toleration strictly understood as a moral attitude.

The case of toleration is, unsurprisingly, a central one for distinguishing between a strongly moralized conception of liberalism as based on ideals of individual autonomy, and a more skeptical, historically alert, politically direct conception of it as the best hope for humanly acceptable legitimate government under modern conditions. The first of these conceptions has been dominant in American political philosophy in the last twenty-five years. The present arguments, such as they are, favor the second conception, one nearer to what the late Judith Shklar called "the liberalism of fear."[9] But, as Judith Shklar herself would have been the first to point out, it must itself always be a political and historical question, how far conditions will allow that form of liberalism, or indeed any other, to exist or to achieve anything.

Notes

1. For an analysis of these problems see D. Heyd (ed.), *Toleration: An Elusive Virtue*, Princeton, 1996, and the particular contribution by B. Williams ("Toleration: An Impossible Virtue?"); G. P. Fletcher ("The Instability of Tolerance"); T. M. Scanlon ("The Difficulty of Tolerance").
2. T. M. Scanlon, "The Difficulty of Tolerance," in: ibid., p. 226.
3. Ibid.
4. T. Nagel, *Equality and Partiality*, Oxford, 1991, p. 156.
5. J. Rawls, *Political Liberalism*, New York, 1993.
6. T. Nagel, *Equality*, p. 24.
7. I hope to delve into some of them in a study appearing on political liberty.
8. This is one of the reasons for which the idea of satisfying the Basic Legitimation Demand does not coincide with this insatiable ideal of many a political theoretician: universal consentment.
9. J. Shklar, "The Liberalism of Fear," in: N. Rosenblum (ed.), *Liberalism and the Moral Life*, Cambridge, Mass., 1989. See also the collection of essays on Judith Shklar's work in: B. Yack (ed.), *Liberalism without Illusions*, Chicago, 1996.

Interlude[*]
"The Others"

Octavio Paz

My deepest and most enduring impressions of the summer of 1937 do not concern my encounters with writers or the political discussions that kept me and my companions awake long into the nights. It was the encounter with Spain and her people that shook me: seeing landscapes and historical sites with my own eyes, touching stones with my own hands, that I had known in books since childhood. It was also, and to be honest, above all, my meetings with simple soldiers, farmers, workers, school teachers, journalists, boys and girls, old men and women. With and through them I learned that the word *fraternity* was no less precious than the word *liberty*; it is the daily bread, the shared bread, of humanity. I do not say this as a mere literary figure.

One night, while Valencia's anti-aircraft batteries held off the enemy's advance, several friends and I sought refuge in a nearby village in order to escape the bombs that were being dropped along the road. When the peasant who offered us shelter learned that I was from Mexico – a country that was helping the Republican cause – he ran out into his garden in spite of the bombardment and retrieved a melon, which he promptly shared with us, along with a loaf of bread and a jug of wine.

I could of course tell other stories but I prefer to conclude here with the memory of an incident that profoundly affected me: as part of a small group (and Stephen Spender will remember this, for he was one of our number), I had the opportunity to visit the campus of the University of Madrid, which was located on the

---

[*] This Interlude is an excerpt from a presentation by Octavio Paz on 15 July 1987 at Valencia. The meeting commemorated the Second Congress of Antifascist Writers held at Valencia in 1937.

front lines. Led by an officer, we passed through buildings and rooms that had formerly served as libraries and lecture halls but were now used as trenches and military blockhouses. Reaching a huge enclosure, which was protected on all sides with sandbags, the officer signaled us to remain silent. On the other side of the wall we could clearly and distinctly hear human voices and laughter. In a low voice I asked, "Who's that?" "It's 'the others,'" the officer replied. At first his words simply stunned me; then my shock turned to immense pain. This was the instant that I realized – and it was lesson I would never forget – that our enemies too have human voices.

Tolerance, Rights, and the Law

Paul Ricœur

Tolerance cannot *not* be concerned with the law, once it takes up in its concept the relationship between truth and justice. And there are several reasons for this. To begin with, the word *right* enters into many definitions of tolerance: the right to difference, to liberty, to those fundamental public freedoms that constitute human rights. Moreover, law, as opposed to morality, is the public instance where obligation is coupled with legitimate coercion. Finally, juridical institutions offer an excellent vantage point from which to observe the transformations of the idea of tolerance and scan the history of the struggles carried out in its name.

It was thus appropriate to begin with an historical review of the formulation of the 1789 Declaration of the Rights of Man and Citizen, and to reconstruct the arguments touching on the relationship between tolerance and liberty. As the author of the first article sees it, the crucial historical fact of the modern history of tolerance was the inclusion of restrictive legislative within the confines of a constitution. Following this line of reasoning, it becomes necessary to investigate, on an international scale, the historical dialectic between simple declarations of intention and the adoption of restrictive legislation. If we take the right to apostasy as the touchstone of tolerance, then it must be admitted that even to this day the canonical texts of the world's international organizations have failed to sanction such a major concession, in the sense of moving from declarations to acts. Returning to the domestic law of democratic countries, one is surprised by the gap existing between recent developments and the actual historical state of affairs on a planetary scale, in which the freedom to choose one's religion – including the right to change it – remains the major challenge.

According to the author of the second article, the West is now facing new challenges. The biggest among them is less the existence of beliefs deemed heretical by dominant spiritual authorities than in forms of individual behavior that endanger these individuals themselves. At the same time, the public's sense about what constitutes unacceptable behavior has also changed; in the absence of institutions embodying ultimate truth, judges are seen as the only available legitimate arbiter; equally, the law-based State can no longer declare itself judge but rather can act only as tutor, replacing its symbolic function.

With the author of the third article we return to the question of new international challenges, in particular those resulting from the acknowledgment of a right to humanitarian intervention that includes the use of compulsory measures. In this case, resistance is based not on religious beliefs or convictions but on the long-standing political principle of state sovereignty: from this point of view, the right to humanitarian intervention constitutes an actual violation of the principle of non-interference in the internal affairs of a state. How does this consensual limitation on the principle of sovereignty relate to our problem of tolerance? It relates to it in the sense that the cry of victims calling out for help constitutes the ultimate legitimation of this still gestating right. For if tolerance means more than merely enduring, if it actually implies helping, then coming to the aid of persons in danger is indeed a new stage in the progress of tolerance, one stamped not only in vague declarations but in ratified agreements that compel and constrain.

Human Rights and the Fate of Tolerance

Ghislain Waterlot

Original versus Modern Tolerance

The meanings of tolerance nowadays form a complex and ambiguous maze that far exceeds the scope of this essay. To clarify the following pages, however, we propose a preliminary distinction between *original tolerance* and *modern tolerance*.

> By original tolerance we mean the attitude that consists of putting up with, or not preventing, that which should not by law take place. It is motivated by prudence or condescension with regard to human failings. It is a sort of last resource. In any event, it is neither a permission nor an authorization: it is a favor, subject to revocation. As far back as one goes in human history, one finds traces of this elementary social practice.
>
> By modern tolerance, we mean the form of tolerance that has developed in modern times and is formulated by Castellion, Spinoza, Locke and in particular Pierre Bayle. To tolerate is to consent to the idea that in the name of freedom, in principle recognized by all, other men think and act according to principles that we do not share or with which we do not agree. In other words, tolerance is the corollary of freedom.

This essay will deal exclusively with modern tolerance. Our intention is to show how this tolerance was progressively included into the different Declarations of Human Rights (and the corollary texts) which sanction it politically. We shall also analyze the opposition it encountered and the setbacks it suffered. The prism of international law singularly highlights the underlying stakes of this notion, which is still of present concern.

The Declaration of Human Rights

In 1787, the king of France finally granted the Protestants an edict of tolerance. It was conceived along the lines of the edicts of the sixteenth century; the Protestant faith was yet to be considered licit, *it was not supposed to exist*, yet was nonetheless tolerated in the lands of the kingdom since it could not be otherwise. The Protestants still did not have the rights of the Catholics, and their public worship was not free; it was limited to its barest and most simple expression. This form of tolerance no longer corresponds to the human aspirations, since it becomes unbearable to see one-self considered a second-class citizen based solely upon a profession of religious faith different from that of the majority. But this edict was one of the last official acts of a tired regime on the verge of collapse. The convening of the Estates General and the beginning of their work on 5 May 1789 marks the beginning of the French revolution for us and the end of a era. Our interest in this great upheaval lies specifically in the drafting of the Declaration of Human Rights of Man that the deputies decided to insert, after much wavering, at the beginning of the kingdom's Constitution. As we know, the drafting of this declaration took place in the month of August 1789[1] precisely from the 20 to the 26 of August. The most fiercely debated articles were articles X and XI from the sessions held on the mornings of August 22, 23, and 24. After these sessions the atmosphere was exceptionally agitated:

> 'The Assembly was very tumultuous,' noted the national Courier, 'and one would need a whole book to take stock of all the amendments and sub-amendments, particular details, and personal debates.'[2]

The president of the Assembly, the count of Clermont-Tonnerre, exhausted and vexed by the heat of the debates, went so far as to tender his resignation, which was refused. Finally in a little more than two days, a vote was taken on the two articles. These are the two articles of essential interest to us, since they posit *modern tolerance* or the consequence of the freedom of conscience. Rabaut Saint-Etienne and Mirabeau, whose participation in the debates was decisive, insisted on the fact that as far as the freedom of expression was concerned, it was not a matter of tolerance in the traditional sense of the term. The difference of faith and conviction must no longer be accorded as a favor, but granted in the name of a single freedom. Let us cite the contents of these articles:

Article X: No one must be disturbed for his convictions, even religious ones, provided that their practice does not disrupt the public order established by law.

Article XI: The free communication of thoughts and convictions is one of the most precious rights of man; all citizens may therefore speak, write and publish freely, except in the abuse of this freedom in the cases determined by the law.

As for Article X, we note that the word *freedom* does not appear and that the formulation is doubly negative. Rabaut Saint-Etienne proposed writing:

All men are free in their convictions: every citizen has the duty to profess his faith freely and no one should disturb him because of his religion.

His colleagues did not follow suit, contenting themselves merely with the prohibition of the persecution of convictions – without asserting the freedom; furthermore, they placed a kind of restriction on religious convictions. Certainly they all agreed that these should no longer be persecuted, but such convictions became all the more susceptible to being so. Were this not the case, how should we interpret the need to single out religious convictions with the adverb *even*? Here it is as if we see a residual condescension, the favors of the majority. But we note in particular the fact that the idea of a dominant faith is no longer entirely excluded, although it does not appear specifically in the drafting of article X. We should note here that the Declaration is not exempt from traces of the historical interests of the men who drafted it. Some jurists[3] draw attention to the *miracle* of the Declaration, given that the deputies, in spite of the stormy nature of the debates, had enough foresight to make the articles of the Declaration have bearing not only on a specific epoch, but throughout the centuries as well. Nonetheless, a few *blemishes* still remain. One of them appears in the wording of article X, in the way in which the constituents grant freedom of religion as if it were a favor. To be understood, this formulation cannot be separated from a pressing and serious question in the minds of the men who drafted the Declaration, the question of ascertaining whether or not a civic religion should be established. This is why the *side of the tolerants* quarreled so fiercely with the *side of the clergy*. To understand this struggle, we should recall that the groundwork upon which the members of the Assembly were working, which is to say the draft of the Declaration known as that of "the sixth division," included a specific mention of an obligatory public faith. In fact, the draft of the sixth division produced three articles on the question of religion:

> Article XVI: Since the law cannot reach unseen offenses, it is up to religion and morality to broach them. It is therefore of utmost importance for the common good that both of these should be respected.
>
> Article XVII: The upholding of religion requires a public faith. Hence respect for the public faith is indispensable.
>
> Article XVIII: Any citizen who does not disrupt the established public order should hereafter not be disturbed.

Herein lies the origin of all the reflections that were to follow. After a rough oratory joust, the *side of the tolerants* succeeded in making its adversaries accept that the idea of a civic religion should be placed, were there a specific place for it, in the body of the Constitution of the kingdom and not in the Declaration, which was by nature more universal.[4] Nonetheless some of them extolled the idea of a civic religion as universal.[5] Perhaps, retorted the others, but *the duties* it would immediately imply could not figure into a declaration setting forth *the rights of man*. The necessity of a civic religion was therefore separated from the Declaration of Rights, and articles XVI and XVII of the draft proved null and void. But just after having been shown to the door, civic religion burst forth anew, as we shall explain. The second part of article X: "provided that their practice does not disrupt the public order established by law," must be explicitly tied to the shadow – menacing for some, reassuring to others – of a civic religion. For by the term *public order* we are led to understand – as in article XVII of the sixth division's draft – *public worship*. This means that for the practice of religious convictions to be tolerable (and we are obliged to note that atheism is *still* implicitly condemned), it must not in any way disturb the officially established religion. Is this the influence of Rousseau and the civic religion of *Le Contract social* (the Social Contract)? Certainly not, for all the deputies knew full well that the civic religion under the circumstances would be the Catholic religion, proclaimed the religion of the French State. The deputies of the clergy were fighting in this direction. The count of Castellane underscored in vain, against the preeminence of Catholicism, that "France in truth is Catholic but the French are not"; he was well aware that the cause was difficult to negotiate. Certainly with the distance of time comes the difficulty of understanding that the restriction of article X was interpreted as a victory for the Catholic or traditional party over the tolerants or innovators. Nonetheless it was in fact in these terms that the press of the time reported the conclusion of the debates:

> 'After having decreed this article,' tells the *Journal des Etats généraux*, for example, 'the members of the Assembly retired tumultuously, some with heavy hearts, at being unable, in spite of their resistance, to prevent it; others, and in particular the members of an order that is not an order, withdrew triumphantly for having passed a decree which, in a century other than our own, could have served as the basis for the Inquisition.'[6]

The idea that the practice of religious convictions could be contrary to the public order is thus considered a victory for Catholicism. In this context, article XI cannot be separated from article X. Debated the day after the memorable session of August twenty-third, to some extent it reestablishes equilibrium by insisting very strongly on *the freedom* of communication and the expression of ideas, using an affirmative wording: "The *free* communication of thoughts and convictions is one of the most precious rights of man: all citizens may therefore speak, write and publish *freely*." Curiously, the deputies did not interpret the restriction of article XI unaminously ("except in the abuse of this freedom in the cases determined by the law") as a victory for the side of the clergy. They felt strongly, in a great majority, that freedom of expression could not be absolute. Only Robespierre and three other deputies pleaded in favor of an unlimited right of expression, relegating the notion of *abuse* to the discretion of the penal code. But this opinion was held only by a small minority. We should therefore ask ourselves why that which is challenged on the one hand (article X) seems taken for granted on the other (article XI). The answer that comes to mind is that the restriction of article X is understood as a paring of freedom whereas that of article XI as a simple limitation necessary to guarantee its exercise in concrete terms. In other words, the *public order* of article X is framed within the perspective of a Catholic religion that continues to lobby against the practice of other religions (especially the Protestant and Jewish faiths at the time). The *abuse* of article XI is the expression of an opinion that challenges the rights of others (inciting to violence, defamation, lies, etc.). For the people of the time, it is important to differentiate between two entirely different things. For we who no longer live in a world dominated by the Catholic faith, it is a question of a sole and same limitation necessary to freedom. For we must not forget that freedom of conscience and freedom of expression relate as naturally to freedom as parts that fit into the whole that includes them. Freedom, one of the four "natural and indefeasible rights of man," contains within itself the necessary limitation:

> Freedom consists of being able to do everything that does not harm another, just as the exercise of the natural rights of each man is limited only by those that assure the enjoyment of these same rights by others. These limitations can only be determined by the law.

Thus the limitation of freedom is inherent to the essence of freedom, which is another way to say that freedom must be by definition capable of universality, since the absence of universality destroys freedom. This requirement introduces the limitations represented by the real law within the community or political society. Hence one should not be surprised that, in articles X and XI, the law reappears and reminds us of the necessary limitations – without however determining them: only *the* real laws can determine *any given* limitation. For those of us who are detached from the debate of August twenty-third 1789 the limitation of tolerance in article X is perfectly understandable in as far as its necessity is concerned; it does not shock us. The *practice* of a religious principle, which we can legitimately interpret as the act of expression of worshiping,[7] has the requirements of public order as its limitations, meaning the order established by the Republic whereby the freedom of everyone – both individuals and groups – should be respected. The same goes for other, non-religious convictions, such as political or aesthetic opinions: they cannot be absolutely free of any limitations, precisely because of freedom's inherent universality. Some expressions of conviction and some types of practices are harmful either to the community as a whole or for certain individuals in the community (such as children). In this regard, each epoch introduces new restrictions that change the limitations: "Other times, other customs," as the proverb says. At each moment of the history of a community, what must be tolerated or not in the name of freedom and what surpasses these limits must be reconsidered. This task is given to the legislator, who must, *prudently*, constantly redetermine *the many* limitations of the freedom of expression. But *the* limit will never disappear as such, for this is what guarantees freedom.[8]

Toward a Juridically Restrictive Norm

The Declaration of 1789, by setting forth the principle of freedom and its consequences, was not able to fulfil its function as a Preamble to the Constitution during the French Revolution, since the troubles of the time condemned all the Constitutions (1791, 1793, 1795) to remain inoperative. Since 1946, however, it has been applied rigorously in France and has fulfilled its function. Certainly the constitutionality of the Preamble to the Constitution of 1946 was debated for some time in the juridical world,[9] but the full inclusion of the Preamble into the Constitution in its entirety took place thanks to a decisive argument: article 81 of the Constitution refers explicitly to it. Furthermore, with the new Constitution of 1958, all ambiguity disappeared: the Preamble is partially numbered and included in the first section of the Constitution. The Declaration of the Rights of Man of 1789 is therefore much more than a profession of political faith, it has become a juridically restrictive text. In fact the Constitutional Council passed the laws of the Republic through the filter of the seventeen articles of the Declaration, raised to the status of a *yardstick*. Many times the articles of the law were rescinded or revised after just such an examination.[10] It is noteworthy that the history of the Fifth Republic shows it to have been in favor of more and more democratic recourse to the Constitutional Council. Beginning in the Fifth Republic, only a parliamentary majority could refer to the Council; in other words the verification of the constitutionality of laws was the privilege of the same men who voted. Under the presidency of Valèry Giscard d'Estaing, (1974-1981), a livery of seisin through parliamentary opposition became possible. Finally, on 14 July 1989, president François Mitterand proposed that the simple citizen have access to the seisin of the council. This marked evolution toward a greater democracy in institutional appeals indicates that tolerance (written into articles X and XI of the Declaration) must inspire the legislator's actions all the more. Indeed since a legislator's decisions are more subject to the verification of their conformity with the fundamental principles set forth in the Constitution than in the past, it is clear that the demands of tolerance are more strictly imposed on him.

The International Charter

It would, however, be singularly reductive to confine ourselves to the sole example of France. Today the requirements of human rights are written into the legislations of many countries. Furthermore human rights have been considerably elaborated through the development of international law following the Second World War. We shall skip over their concrete presence in various national legislations (even a cursory glance would take much too long), and follow the progress of the references to tolerance in the principle instruments of international law. The first and the most important of these instruments is the Universal Declaration of Human Rights promulgated in Paris on 10 December 1948. Here tolerance is more precisely set forth than in its predecessor of 1789. On the one hand it is the central focus of articles 18 and 19 that correspond very exactly to articles X and XI of 1789; on the other hand, tolerance is expressly affirmed as the goal of education in article 26. Let us first analyze articles 18 and 19:

> Article 18: All persons have the right to the freedom of thought, conscience and religion; this right implies the freedom to change religion or conviction as well as the freedom to practice one's religion or conviction, alone or in a group, in public or in private, through the teaching, practice, worship and the fulfilling of rites.

> Article 19: All individuals have the right to the freedom of conviction and expression, which includes the right not to be disturbed for one's convictions as well as right to seek, receive and distribute, without boundaries, information and ideas by any means of expression whatsoever.

At first glance, the reader notices the differences and the progress in the determination of tolerance. In article X of 1789, it is only a matter of *convictions* and *practices* of these convictions, with no qualifications other than the case of the religious nature of these same convictions. In article 18 of 1948, it is a question of freedom of *thought, conscience and religion.* This last term is associated with the word *conviction.* This association implies that atheism is now recognized and affirmed as a legitimate possibility for humans. It is permissible to be an atheist. As for freedom of thought, it implies the right freely to profess philosophical ideas adopted conscientiously. It is no longer necessary to hide or keep to oneself or to a few close friends choices of a philosophical or metaphysical nature. The idea of *practice* is, furthermore, quite precise. To practice one's religion (or conviction), means first of all to teach it. This right to teach pertains not only to the adepts wishing to deepen their spiritual formation, but also, implicitly, to people outside the religion being taught, to whom the preaching believer undertakes measures in the spirit of proselytism. In as much as these contacts are not imposed they are recognized as legitimate. This means recognizing a fundamental demand of the religions of which the majority are today founded on public preachings and proselytism. Hence the right to worship and practice publicly is explicitly recognized. In short, and perhaps in particular, article 18 clearly accentuates the *personalized* characteristics of the Declaration, since it introduces the fundamental idea that an individual always has the right to change religions should he see fit to do so.

Such an arrangement puts into effect, in the religious context, the fundamental principle of all the Declarations of Human Rights: the primate granted to individual conscience over collective pressure. According to the Declaration, the community is organized in such a way as to make the freedom of individuals a reality. In this frame of mind, the community has the right to impose duties and restrictions on the individuals that compose it. But the ultimate goal remains the personalization of the individual. The community is the means, the personality the ultimate goal. Nonetheless this last idea is deceptive, in as much as it leads one to imagine that once the goal is met the means disappears. Yet here the goal will never be met, since the work of liberating the individual with regard to both external and internal nature (his rough nature as an individual) must be taken up anew during each human generation, that is, incessantly. The community will therefore always remain the element within which the human individual personalizes himself. Nevertheless *personification*[11] is prized, at least in the modern Western world; it is the ultimate goal. If we transpose this principle into the religious sphere, this would imply that the individual expansion of spiritual life would be considered the ultimate requirement to which everything else is subordinate. Certainly churches and religious communities are implicitly recognized as indispensible: a deep religious life can never be conceived in the absence of a communal framework. To believe is to believe along with others, in a group, by inserting oneself into a given tradition and heritage. The idea of a purely individual faith is an abstraction. But the requirements of the group, of the *ecclesia,* can never include the repression of apostasy. The enrolment into a faith by birth cannot constitute a *destiny.* All spiritual undertakings are open to revision by the individual in the name of freedom.

It is helpful to note that the articulation of this consequence of tolerance with regard to religion constitutes a *high point* of the Declaration. If indeed there is something that religious movements have difficulty admitting, it is the legitimacy of apostasy.[12] The message of salvation that such movements for the most part convey is hard to reconcile with the possibility of a revision or personal evaluation. Often the initiators and founders (the prophets) of religions are situated so high above the rest of humanity that it is difficult to accept, within a religious community, that a simple member of the congregation might place himself above the position of the founder (at least implicitly so), by judging the pertinence of his message. Who believes himself capable of judging what comes from God or the divine? All religions (or almost all) voluntarily welcome the faithful who renounce their first beliefs to join their ranks; it bears witness to the superiority of their beliefs. On the other hand they have difficulty accepting people leaving them. Hence the Declaration articulates a demand that imposes an almost *unnatural* effort on religions. We shall soon have occasion to appreciate the extent to which this requirement of the Universal Declaration drew opposition.

To consider article 19 for a moment, we see a singular movement toward greater precision. First of all, the "free communication of thoughts and ideas" of 1789 (article XI) becomes the right "to seek, receive and distribute, without boundaries, information and ideas." Thus the Universal Declaration requires tolerance not only of the diffusion of ideas, but also of a citizen's active search for ideas or information that do not come to him through the intermediacy of a customary organ of diffusion. The Declaration argues directly in favor of the abolition of the rule of secrecy, that is, the promotion of clarity, accepted with such difficulty by the organs of powers, whatever they may be. Next it outlines the consequences of its universal extension, since it posits that boundaries should not be considered a potential stopping point for communication. No government can legitimately refuse the introduction of foreign ideas into the country in which it conducts its business. Indeed, the practice of closing off a community to foreign ideas judged potentially subversive is a traditional practice of long standing whose use was (and still is) common. In short the accent is quite clearly placed, in both articles 18 and 19, on the *affirmation of freedom.*

Within the framework of the Declaration, each individual may think freely, adopt a religion, practice it, teach or promote it, and eventually change it. Anyone may, without fearing the invervention of any power whatsoever, freely communicate thoughts and information, or freely seek them out. From these freedoms for all a corollary is imposed on each individual: *to tolerate the exercise of these freedoms in others,* even if they are found to be distasteful, annoying or even harmful. This last aspect makes the practice of tolerance very difficult and gives it a manifestly moral dimension: to be tolerant is a virtue. As for the restrictive clauses, they are absent in articles 18 and 19. In Articles X and XI of 1789, the limitation on freedom (to practice a religion and to express oneself) is clearly affirmed. In 1948, the men drafting the Declaration no longer thought it necessary to recall the indispensable limitations each time. These limitations have been moved almost to the end of the Declaration (articles 29, line 2), where they are set forth in quite laconic and general terms:

> In the exercise of his rights and the enjoyment of his freedoms, each individual is subject only to the limitations established by the law with the exclusive aim of assuring the acknowledgment of and respect for the rights and

freedoms of others and in order to satisfy the just requirements of morality, the public order and the general well-being in a democratic society.

At the same time as the limitations are set forth, the aspiration universally to found *democratic* societies is affirmed. And this corresponds in article 26, to the promotion of *education* and the call, this time direct, for tolerance considered as a major educative objective:

Each individual has the right to education (...) Education must strive for the full blossoming of the human personality (...) It must favor the comprehension, tolerance and friendship among all nations and all racial and religious groups ...

Hence the universal Declaration salutes tolerance and associates it with education along with a few other cardinal virtues. As for tolerance, it is the highest point. After having been conceived in the sixteenth and seventeenth centuries, after having been demanded in the eighteenth century, today it is officially proclaimed and heralded as a requirement to be taught to all humankind. It imposes itself as a requirement for each individual in recognition of the freedom of all. Nonetheless the Declaration in and of itself is nothing more than a profession of faith. Signed by almost all the countries in the world – with a few noteworthy exceptions – and thereby recognized theoretically, the Declaration has no juridical power: nothing guarantees its application. This is indeed a shortcoming, upon which the jurist Jacques Mourgeon insists, since "the insolvency of Power voids the affirmation of rights of every substance and meaning. Be it juridical or material, voluntary or the result of a real obstacle, it reveals the virtuality of the rights affirmed, if not the vanity of their affirmation."[13]

It would, however, be wrong to content oneself with such an observation, for the Declaration of 1948 is a founding *charta* for other international institutions which, for their part, are endowed with a restrictive nature. These include the International Pact On Economic, Social and Cultural Rights, or the International Pact On Civic and Political Rights, both of which were proclaimed in 1966 and put into effect in 1976. The countries that signed agreed to modify their national legislations in terms of the stipulations of these Pacts. In this way a process of control was put into play, as J.-B. Marie notes: "the participating countries agree to make (reports) at various intervals concerning the measures taken and

the progress made in order to assure their respect for the rights recognized in the contract; these reports may be examined by an organization made up of independent experts who make observations
or criticisms and are able to ask for precise explanations from a
country concerning the way it assures (or does not assure) the
enjoyment of the recognized rights."[14] Furthermore, an optional
Protocol relating to the International Pact On Civic and Political
Rights obliges the signing countries to recognize the intervention
of an International Committee of Human Rights in the case of a lit-
igation between the country and a citizen.[15] A relinquishing of sovereignty, as limited as it may be, is always accepted by a country
with difficulty. Hence no one will be surprised that the countries
signing these Pacts are far less numerous than those signing the
Universal Declaration.[16]

International Resistence or the Risk of an Impass

As far as tolerance is concerned, it is remarkable that going from
the Declaration to the Pacts represents a marked setback. Particular attention to this point is worthy of note here. We have emphasized, in fact, that the freedom recognized in individuals to
change religion constitutes the highest point of the Universal Declaration. In the corresponding article of the Pact On Civic and
Political Rights (likewise numbered 18), this explicit mention has
disappeared. It has been replaced by:

> Each individual has the right to the freedom of thought, conscience and reli-
> gion; this right implies the freedom to have or adopt a religion or a conviction
> of choice, as well as the freedom to practice this religion or conviction, etc.

One might say that the difference is insignificant and that *freedom
to adopt* is another way to say *freedom to change*. In fact this is not the
case, for the freedom to adopt retains only the idea of *entering* into a
religious order, it does not include the idea of *exiting*. The double
movement associated with the idea of changing has here been cut in
half. Furthermore, bitter debates between the representatives of different national delegations are hidden behind these wordings. Pressures were exerted, particularly by the Islamic countries, to restrict if
not erase the freedom to change religion, which is nonetheless

inherent to tolerance. Whereas almost all the wording of the Declaration was reused in the International Pacts, it is significant that this
one was modified. And this is not all. Apropros of religion, a *Convention on the elimination of all forms of intolerance and discrimination
based on religion or conviction* was initiated as early as 1955. It would
take twenty-six years of work and negotiations for the Convention
to lead to ... a simple Declaration. In 1972, in fact, "The General
Assembly (of the United Nations) agreed to grant priority to the
elaboration of a Declaration since the adoption of a Convention no
longer seemed possible, by reason of a multitude of obstacles of a
political nature."[17] This means that a text that would have had a
somewhat juridically restrictive nature was officially renounced.[18]
Apropros of world religion and the violence it can ignite, which
must be combatted, the United Nations was forced to make do with
an international declaration. As far as we are concerned, the terms
themselves are still altered with regard to the Pact On Civic and
Political Rights. What does one read in the Declaration against intolerance that was finally adopted in 1981? It is the following:

> Every individual has the right to the freedom of thought, conscience and reli-
> gion. This right implies the *freedom to have a religion or any other conviction what-
> soever of choice*, as well as the freedom to practice this religion or conviction ...

If we wanted to play guessing games, we would ask: what
word is missing? Quickly the reader would notice that the verb *to
adopt* has disappeared from the text which, otherwise, faithfully
repeats article 18 of the Pact On Civic and Political Rights.[19] This
disappearance is not harmless. It suppresses any mention of the
idea of entering or leaving a religion. The dynamic gives way to
the static: "I have, you have, he has a religion ..." The mention of
choice has not disappeared, but any reference to modification or
change has been erased. The forces that tend to make religion an
individual's *destiny* are in full force here. Of course the specialists
on international law insist on the fact that the second paragraph of
the same article 1 affirms:

> No one shall be constrained in attaining the freedom to have a religion or a
> conviction of choice.

The mention of *choice* of religion and the condemnation of constraint seem to imply that the individual has the right to change

religion. This is true. But what counts as far as we are concerned is the effort the delegations made in order to reduce as much as possible (and even to erase) all explicit references to the changing of religion and consequently to combat all that tends to affirm apostasy as an individual right:

> The Western negotiators came up against the opposition of the Islamic countries (forty in all) with regard to a portion of this text. The group's spokesman finally remarked that while they considered the Declaration as a whole an important document, it was no less true that the Coran does not permit a Muslim to change religions.[20]

In fact, their resistance to the text was such that the representative of the Islamic countries finally asked that the text be adopted by the general assembly of the United Nations *without a vote*. Were there a vote, they said, they would not be able to support such a text. In this way reservations became officially formulated in the United Nations with regard to the "possibility of applying any specification or decree of the Declaration that might be in opposition to Islamic law (Chari'a) or any legislation or juridical act founded on Islamic law."[21] The core of the resistence is always the same: the non-dissociation of the political and the religious. In a country where religious dogma and laws are intermixed, tolerance is concretely impossible. It is indeed obvious that one cannot ask religions to accept apostasy as such. All condemn it out of necessity and consider the apostate to be someone on the road to damnation, if he is not already damned. The faithful can pray for his return, but they cannot acknowledge his behavior. If a religion recognized the legitimacy of apostasy, which would admit tacitly that it is not essential to be counted among its ranks, it would weaken itself, rendering itself relative. On closer examination this is not what is being asked in the name of tolerance. It is asking only that each religion renounce the exercise of the power to restrict individuals when these individuals opt for apostasy. The apostates can be blamed among the ranks of the faithful as much as one pleases, as soon as one admits that it is wrong to engage in the slightest pursuit of them, whatever its nature. But in a country where the religious dogmas receive the support and sanction of the civic laws, it is impossible really to prevent persecution. In a way the problem lies here: human rights presume a recognition of a lay political perspective, above a religious one, in the public space, which guarantees the rights of individuals against the inevitable pressure of different groups. In all the countries in which this separation of the religious and the political has not taken place, the rights of man cannot be recognized in concrete fashion.

This is why on an international scale human rights are not so much admitted as discussed. In the eyes of certain writers, the *tensions* and even the setbacks we have mentioned justify pessismism.

> The Universal Declaration of Human Rights should not create illusions. At the time of its adoption by the United Nations (in December 1948), it reflected an international society of which the great majority of its members,whatever their reserves, accepted personalism. The current majority are followers of Islam, Hinduism, Buddhism or Animism. These currents of civilization, still very powerful, are certainly not negators of certain prerogatives of the individual, but rather situate them in the perspectives of the political relationships that are specific to them and which differ profoundly from ideas of a Christian nature.[22]

This anxiety can be justified by the current tendency, in the Far Eastern countries that are not Islamic, for example, to question "the formal logic of liberalism and individualism of modern Europe," in favor of a "new world order (consisting) of allowing each people and each nation to reaffirm their positions as tied to their historical traditions and regional idiosyncrasies."[23] This basic hostility cannot be overlooked, especially since it is at times underscored by disturbing political demonstrations. In any case it forces us to note that nothing has been done on an international level, that the promotion of the human rights and hence of tolerance which, as we have seen, constitutes one of its central points, remain the focus of a struggle whose stakes are essential. It is not so much a matter of opposing sporadic and even repeated violations of the rights of man, as of fighting against the refusal of a certain number of groups and even governments to accept it in principle. This is the essential point. When the whole world agrees on these fundamental values, the worst will be over. Next it will be necessary to try to reduce, on a daily basis, the rift between words and action, saying and doing. With human rights, on the scale of international relations, things have not really reached this point yet. "The goal of the international contracts," recalls Jean-Bernard Marie, "rests upon values that are perhaps not as universally accepted by the world as these texts imply. It is not simply a matter of the distance that always separates the ideal from reality which is in question here, but a distance with regard to the principles themselves and the specific norms formulated on a universal level."[24] One must not therefore underestimate the following point: if tolerance is one of the fundamental principles of modernity, this modernity is not one that has been agreed upon on a global level. It is exposed to contradiction and opposition: in short, it is subject to tensions according to which its future and its fate shall unfold. The idea of modernity as the definitive and happy culmination of the history of humanity, has not yet found its way onto the current agenda.

Notes

1. On the Declaration of the Rights of Man and the conditions of its drafting, see, among *others, M.Gauchet, La Révolution des droits de l'homme*, Paris, 1989; J. Morange, *La Déclaration des droits de l'homme et du citoyen*, Paris,1988. As the latter is a jurist, he gives us interesting insights into the juridical signification and bearing of the Declaration, from the time of its proclamation up to our day.
2. Quoted in: M.Gauchet,*La Révolution*, p. 170.
3. Such as J.Morange, *La Déclaration*.
4. Rabaut Saint-Etienne, Mirabeau, Pétion, Bouche and especially Talleyrand expressed such an opinion, with the latter using a remarkable eloquence whose effect was reinforced by his status as a prelate.
5. The marquis of Clermont-Lodève in particular.
6. Quoted in: M.Gauchet, *La Révolution*, p. 172. Marcel Gauchet's text demonstrates very well that at the time the article was generally interpreted as a victory for the clergy. See also B. Kriegel, *La Politique de la raison*, Paris,1994, and in particular, "La Déclaration des droits de l'homme et la liberté de conscience."
7. Of course this is not the only manifestation possible.
8. Hence the radical absurdity of the 1968 slogan of: "Il est interdit d'interdire" (It is forbidden to forbid); this is absurd not only from a logical point of view (if it is forbidden to forbid, it is forbidden to forbid to forbid), but also from the point of view of reason: there is no freedom *imaginable* without the forbidden.
9. The exegesis is powerless to delineate the uncertainty. Alternately, the same assembly, the same parties and, at times, the same orators attributed opposing natures to the Preamble, from a veritable juridical text of a constitutional nature, to a simple profession of political faith (See J. Rivero and G. Vedel, *Les Problèmes économiques et sociaux de la Constitution du 27 octobre 1946*, Paris, 1947).

10. For some examples of the decisions of the Constitutional Council, see J. Morange, *La Révolution*, pp. 108-11.

11. The term comes from E.Weil, *Philosophie politique*, 24, Paris, 1956.

12. Krishnaswami, who in 1955 was commissioned by the sub-committee of human rights of the United Nations to draw up a report on intolerance and discrimination notes: "although religions or convictions favorably welcome – and in certain cases even encourage – the conversion of people belonging to other faiths, it is very difficult for them to admit that their own members convert to another religion. Apostasy is judged harshly; it is often forbidden by their religious codes."

13. See *Les Droits de l'homme*, Paris,1978, p.87.

14. J.-B. Marie, "Le Droit international, une ressource pour lutter contre l'intolérance," in: *L'Intolérance et le droit de l'autre*, Geneva,1992, p. 103.

15. The first article of the optional Protocol reads as folllows: "Every county signing the Pact that also signs the Protocol recognizes that the Committee is competent to receive and examine the communications presented by individuals under its jurisdiction who claim to be victims of a violation, by the signing country, of any of the rights set forth in the Pact."

16. The United States signed (in 1922) only the International Pact on Civic and Political Rights. To our knowledge, the Pact On Ecomonic, Social and Cultural Rights has not yet been signed by the United States.

17. See J. Walkate, "Aperçu historique sur la Déclaration des Nations-Unies sur l'élimination de toutes les formes de l'intolérance et de discrimination," in: *Conscience et liberté*, No.43,1991, p. 14.

18. A Convention, like a Pact, shares a juridically restrictive character; a Declaration, in international law, is a simple profession of faith.

19. It also adds the expression "any ... whatsoever" before and after the word *conviction*. The insertion of the indefinite pronoun here reflects a pressing demand from the countries of the former Communist black to underscore the legitimacy of atheism.

20. See J.Walkate,(note 17 above), p. 15.

21. These observations were formulated by Iraq (in the name of the organizations of the Islamic Conference), Syria and Iran. We should add that certain Eastern European countries and Russia expressed reservations of a similar sort, insisting on the incompatibility of certain specifications of the Declaration with their national legislation.

22. J.Mourgeon, *Les Droits de l'homme*, Paris,1978, p. 55.

23. As suggested by Iwo Kôyama, cited by Bernard Stevens in his article "Ambitions japonaises, nouvel asiatisme et dépassement de la modernité," published in the magazine *Esprit*, No. 213 (July 1995). Iwao Kôyama was one of the leaders of nationalist thought in the 1930s in Japan. His ideas have been revived today, according to Bernard Stevens, by a significant number of Japanese intellectuals.

24. J.-B. Marie, (note 14 above), p. 10.

The Law and the
New Language of Tolerance

Antoine Garapon

The history of the idea of tolerance is marked by a rift between its original meaning and its modern one.[1] At first tolerance was understood as the effort made to put up with certain reprehensible acts or lapses with regard to society's values, since rules can never be respected at all times without life becoming unbearable. Conceived originally as a discretion on the part of authority, it progressively acquired the meaning of a "right to differ." "The idea that a free space must obligatorily be assured to each member of the community," writes Ghislain Waterlot, "is a relatively new idea that is fundamentally very modern."[2]

We have perhaps come to the threshold of a new stage of this history, in as much as today tolerance is facing new challenges. "Classical" tolerance, which posits one definition of societal good against another, continues to be put to the test, as we see in the issue of the Islamic veil.[3] But this type of conflict – which is perhaps in the process of increasing in countries with immigrants – should not mask the magnitude that the question of tolerance represents in a democratic society. A democratic society is often considered more tolerant than others not because it is more virtuous, but because it is not content to put up with differences, but rather encourages or even engenders them. The difference is not merely external, such as the clash of foreign cultures, but also, if not especially, internal, with a society's own members becoming more different from each other by the day. It no longer involves conflicting institutionalized cultures, but also those individuals claiming to emancipate themselves from any dominant culture, be it national or foreign. Not only do communal customs begin to weaken in a democratic society, but they lose their hegemonic pretensions in particular, that is, their ability to serve as a reference. Minorities are no longer ashamed, and the problem of tolerance becomes profoundly modified. In order to safeguard against the underlying complexities of a question continuously raised by the effusiveness of the well-intentioned, or the coldness of abstract reasoning, we would do well to begin with the issues currently debated in France. Beginning with a sociology of modern tolerance, what are the new stakes? How do the problems present themselves? On what occasions? How are they resolved?

It is not certain that one can separate the question of tolerance from that of democratic pluralism. The major antagonisms that run through our democracies today call into question not only beliefs, that is, concepts of good, but choices of lifestyle as well. The conflicts they generate are no longer only positive, although many cases do involve the role of arbiter, but also – and this is new – negative, with no one having the authority to solve them. What would be the criteria? It is no easier to come to an agreement on the nature of evil than it is on that of good. Such an uncertainty can be more clearly demonstrated by a shift into a more tangible criterion: the body and its health. This reformulation of the question of tolerance in contemporary society assigns another objective to the struggle for democratic tolerance, which at this point of time is perhaps more in need of mediators and interpreters than prophets or good apostles.

Conflicts in Conceptions of Good or in Choices of Lifestyle?

"Religious tolerance as it was discovered in the sixteenth and seventeenth centuries," writes Paul Dumouchel, "remains the paradigm of tolerance. The various denominations of Christianity were not opposed to each other in an accidental or contingent fashion, but because each conceived of itself as the true interpretation of a universal religion."[4] Can we still think of modern tolerance as based on religious disagreement? When it opposed two rival versions of the same Christian faith, the trouble arose perhaps more from their similarities than from their differences. They might debate the practice of mass or last rights, but they remained in agreement on the manner in which to eat, dress or love, that is, customs. This agreement has more to do with dogma than with the role of belief. In other words, the definition, scope and breadth of belief have changed. The distinction between belief and behavior has become more and more uncertain: into which category should sorcery be placed? Is it a religious practice? What about excision? It is certainly not tied to a religion – and notably not to Islam – but rather to a custom that certainly issues from a concept of good, but has absolutely no pretense to universality. And yet one speaks vaguely of the community of homosexual, Africain, Jewish or Gypsy minorities; but what do they have in common? Not being the majority? This negative definition is paradoxical, with these minority differences affirming each other in relation to a center that no longer exists, in relation to a majority that has itself lost all exclusive claim to citizenship.

Conflicts between beliefs do not have the same meaning in a society in which the majority professes one same faith; in a society in which the majority of its members are believers, even if not in the same thing; and in a society in which the majority don't believe in anything and do not govern their behavior according to a belief. No reflection on modern tolerance can forego a reflection on the new status of beliefs in our disillusioned societies. Can homosexuality or recourse to abortion be summed up as particular conceptions of good? No, it is rather a choice of lifestyle in which behavior is not necessarily universal, but which claims the same tolerance on the grounds of the same right to differ. The relationship between belief and behavior is not exactly the same today as it was in the eighteenth century; it has perhaps become inverted. Today, belief is less of an inspiration for any particular action than are individual behaviors such as drug use or homosexuality, which lead into particular symbolic universes. What causes the problem of tolerance to take an unforseen turn is that it is confronted with the dislocation of the idea of belief and a diversification of behavior that resist the traditional categories that have previously defined tolerance.

Is it still possible to neatly compartmentalize the questions of multiconfessionalism, pluralism and multiculturalism? To cling to the paradigm of religious tolerance is to refuse to see the manner in which the problems of democratic coexistence present themselves today. Indeed these lie not so much in the clash of many concepts of good, or even in the diversification of lifestyles, but rather in the conflict between these two. This is what the abortion question demonstrates: one side calls for its prohibition in the name of a *religious* good, the other side fights for its legalization in the name of a *political* one. The dialogue is all the more difficult since the sides do not speak the same language and do not situate themselves on the same level. It brings together a concept that lays claim to universalism, and an individual life choice which, like any public freedom, can never be universalized. A Christian can be opposed to the practice of abortion in the name of his personal convictions, but accept that it is permitted to those who desire it.

In a democracy, conflicts do not necessarily involve only the communities of believers, but likewise those groups of people united by the same life choices. The collective or communal nature of beliefs is more fluid since it confirms the phenomenon of the "New Age," which refers more to individual practice than collective belief. "An isolated individual whose concept of good is essentially opposed to that of his fellow citizens does not constitute a political problem, but rather one involving the police,"[5] writes Dumouchel; but when the number of individuals who each have a different conception of good are no longer opposed to a majority but rather to other individuals each with his own way of conceiving good, this becomes a central political problem.

The neutrality of state defined by law translates, on the social level, into a moral equivalency: all behaviors, even those that were still considered deviant yesterday, are now placed on the same level. Democracies are all haunted by a *generalized scrambling of the norm*.[6] Such a moral depressurization is of interest to the question of tolerance in that it produces certain consequences. It should perhaps be compared with a new intolerance (the term is used here in its psychological sense) of delinquency, pushing religious groups to become more demanding and demonstrative.

The evolution of democratic societies is contradictory: the more they liberalize themselves the less they accept transgression. In other words, the more tolerant they are in the modern sense of the term, the less so they are in its original sense. In the new penal code that France has recently adopted, a certain number of infractions of a moral connotation, such as homosexuality between an adult and a minor, have disappeared, which might appear to qualify it as more liberal. But at the same time it includes other infractions such as sexual harassment, the aggravated incidence of domestic violence, or other serious incriminations such as putting other people into danger, which counterbalance this first impression. It shows itself to be more tolerant with regard to certain behaviors concerning individual freedom, but is more intransigent with others. It is both more liberal in reducing the number of general incriminations and more repressive in increasing the penalties. The history of intolerance would therefore not include its disappearance, but rather its migration toward new behaviors that are no longer accepted. While adultery is now socially tolerated, tobacco is becoming less and less so. Likewise all the richest and freest societies both in the north and in the south, and on both sides of the Atlantic, are showing a harsher and harsher attitude toward deviancy and delinquency. This is what the Americans call *Tough Penology*, that is, harsh criminology. Everywhere the prison population is rising in number and everywhere one sees a tendency to criminalize the social problems that society cannot otherwise control.[7] One even sees our societies returning to reactions that have the look of sacrificial expiations, a return of the mechanism of the scapegoat in matters of sexual crimes in which children are the victims. In the repression of adultery, people used to condemn immorality; today they seek to exorcize the impulse to monstrosity. Child murder remains the last figure of absolute evil in a society that doubts it own values: "he at least was innocent!" cries René Char. This horror alone proves capable of raising the doubt that sets in with the identification of the offending and the offended parties, halting the indifferentiation into which the aggressor and the victim are usually plunged. In our society, which is slow to rise up in indignation, one must seek the spark of a shudder in such extreme cases of suffering and intolerability in order to find a consensus. Belgium was recently the theater of a particularly atrocious crime whose victims were three little girls. A large crowd gathered at the funeral, in a gesture of solidarity that hadn't been seen since the death of king Baudouin ...

Just as religious freedom is broadening, a new political demand is taking shape: that of publicly demonstrating one's faith. This demand does not bear solely on one's right to base one's conduct on one's own conscience, and thus on an abstention of the state, but on the possibility of proclaiming one's convictions and belonging to a community, that is, a positive recognition of one's uniqueness by the law. It used to be that people demanded to be heard by the state, now they demand to be recognized. As freedoms begin to become more established, what was once considered a freedom becomes converted to a right to differ. "One has the feeling that it is no longer conscience that must make its own way against the dominant norms, but that the norms must adapt themselves to the diversity of conscience."[8] By changing the meaning, tolerance also changes language: it progressively abandons the moral register for the legal one. In so doing, it merely follows the movement of Western societies which no longer see themselves religiously or politically, but juridically. But doesn't this confusion with subjective rights risk killing the idea of tolerance? If a tolerated behavior is only conceived as a preamble to a recognized right, what remains of the political virtue of tolerance? How can we analyze this tolerance's linguistic progression from the moral, psychological and political ... to the juridical?

Positive or Negative Conflict?

The metamorphosis of the idea of tolerance follows the mutation of the political, that is, the conversion of a monarchy based on faith in a government, to rights founded on another idea of justice. In both cases, justice is the ultimate point of reference, but it does not mean the same thing. It evolves from a substantial content toward a more procedural definition. "Before the law, individuals are reputed to have beliefs, convictions and interests that define the *content* that justice is unaware of, since it is only justice, the arbiter of rival claims, not the tribunal of truth. Invalid as an instance of truth, civic power assumed the status of the state of law. Whereas divine right defines itself by a claim to truth, the right of the state of law is agnostic in the proper sense of the word."[9] Paul Ricœur defines democratic intolerability as the confusion between justice and truth on an institutional level. But is it not a bit illusory to believe that communal life can be limited to pure procedure? Can a political community forego substantial communal values organizing its relationship to the world? Can one limit the government's role in a democracy to arbitrating between two opposite conceptions of good? Should it not substitute itself for the absence of a communal concept of good? Problems arise as much from the excess of meaning as from the lack of it. Religious tolerance was tied to a universe still steeped in meaning; this is no longer the case in a world in which the heavens have been emptied. The problem is not limited to a *positive conflict* between two rival concepts of good: it takes the unexpected turn of a *negative conflict* in which no one is authorized to intervene in the realm of mores.

The absence of an instance of truth increases conflicts and ultimately reinforces the status of a third party, which is passed on to a new actor: the judge. In as much as conflicts are not resolved by tradition or mores, the opposing parties turn to the judge, the only arbiter available. In soliciting a civic authority to free themselves from the hold of a religious one, they paradoxically legitimize a new symbolical domination. Even the fiercest adversaries of the juridical, those who surrender some of their power to it, have recourse to it, simply because it is the only one. Justice is called upon to fill the place left empty by the religious, as if this void was impossible, and this moral silence too difficult to bear. The rise to power of the juridical, which becomes the necessary direction taken by all debates on tolerance, is one of the great events that characterizes the life of all democratic societies these last few years. It is occurring as much on the level of the entire political community, which more and more surpasses the boundaries of nation or government, as within the communities or internal subgroups of the government and among the individuals themselves. In all three domains, the juridical assumes the role once played by the religious.

It is possible to interpret the new relationship between the state of law and justice by transposing, term for term, that which Ricœur says about the relations between the political institution and the Church in the predemocratic configuration: "the political asks the religious for *unction*, that is, the sign of the sacred; in exchange, the ecclesiastic institution asks the political for *sanction* from the secular show of force for that which it considers schism or heresy. This exchange between *unction* and *sanction* constitutes a reciprocal instrumental relationship, in which each of these institutions receives from the other that which it lacks: the spiritual might of the sacred for the political, the physical might of constraint for the religious, or rather, the ecclesiastical."[10] In what domains, indeed, does one see justice intermingling with the consent – if not the intentional request – of executive power? In questions concerning the human being, as in the definition of life and death from the perspective of bioethical issues, euthanasia, as in the Tony Bland affair in England,[11] adoption in India, sexual aggressions in Canada, transsexualism in France, abortion in the United States, the death sentence, as in South Africa, religious conflicts in the temple of Ayoda in India,[12] the crucifix in Bavaria,[13] in short, in all the domains that house the *sacred*.

The final stage in the privatization of beliefs and the liberation from all traditions is the total disaffiliation of the democratic subject. This is because what awaits the individual emancipated from all collective belief is, for the most fortunate, the falling back on his most tangible interests, that is, narcissistic and financial interests – and, for everyone else, the plunge into psychological destructuration. Such is the new picture painted by many people brought before the penal judge. The risk does not come exclusively from repression, but also from exclusion. A society is nothing more than an organized system of differences; it is the discriminating divergences that give individuals their "identities" and allow them to situate themselves in relationship to others. The "excluded" are excluded first and foremost from this system of differences; they are orphans of all social affiliation and therefore of all representation. They are deprived of any participation in a collective action, from the right to have rights and the benefit of any social solidarity whatsoever. It is therefore no longer possible to limit oneself to seeing delinquency as a simple form of asocialness; it must be recognized as a problem of socialization, as the number of contemporary pathologies (urban delinquency, drug addiction, suicide etc.) bears out. The state of law should no longer merely make itself arbiter, but also tutor, a substitute for a failing symbolic function. Its difficulty no longer lies in showing itself to be tolerant and structuring. In truth, never has moral freedom been as great as it is today, but in turn never has public intervention into the lives of citizens – and notably into their internal life – been as strong, which is not the least paradoxical aspect of our day.

Another paradox of the current demands on the law consists of the use of legal proceedings as a symbolic instance of social recognition. The most patent example is that of the contract of civil union demanded by the homosexual community. In France, the relationship between two concubines, that is, two people of the opposite sex living together without being married, is a source of rights, notably social rights. How is it that someone can have Social Security take care of his concubine if he is heterosexual and not if he is homosexual? This undermines the equality of citizens before the law, which is an essential principle of justice. But in claiming the institution of this new statute of marriage, and under the pretext of fulfilling the democratic dogma of equality and impartiality, is not the homosexual community asking for a certain recognition by the juridical order? Is this the role of the law? Should it not rather limit itself to the preservation of free spaces in which people have the right to live as they wish to live, and restrain itself from according any moral sanction? It is not its role to pass judgment – even a positive one – on sexuality. The moral appreciation of homosexuality – ever since it has ceased to be repressed by the penal code – is nevertheless the domain of individual conscience and not the law. Herein lies the ambiguity of the claims for positive rights, and not merely for the freedoms for minorities. With regard to the claims made by minorities in the United States, Philippe Raynaud comments on, "the redoubling of the politics of special interests by a politics of recognition; the main goal is to make people admit that any given group, with its particular nature, is indeed part of the national community, whose internal diversity includes the secret counterpoint that it is not enough to be a formal citizen of the United States to be fully 'American.'"[14] The juridicalization – and worse still the constitutionalization – of public morals risks further straining the moral conflicts of a society, with the victory of one position calling for the disqualification of the opposing party, which is seen as contradicting the fundamental values upon which the Constitution rests. The value of "conviction" of the weaker party risks no longer being recognized.

A Consensus on Evil

Democracy agrees more easily on the definition of absolute evil than on a concept of good, as the debate on revisionism currently stirring public opinion in France demonstrates. Must one tolerate the negationist discourse that contests the reality of the Shoah? French law – called the Gayssot law after its founder – restricts

> "those who would contest the existence of one or more crimes against humanity such as they are defined by article 6 of the statute of the International Military Tribunal of Nuremberg, that is, the assassination, extermination, reduction to slavery, deportation, and any other inhuman act committed against civilian populations before or during wartime, or persecutions for political, racial or religious reasons, when these acts or persecutions, whether or not they constituted a violation of the rights of the countries within which they were perpetrated, were committed following any of the crimes recognized by the Tribunal or in conjunction with any such crime."

The extreme right has fought unceasingly against this law, deemed "totalitarian." A representative of the National Front[15] publicly accused the creators of this amendment of being incapable of demonstrating the reality of the Shoah scientifically.

How to justify this exception to the freedom of expression that restrains the *contents* of speech, with which, in principle, democracy should not concern itself? Is it out of concern to protect a minority, in this case the Jewish community? The protection of the memory of the Shoah is part of what Ricœur calls a conflictual consensus on the part of all religions, notably among Jews and Catholics, even though some points of disagreement remain, as the issue of the Carmelites in Auschwitz demonstrates.[16] Did not the Episcopal Conference of the Catholic Church in France just recently refer to the Jewish genocide as an "incontestable fact," "an *indisputable* established fact"?

In departing from the principle of tolerance of all opinions, the law marks the importance of this event in a symbolic fashion, to some extent separating it from history in order to recognize its unique place. Genocide has not been directed at the Jewish people alone, and the limitation of the Gayssot law to the events of the Second World War alone is one of its weaknesses. This century's genocides – Armenian, Gypsy, Jewish, and, closer to home, Tutsi – of which the most extreme was the Jewish Holocaust, have allowed countries to come to an agreement on that which they do not want, in a sort of negative natural right. The parliamentary debates of the new penal code showed the capital importance that the crime against humanity has assumed in the contemporary juridical consciousness. The still recent memory of the Shoah has inspired the great texts on the human rights of the immediate post-war period, starting with the Universal Declaration of Human Rights of December 1948. A crime against humanity is a fundamental crime in that it symbolizes the extreme instance of intolerance of the other, that is, his systematic elimination as scientifically organized by a modern government. It embodies the modern evil of societies without transcendence, which is no longer the murder of the father, the Other, but of the other, the brother. In order to prevent its recurrence, nations founded the New International Juridical Order on Human Rights.

But this law has another, less obvious, justification: it also aims at preventing this crime from perpetuating its maleficence. The crime against humanity is a continuous crime,[17] which still produces effects today. To deny the Shoah, indeed, is not merely an historical opinion; it continues this same crime by perpetuating it on the survivors, thus making the denier the posthumous accomplice of those who organized the Shoah and who left no traces with this goal in mind: indefinitely prolonging the suffering of the survivors. Negation, in fact, is part of the crime against humanity. Murder contains an intrinsic element of its own denial: this is also the reason that it is not an ordinary crime. The other is not only killed but destroyed, denied, made to vanish. Even his death disappears. Denial is the enabling factor of the crime against humanity. The premeditated destruction of proof that characterizes all these types of crimes does not stem from the very human desire to escape punishment, but rather from the desire to complete the crime by making its proof impossible and thereby its torture indefinite for those who know that their forefathers were victims but cannot prove it. As the crime takes place it precludes any justice, that is, commemoration. It kills memory and prohibits mourning by making the injustice committed seem improbable, uncertain in both senses of the term, and, most importantly, unprovable.

The proof lies in the suffering of the survivors. They are condemned to bear an injustice that prevents them from living for generations. The initial crime is not only denied but it becomes immaterial, and the victims are transformed into non-beings. This produces the result of making survival difficult – if not impossible; such is the extent to which the children are victims of psychic confinement, without the possibility of symbolization. "Hence," says a survivor of the Armenian genocide, "there cannot be any real intersubjective exchanges between the child and his surviving parent, who has become doubly 'clandestine' to himself: since he cannot integrate an important part of his life experience, but also because this has been erased from the world's consciousness."[18] One might remember the moment of intense emotion at the trial of Klaus Barbie,[19] when a victim told the court that at last she could sleep at night; having finally looked Barbie in the face her suffering had at last been given a name. The legislator's concern is not the memory of past victims, but the protection of current victims, that is, the actual suffering of the children of survivors.

Hence the law does not defend an official version of history that would need assistance from justice to resist the proofs accumulated by an opposing party. But in fighting against the self-destructing mechanism of the material proof of a crime that its perpetrators organized to protect their own memory, it protects its own reference point.

The Body as Absolute Criterion

The question of tolerance is curiously raised most often in our societies when the body is at stake. One thinks at once of the question of abortion, which is one of the most important debates in

Western society today, or of the Islamic veil, which has provoked passionate debates in France, the Jehovah's Witnesses's refusal of blood transfusions during surgical procedures, and more generally the infinite number of bioethical questions raised by a medicine that catches all schools of thought off guard, subjecting them to radically forbidden problems. There is an unquestionable consensus around the integrity of the body. Beliefs and behaviors are tolerated on the condition that they don't compromise the integrity of the body. More precisely yet, it is with regard to the body of the child that the liveliest debates take place today. In a liberal government, the difficulties that cannot be resolved with regard to adults are done so through children. The issue of the Islamic veil has caused debates on integration according to the French model well beyond the case of young girls. The child constitutes the stake of power all the more since it is to him that the perpetuation of beliefs will be passed on, and since he cannot express an opinion himself. Never do the differences between cultures appear more clearly than in the places that respective cultures reserve for children. How many parents – foreign or not – are surprised if not shocked by the place justice grants to the words of children today.

Such an entrance into the debate does not perhaps favor tolerance. First of all, emotion gives bad council. Secondly, antagonism is not broached as such, but by its consequences. In a way one enters through the exit. It is always when lacking one of its aspects that people will argue a cause. The concentration on the body allows one to skip over deep motivations, failing to draw ties with a certain relationship with the world. Our societies have a hard time believing in beliefs, in imagining that they can inspire behaviors so heavy with consequences. While religious tolerance focuses – perhaps too much so – on ideas, today people think only of the body, without considering what conception of the world it sets into play. In short, this entrance suggests an exit on the same level, that is, physical or psychological health. People are more likely to seek assistance from scientific expertise than from philosophical reflection, and rather than Voltaire or Pierre Bayle, it is Professor Montagnier or François Dolto who are sought out.

The question of excision concentrates all these difficulties. It embodies the modern figure of the intolerable. We are far from the

days when World Health Organization, considered that "ritualis-
tic operations ... are the result of social and cultural beliefs"[20] and
therefore not within its jurisdiction. The practice is not broached
as a whole, but only through the visible, that is, the marking of the
body (would it be conceivable to discuss Western surgical practices without linking them to our concept of science?). It should be
possible to contest this approach without immediately incurring
the accusation of defending such practices. Would it be intolerable
to denounce this diabolicalness? The debate is indeed paralyzed
by the phantasms it awakens. Emotion brought to the extreme –
what could be worse than the cold-blooded mutilation of a child –
paralyzes any debate and hence encumbers any evolution through
pedagogy and conviction. In highlighting the obviously intolerable mutilation while concealing, for example, that it is first and
foremost a celebration organized in the hope of integrating the
child, one precludes any internal evolution of the ritual. Without
taking the time to listen, for example, one does not learn that in
certain countries the women themselves draw the practice toward
its end by limiting themselves to a simple prick, beading up a
drop of blood, retaining only the social ceremony or the identifying benefit to the child.

The body remains the last stake of people who no longer believe
in anything. This sacralization of the body is perhaps not without
ties to the de-symbolization of current society and the challenging
of beliefs in a general way. In the face of this consensus, devoid of
any organizing principles, the legislator is thus condemned to
limit himself to the *vital*, that is, to life pure and simple, held up as
a value in itself, or more precisely, as a new subject of political
concern. Biological life becomes the sole common denominator
among men to whom the democratic consensus has given the
freedom to be themselves, that is, different, but who can only
remain so on the condition that they keep something in common.
This is what Phillippe Raynaud calls the *new hygienics*, a "new
configuration in which the norm presents itself, independently of
all moralizing injunctions of the 'traditional' or 'moralizing' type,
as the simple result of the taking into account of self-evident public interests and values that can be universalized: the forbidden
arises from an objectively discernable danger."[21] Nevertheless, it

is the living that forms consensus. Life is the lowest common denominator among living men.

Will *bios* win out over *logos*? Certainly not, but it is its condition. This consensus on bodily integrity is indicative of the sole substantial principle of democracy: respect for the human individual. This principle, which is higher than all others, federates the consensus on evil and that which ties it to the body. "We have," writes Durkheim, "a cult of personal dignity that, like all other cults, has its own superstitions. It is thus a common faith, if you will, in as much as it is shared by the community, but it is individual in its object."[22] The body is protected as a site of consciousness, the seat of general and therefore sovereign will. The capable man is both the condition of social intervention but also its ultimate goal. This is because without a subject of the law, without citizens, there is no general will, no deliberation and no space for collective action, no State. Is not the most intolerable aspect of excision not mutilation but the fact that it is practiced on someone who cannot consent freely? Would one have the same repulsion with regard to an adult woman freely accepting this rite (as is the case with young immigrants re-entering the country)? Probably not, since the intolerable in the excision of a child is more like the rape of a consciousness than a body.

Mediators and Interpreters

What distinguishes all forms of tolerance from its principle enemies, indifference and relativism, is the constant effort it demands.[23] "Tolerance," writes Joël Roman, "is not the reign of indifference, but rather the reign of democracy, not a moral posturing, but rather a civic contract, which requires not psychological predispositions but confidence in procedure and institutions." We find the same concern in Ricœur, who writes that "when one assesses what the State of law signifies by contrast, the theological void it implies, one should not be surprised at the lateness of its appearance in history, nor by its incompleteness. This is why I introduced it as the ideal type of modern liberal government. To tell the truth, it's a *veritable abstention of power* which is needed here."[24]

How does this task present itself in concrete terms today? The difficulties no longer involve traditional examples, such as that of the parliamentary debate, which loses importance without, however, disappearing. The most crucial questions of democratic coexistence are decided by judges – notably constitutional judges – or by mediators or other experts on life sciences, given the importance of the body. Conflicts of values are thus resolved in our societies by the two least democratic branches of power, that is, by the administrative and judiciary powers. The attempt sketched here better to focus the modifications with which democracy colors the question of tolerance makes no theoretical claim, but has as its goal to outline the parameters of this new democratic task. This entails new actors, the learning of a new language and the institution of new sites.

What prevents religious tolerance from serving as a reference in our contemporary debates is that it speaks the language of morality and not that of the law, which has become the new grammar of democratic relationships. The juridical rises as common culture declines. The invasion of the law confuses registers and risks eventually suffocating all other points of view. No longer daring to speak of morality, the great principles of the Republic – Human Rights or the Constitution – are invoked. But this mixture of many political, moral and historical discourses into a single juridical language is dangerous. First of all it invites people to learn to speak the language of law in order to formulate political problems arising from democratic coexistence. The learning of this language is all the more pressing as it is the only way to block the new imperialism of jurists that is taking shape today. This will be better combated by recognizing its virtues and possible uses rather than by confronting it directly.

Hence the concern to give the floor back to its recipients, that is, the citizens. More than needing experts, the citizens need *interpreters*, not only to understand others, foreigners, but also to understand themselves. A multicultural society needs both linguistic and cultural interpreters. This is why one sees cultural mediators entering the children's court in Paris. Neither social workers nor jurists, they perform the task of helping the judge understand a given situation. Probably their work should be expanded, their role clarified and a status created for these new interpreters, who make it possible to decipher a meaning, an invisible link that no longer has currency in our modern societies, in practices that initially shock us. But the society also needs interpreters for itself, to make a link with its invisible self. The democratic society that claims to be transparent is in reality more and more opaque. The visibility of every moment reinforced by the media diverts and often blinds it. It understands foreign cultures better than its own actions. This is because in a democracy, perhaps more than in any other society, recourse to the invisible is essential. For all societies, as for man himself, the beginning is as mysterious as the end. This is why it must be celebrated with a creation myth, epic, fable, or myth. What then is the social contract, the republican pact, if not a fictitious moment of democracy? What is deliberation if not the clarifying of common goals?

What does the close examination of the solutions that the jurists bring to major conflicts reveal? If one discounts the larger questions – most often solved by the constitutional process that calls for binary responses (authorization or prohibition of abortion, for example), one notices that justice often resorts to internal negotiation, discussion of each individual case. What demonstrates that the practice of law is less antidemocratic than it seems at first glance is that justice is more for than against the participation of the citizen. Indeed, justice proposes more the displacement than the resolution of the sites of confrontation. For example, one juridical determination specifies that authorizations of absence for religious celebrations not given as holidays may be granted by a departmental head on condition that this absence "remain compatible with the normal functioning of a department." In another case pertaining to a request for exemption from scholastic obligations for the Sabbath, the Council of State, in a conciliatory frame of mind, decided that such exemptions were possible on condition that they remain compatible with the tasks inherent to the studies and respect for the public order of the establishment. Who in fact will make such decisions? Don't we in fact run the risk of being at the mercy of the whims of a departmental head if the procedures to be decided upon are not formulated conjointly? These solutions are only really satisfying if at the same time one considers the conditions of a true democracy in the institutions. Why not generalize the council chambers to make such decisions collectively? This practice is spreading in schools, hospitals and numerous institutions. One thinks of the committees on medical ethics in each hospital, the school board and why not, one day, collective decisions in penal establishments as well? This is how tomorrow's democracy will evolve, by offering everyone, children, parents, religious authorities, and citizens, to participate in the respect for tolerance on a daily basis. This is no longer a matter concerning interpreters, but *mediators*. All that we have described no longer concerns a centralized, dramatized debate, settled by far-off representatives, but rather a proliferation of small interrelated deliberations to be sent to a judge in cases of disagreement, who in turn will send them back to the interested parties. This is the form assumed today in the struggle forever required by the idea of tolerance as a virtue to be rescued from the automatic turning back on oneself, from indifference, from skeptical relativism ... or from its diversion by the jurists!

Notes

1. G. Waterlot, *Tolérance et modernité, généalogie et destin d'un concept,* unpubl. thesis, Lille, 1996.
2. Ibid., p. 8, n. 11.
3. This issue, which is still alive in France, raises the question of whether or not public schools may accept young muslim girls who come to class wearing the Islamic veil.
4. P. Dumouchel, "La Tolérance n'est pas le pluralisme," in: *Esprit,* 8/9 (1996), p. 175, n. 17.
5. Ibid., p. 181, n. 28.
6. On this question see the debate between D. Moynihan and C. Krauthammer in: *Le Débat,* 81 (1994).
7. On this subject see A. Garapon and D. Salas, *La République pénalisée,* Paris, 1996.
8. D. Lochak, "For intérieur et liberté de conscience," in: *Le for intérieur,* Paris, 1995, p. 200.
9. P. Ricœur, "Tolérance, intolérance, intolérable," in: *Lectures I,* Paris, 1991, p. 300.
10. Ibid., p. 296.
11. In this case, judges had to decide on the stopping of a respirator for a young victim of the collapse of a stadium in Sheffield, England.
12. In this case, the executive powers asked the supreme court to take a stand on the ownership of a mosque constructed over an ancient Hindu temple and

which had become, over the course of the years, a focal point of communal tensions in India.

13. Regarding the contested presence of the crucifix in Bavarian state schools.
14. P. Raynaud, "La Démocratie saisie par le droit," in: *Le Débat*, 87 (1995).
15. Which is to say, the extreme right of nationalistic and xenophobic France.
16. This conflict set into opposition a Catholic congregation wishing to erect a convent on the edge of the former concentration camp and provoked the wrath of Jewish groups.
17. Jurists distinguish between instantaneous infractions whose effects are immediately spent, such as murder, and continual violations which are repeated over and over, such as the possession of stolen goods.
18. J. Altounian, "Porter le nom d'ancêtres clandestins (trauma d'un génocide 'secret' chez les descendants des survivants arméniens)," in: *Violence et politique*, Paris, 1995, p. 155.
19. Klaus Barbie, head of the Gestapo in Lyon during World War II, was condemned for crimes against humanity in a trial 40 years after the fact (1987).
20. *Le Monde*, 22 August 1996.
21. P. Raynaud, "L'Hygiénisme contemporain et l'écologie: une permissivité répressive," in: *La Nature en politique ou l'enjeu philosophique de l'écologie*, Paris, 1993, pp. 138-49.
22. E. Durkheim, *De la division du travail social*, Paris, 1978, p. 48.
23. See G. Waterlot (note 1 above), pp. 39-41, 548.
24. P. Ricœur (note 9 above), p. 301, with my emphasis.

The International Community and Limitations of Sovereignty

Mario Bettati

Public international law is entirely a product of consensualism. The State, which is both the legislator and subject of the world juridical order, only agrees to comply with exterior norms to the extent that it approves of their content. Any treaty, in its contractual nature; any custom, in its consensual nature; any decision of an international organization, in its ability to be enforced, expresses the agreement of the concerned States, whether on a case by case or global basis. National sovereignty is in this way safeguarded. Nothing can be imposed on those who govern without their consent. Indeed, until the middle of the twentieth century, States had succeeded in juridically protecting their free will; or more precisely, their free willfulness. International law required no behavioral norms, and no obligation of tolerance, in regard to a State's own nationals.

The shock of World War II, the trauma inflicted by Nazi atrocities, and the progress of democratic ideals were instrumental in the adoption of the first set of international judicial principles aimed at limiting the prerogatives of national sovereignty. The international community won the right to intervene in the internal affairs of a State when the aim was disinterested. The defense of human rights inspired increasing efforts by diplomats and nongovernmental organizations to bring an end to all forms of intolerable behavior. To this day, however, most of these efforts remain verbal. An embattled State must account for its actions, must allow inspections, must on occasion suffer condemnation and punishment. Yet this last is usually of a rather gentle nature. Punishment is either political, as in the case of the United Nations, or judicial, notably by the Council of Europe or the Organization of

American States. These sentences are rarely accompanied by an instrument for their forced implementation. Moreover, the few cases of economic embargo have proven to be both ineffective and controversial. Nevertheless, intolerance has come up against a dogged foe: the international community now possesses a universal conscience. It opposes oppression and tyranny everywhere. However, because lacking a permanent public force to guarantee that its decisions be carried out, the international community has not managed to stamp out all manifestations of injustice. Still, its constant pressure is gradually breaking down the fortress of national sovereignty.

A second set of principles has been produced as a result of the activities of humanitarian organizations. Their actions "without borders" bring them face to face with human suffering. These organizations, physically present on the territory of a State – with or without its knowledge, sometimes with its tacit approval but rarely with its formal authorization – break established rules and work without juridical constraints. Their intervention, which is sometimes illegal, is nevertheless legitimate. The justice of their cause reveals and underscores the gap between law and morality. The indignation felt by many is caused by the fact that the former always lags behind the latter. Work has been done to reduce this troubling gap, although much remains to be done. The right to intervene in order to lend material support to those in danger is in its infancy. It has been called the "right of humanitarian intervention."[1] Such intervention irritates and it bothers – especially the dictators. However, lacking a permanent military force, the international community finds it difficult to decide on what course of action to take when it determines – in the face of intolerance and the intolerable – that it must do something to overcome the obstacles preventing help from reaching the victims of an intolerable situation.

The Development of Non-Material Limitations on Sovereignty

For a long time international law regarded the nationals of a sovereign State to be that State's goods. In a sense, its property. The state had exclusive jurisdiction and free reign over its nationals. A telling example of this principle is contained in the story of Bernheim. In 1933 this German Jew went to the League of Nations, seeking condemnation of Nazi crimes committed against his people. However, convinced by the arguments of the German representative, this Genevan body turned down his request. Here's what this representative said: "Ladies and gentlemen, a man's home is his castle. We are a sovereign State: nothing that this individual has said concerns you. We will do what we want with our Socialists, our pacifists, our Jews; we will not accept the control of either humanity or the League of Nations."[2] The man who expressed this opinion went by the name of Joseph Goebbels ... and his logic was in harmony with the international law of the period. It was Bernheim who was in conflict with reigning principals and beliefs. His suit was dismissed. There was no limitation in law to absolute sovereignty. Nor to intolerance. The path was clear for Hitler.

The cowardice of the League of Nations and its member states was concealed behind the façade provided by the principle of non-interference, resolutely upheld by fundamentalist jurists. René Cassin, who was not of their number, made mention of this sinister episode in a speech he gave to the General Assembly of the United Nations in Paris in December 1948, the subject of which was to vote the Universal Declaration of Human Rights: "Thus the first great crime went unpunished; this crime against German human rights became a crime against the human rights of peoples of all nations, and soon after that the supreme crime, universal war, was committed." In a famous article written for *Nouveaux Cahiers*, and published in April 1940, Cassin explained that the Covenant of the League of Nations "did not dare to challenge directly the principal of national sovereignty: two direct consequences of this decision are the rights to war and neutrality ."[3] By defending the principal of sovereignty, the Leviathan states lend mutual support to one another in the battle against what Hitler, in *Mein Kamf,* called "the subversive power" of individual criticism. Sovereignty thus serves as a mutual guarantee for the torturers.

The victory of the allies was expected to bring about a decisive change in the concept of sovereignty as well as the creation of an organization capable of defending human rights. The occasion of the drafting of the United Nations' charter added to that hope. However, it proved to be another lost opportunity. The San Francisco text makes only brief mention of the idea of basic rights. It says that these rights should be "promoted," "developed," "encouraged" and "fostered": a rather feeble resolve in the face of the Holocaust. There was nothing obligatory here, nothing compulsory, nothing authorizing an outside authority to investigate incipient, existent, or flourishing barbarism. Nor was there a mechanism by which mass cruelty, brutality, or sheer horror could be immediately stopped. From Yalta to San Francisco, it was but the sovereigns themselves who gathered. Could they have been expected to organize anything other than a mechanism for guaranteeing their mutual security? As Professor Jean Combacau wrote, "I am in my own house, they belong to me."[4]

Following the second world war, the international community adopted the principle of defending human being *as* human beings. It did so by addressing them not as members of a group or citizens of a State but as individuals. It was believed that one way of averting the resurgence of Nazi-like atrocities was to have the world's most representative body proclaim certain basic, universally valid norms: this organization was the General Assembly of the United Nations. Gradually, under the leadership of intellectuals and the pressure of public opinion, individual States agreed to acknowledge the right of the international community to monitor the living conditions of the world's citizens; next came a ban on certain kinds of behavior incompatible with a few basic democratic principles. Still later the member states agreed to prohibit the subjugation of entire peoples to colonial rule and to promote the liberation of States still subject to it. Henceforth, sovereignty was to be exercised within the framework of international law, the role of which was to limit the arbitrary exercise of power. The idea of democratic intervention – which is a consequence of the universality of human rights – both authorized the international community to demand that governments they justify their treatment of their citizens and allowed for the collection of information in this regard.

One needs only to observe the proceedings at the United Nations to realize that the claim of sovereignty no longer permits governments to do whatever they want without having to answer – at least politically or diplomatically – for their actions. Each autumn, entire sessions of the Third Commission of the General Assembly are taken up with discussions of basic freedoms. The Commission on Human Rights devotes long hours to this subject too. And so does the Subcommision on Minorities. While public opinion may not be much informed on the nature of the discussions that go on here, international institutions react to the demands of governments and non-governmental agencies. Although this kind of intervention is political, ethical, and verbal rather than material in nature, it nevertheless provides a solid base of support for opposition and dissident figures. Its focus is more on the ethical than judicial plane.

Universality and Ethical Limitations on Sovereignty

In trying to overcome the obstacle of sovereignty, the international community began by making moral and political pronouncements aimed at disconnecting, at least in part, the individual from the State of which he or she was a national. The goal, however, was not to strip the individual of his or her nationality. Nationality was ascribed as a human right and the powers of those who govern were accepted as an indispensable element in social organization. The aim was rather to establish the individual as an object of law, existing in part outside the control of the State; in a sense, to internationalize the individual in order to legitimate the right of other States to act in the individual's best interest. "They are mine," says the state: "They are also ours," says the United Nations, as part of humanity's common patrimony.

This *universality* of human values demands that each individual feel compelled to protect those values, even when the threat to them occurs beyond one's own national borders. This is the foundation of René Cassin's Universal Declaration of Human Rights, which he co-authored with Eleanor Roosevelt. Here, for the first time, the principle of non-interference was called into question in the name of another, still more fundamental axiom: the individual's belonging to the human race or the transnational identity of the human person. According to Cassin, the characteristic "universal," which the Declaration substituted for "international" on 10 December 1948, was necessary in order "to protect people everywhere, of all faiths and viewpoints, without regard to the nature of the State or the other human groups amongst whom they live."[5] He also insisted that there should be no distinction between citizens of one's own country and foreigners: "We are not afraid to assert that there exists territorial universality. France, when it worked on the Universal Declaration, never thought for a moment that these basic rights could be denied to any human beings, no matter where they lived, and especially not to people living in countries without self-government."[6] Addressing these people directly, he said: "Before your countries are allowed admission to the United Nations, you too should enjoy fundamental liberties and rights. Our work was not for ourselves alone: we have fought for all humanity."

At the same, in the convention adopted the day before the Universal Declaration itself, genocide was declared a "crime against human rights, whether committed in time of peace or war. It is a crime against humanity. The individual nations are committed to its prevention and elimination."[7] Anxious to underscore even more strongly the ecumenicalism of his text, René Cassin addressed the world's leaders at the Sorbonne, in February 1949, in the following terms: "It is up to us," he said, "to see to it that the Universal Declaration of Human Rights becomes the Universal Declaration of the citizens of the world."[8] The international community thus laid the groundwork for an ethical limitation on sovereignty: a common conception of the individual and of his or her basic rights. The successes of decolonization, the victories of democracy, and the fall of the Berlin Wall seemed to make progress inevitable. However, our facile hopes in this regard were soon dashed.

Has the principle of the *universality* of human rights been definitively accepted in the international arena? If the arguments heard in the General Assembly of the United Nations in 1994 over the death penalty are any indication, then the signs are not good. The question, which was raised at the request of the Italian parliament, was a source of embarrassment for more than one United Nations' delegation. The abolitionists [9] found themselves opposed by many countries – notably the Islamic nations – asserting that the United Nations had no legitimate right to take up the matter: the death penalty was a matter of divine law and could be neither debated nor challenged. Obviously, the proponents of this position advanced notions of sovereignty and cultural specificity in order to reject the Italian proposal. Singapore, which has become the spearhead for the rejection of universalistic notions, declared itself "unalterably opposed to countries which try to impose their views on other member states of the United Nations. In some of the world's countries capital punishment is a necessary ingredient for the maintenance of public order. This question can not be decided on the basis of consensus."[10] Mr. Chew Tai Soo added: "the particular situation of each country must be taken into account and the right of each country to promulgate its own laws respected. In Singapore, for instance, it is thanks to the death penalty that the general interests of society itself are protected." As for Malaysia, it rejected the abolitionist position on the death penalty because "it attempts to impose values that not all consider universal, without considering the efforts made by those States that have the courage to protect their societies."[11] Thus national sovereignty has many happy days ahead of it.

Samuel Huntington, a professor at Harvard University, has pointed to the clash of civilizations within the international arena.[12] He emphasizes that concepts such as individualism, liberalism, constitutionalism, human rights, equality, liberty, the rule of law, democracy, and separation of church and state carry very little weight in Islamic, Confucian, Hindu, Buddhist, and Orthodox cultures. "The attempts to transmit these kinds of ideas provoke a counter-reaction against what is perceived as 'the imperialism of human rights' which they resist by a reaffirmation of indigenous values."[13] He believes that the notion of "universal civilization" is a Western idea, completely foreign to the particularism of the majority of Asian societies.

The reason that these claims have been called the "Singapore" solution is, as is well known, related to the practices of Singapore's leaders, especially its former Prime Minister, Lee Kwan Yew, and to the arguments advanced by two high-ranking officials in the Ministry of Foreign Affairs, Kishor Mahbubani and B. Kausikan.[14] In order to re-legitimate the idea of unlimited sovereignty, they counter the United Nations' universalistic claims with three arguments. Their first is that, for Asia and generally for the countries of the South, democracy follows economic development. This latter thus has priority, requiring a transitional period characterized by a strong government. Their emphasis on economic development makes efficiency in this area – not the promotion of democratic values – the standard by which a government is judged. Finally, by trying impose the Western concept of democracy on the countries of southern Asia, the West alienates them and behaves like "human rights' imperialists."

Does this mean that these countries acknowledge no norms? Do they deny universal validity to all of the basic principles affirmed in the Universal Declaration of Human Rights of 1948, or in subsequent international agreements on human rights (such as the accords of 1966)? The answer to these questions must be nuanced. The aim of the Singapore School is less to reject these principles altogether than to reduce the number of those considered sacrosanct. The Singaporians assert that the core of authentically universal human rights is considerably smaller than the Westerners claim. Although they accept the international consensus in regard to the prohibition of genocide, torture, and political assassinations, they do not go much beyond that. Kausikan writes: "The Universal Declaration of Human Rights is not the ten commandments that Moses brought down from the mountain: it was created by mortal men. International norms must be developed bearing in mind that they are conceived differently throughout the world." The Malaysian Prime Minster, Datuk Mahathir, an ideological, political, and geographical neighbor of Kausikan, declared in 1994: "We value our independence very much. We do not want to be dictated to as to how we should interpret various values in this country, including, of course, human rights and democracy."[15]

Normative Limitations and the Right to Monitor

"In any case, humanity's right to monitor relations between the State and individual must be affirmed." These were René Cassin's words as published in the *Journal de Genève* on 10 December, 1947. And premonitory they were, spoken exactly a year to the day before the adoption of the Universal Declaration of Human Rights.

Originally, state sovereignty had been limited by the concept of natural law. The word sovereignty, in its usual acceptation, was defined as 'supreme authority.' Jean Bodin speaks of *"summa potestas."*[16] This expands the powers of the State on two levels. First, internally, it expresses the state's authority over its territory and its absolute dominion over its nationals. For Bodin, sovereignty is the highest degree of power. Externally, it implies the absence of any kind of subordination to, or dependence on, foreign states. In law, all states are equal and sovereign, which makes possible the most perfect manifestation of the independence of each state: in the absence of all outside interference, a state is free to constitute itself as it wishes. As the Vienna School of jurists has shown, inherent in this very idea of the state is a conception of sovereignty that tends to provide the state with the capacity to exercise unlimited authority in all areas of human activity.

Is this supreme and unconditional power unlimited? The founder of the theory of sovereignty himself admits that the sovereign authority is limited by the natural law that governs the community of nations. His immediate successors approached the possibility of limiting this power in two distinct ways: either by subordination to a norm outside the State, the authority of which is recognized as superior; or by a voluntarily accepted self-limitation. Contemporary thinking on the subject, which authorizes exterior intervention in defense of the individual, is to some extent rooted in one or the other of these two restrictions. Jean Bodin emphasizes that supreme power is subordinate to divine law, human rights and fundamentals laws. As for the theologians, such as Vitoria: while asserting that sovereign power "is subordinate to no power of the same order and substance,"[17] they at the same time formulate a doctrine compatible with the coexistence of other States and with their own conception of a universal community of States subordinate to law. For his part, Grotius believed that the nature of supreme power was such that its "acts are independent of any other higher power and can therefore be overruled by no human authority."[18] But he later specifies that sovereignty is no less so sovereign when it conforms to "natural and divine law, and even to the idea of the rights of people, to which all the Princes are indebted."[19]

Following this era, with the appearance of the modern State, a host of new theories were proposed to justify the subordination of sovereignty to international law. The German Jellinek saw it as an example of "self-limitation by the State," a voluntary reduction of the extent of its power in relation to other States or to its own citizens. A kind of partial hari-kari or self-amputation of the characteristics of the state or of its sovereign powers.

For the Austrian Kelsen, state sovereignty is limited to the cluster of powers granted it by its own domestic and the international legal orders. These powers are part of a pyramidal system of rules in which each norm derives its legitimacy from its subordination to the next higher one: at the summit of this structure is the fundamental norm. Kelsen's disciples at the normativist school of Vienna, in particular Verdross, made it clear that, because international norms are hierarchically superior to internal ones, only the subordination of the latter to the former guarantees the legitimacy of a state's power. In short, internal sovereignty is subordinate to international law. Moreover, the internal sovereign cannot act arbitrarily since it is obliged to respect this higher norm. Finally, the Frenchman Georges Scelle, who considered human rights to be in the first instance individual rights, asserts that sovereignty does not exist in society since power is always limited by the resistance of the social body. Only law can force its will on all members of society, "only Law is sovereign."[20]

Sovereignty was next limited by the concept of human rights. The international community adopted a series of juridical texts in which various inventories of basic rights of the human person were catalogued. The most important of these texts, in an international sense, were the following: the accord of 9 December, 1948 on the prevention and elimination of the crime of genocide; the Universal Declaration of Human Rights of 10 December 1948; the international accords on human rights of 16 December 1966; the agreements outlawing torture of 1984; and the accords on children's rights of 1989. Among the regional agreements the most important are: the European Assembly of 4 November 1950; the Interamerican pact of 27 November 1969; the Helsinki accord of 1975; the African Charter of Human and Peoples' Rights of 1981; and the Universal Islamic Declaration of Human Rights of 1981.

Common to all these texts is a concept of the human individual, and his or her rights and security, outside of any subordinate relation to a State; the aim of all these various texts is to protect human beings as such. This is the same principle on which human rights' organizations, such as Amnesty International and Human Rights Watch, have developed their strategies of non-material intervention in support of all prisoners of conscience who have neither used nor advocated the use of violence; in support of fair and speedy trials for political prisoners; in support of the abolition of the death penalty, torture and all other forms of inhuman treatment; and in support of the abolition of all extra-judicial executions and forced disappearances.

Using these juridical texts, the Assembly General of the United Nations, as well as its Commission on Human Rights and the Subcommission on Minorities, have launched investigations into various Communist and Fascist dictatorships. Their discussions, and the pressures subsequently applied to these regimes, have played an important role in promoting the return toward – and in some cases, complete embrace of – democracy and tolerance.

By granting the world legal system the right to monitor and intervene, the international community has made it possible to carry out protective and inspectional interventions without – as was the case in the past – treating them as infractions of international law. Based on human rights' treaties, sovereignty is henceforth limited by the rights of other subjects of law: foreign States to begin with, followed by international organizations and individuals. Michel Virally has observed: "the wall of State separating domestic from international law, and internal affairs from international relations, has been breached. International law now reaches to the very heart of the sanctuary of sovereignty; to the relations between the State and its nationals, and, more generally, to the apparatus of the State and the general population."[21]

Effective protection of basic human rights requires specific mechanisms. As of now, other states may use the traditional means of diplomatic pressure, such as political and economic sanctions (the refusal or suspension of a nation's right to participate in an international organization, and embargoes and boycotts) to ensure the respect of individual rights. In 1970, the International Court of Justice found that the prohibition of genocide, as well as the laws concerning human rights, are *erga omnes*[22] obligations, and that the protection of these rights "are the concern of all States."[23] Several other texts, anticipating the possibility of requests between states, created judicial mechanisms to make legal intervention possible in the affairs of states. That same year, the Economic and Social Council of the United Nations, in a now famous resolution (number 1503), granted to the United Nations the right to investigate individual complaints. The agreements of 1966, and the first voluntary protocol annexed to them, which concerned civil and political rights, required the ratifying states periodically to submit reports on the protection of human rights in their respective countries and to answer questions relative to complaints made by individuals or non-governmental organizations. The United Nations' convention against torture, adopted in 1984, created a similar committee, empowered to carry out on-site investigations.

Regional mechanisms also exist, permitting individuals who have been victims of human rights' violations to turn for assistance to supranational authorities, notably The European Court and the Interamerican Court of Human Rights. The European Convention on the Prevention of Torture, adopted in 1987, created a committee to which it granted a general and almost unlimited right to carry out on-site investigations into human rights' violations among its member states (article 2).

Having seen of some of its domestic prerogatives limited by international law in the name of the universality of the human person, national sovereignty has also been subject to external intervention in the name of the ties that henceforth link democracy and law to life, human rights, and peace-keeping. Sovereignty is now subject to material limitations that can include the use of force.

The Emergence of Material Limitations
on Sovereignty

Often, and even frequently in our own day, the international community, using the principle of non-interference in the internal affairs of a foreign state as its justification, failed to come to the aid of endangered individuals. Instead it was satisfied with simple verbal condemnation of a country's massive human rights' violations.

It is true that international and domestic law fundamentally differ on this matter. For example, the French penal code has for a long time contained articles punishing individuals who do not come to the aid of a person unable to protect him or herself. *A contrario*, this obligation of solidarity is deduced by the responsibility of each individual to come to the aid of anyone nearby. It is sanctioned by article 223-226 of the French penal code, which states: "Whoever could have prevented, by his immediate action, and without danger to him or herself or a third party, the commission of a crime or an attack against the physical integrity of a person, but voluntarily decides not to do so, is subject to a penalty of five years in prison and a fine of 5,000 francs. Equally punishable by the same penalties is the action of an individual who voluntarily refuses to come to the assistance of a person in danger, and who could have, without danger to him or herself or a third party, have personally, or by calling for help, come to the endangered person's assistance." The courts clearly defined the constituent elements of this obligation of assistance. There was nothing similar to it in international law. It thus made sense to fill this gap.

Humanitarian organizations had shown the way with their "borderless" approach. It was now necessary to legalize their practice. It also made sense to assure effective support and protection for individual victims of intolerance: this required allowing the use of force, although only when necessary and under strictly defined circumstances.

Limiting Sovereignty by Permitting Free Access to Victims

The adoption, at France's urging, of resolution 43/131 by the General Assembly of the United Nations marked a new stage in the challenge to absolutism. The measure can be summarized in the following terms: in cases of catastrophe the necessity of rapid response mandates *free access to victims*, particularly by international humanitarian organizations.

Free access requires neither abdication nor alteration of the principle of sovereignty, only a simple modification of the way it operates. This is why the right to free access is radically different from all forms of imperialism, even the most innocuous. Not only the purpose of the intervention, but its geographical range and time frame, must be strictly limited and clearly defined. In most cases, the primary aim is to be able to create – in emergency situations – a kind of umbilical cord, like the highway that linked West Berlin to West Germany before the demise of the wall.

It was this goal that suggested to France the idea of applying a generally accepted category of marine law to the kinds of problems faced by groups seeking free access to victims of catastrophes. Thus, according to international law, the State has complete sovereignty not only over its air space but its territorial waters, to the bottom of the sea. This ancient rule of the sea was codified by the United Nations' convention on maritime law, which was adopted in 1982. Article 17 of this convention asserts that ships of all States, that is to say foreign ships, have the *right to make inoffensive passage* over the waters of another nation. This passage must be rapid and continuous. However, the right to stop and drop anchor is guaranteed "in the event of forces beyond the ship's control or in the case of distress, or when aid is being brought to persons, ships, or aircraft in danger or distress."[24]

The General assembly adopted the French initiative on 14 December 1990. This is resolution number 45/100. As described in the United Nations' Secretary General's report of October 1990, it calls for the establishment of humanitarian corridors, through which assistance could be brought.[25] The part that describes these humanitarian corridors largely echoes the French proposals regarding the establishment of the right of free passage through buffer zones. These kinds of zones have been put in place in the ex-Yugoslavia, Sudan, northern Iraq and Rwanda ... However, armed factions – composed of regular or irregular troops – have in some cases shut them down. It is in these cases that the question of whether or not the international community should resort to – or authorize – the use of force to re-open these corridors or directly bring assistance to the victims has been posed.

Limiting Sovereignty by the Use of International Force

This limitation is obviously the one that the authorities concerned have the most difficulty in accepting. Indeed, except in cases of legitimate self-defense, it has for a long time been in dispute. The Security Council's legal foundation for authorizing this kind of intervention merits some attention.

Since the fall of the Berlin Wall the majority of conflicts with which the Security Council has had to deal concern internal conflicts and civil wars. However, the United Nations' Charter explicitly prohibits the organization from intervening in internal affairs that "essentially relate to the national authority of a State" (article 2 \7). It was therefore necessary to find a way around this constitutional obstacle. And a way was found. Since 1991 the Security Council has on three occasions directly carried out – or authorized – intervention in the internal affairs of a state.

The first step in this process was the decision that certain particularly grave humanitarian situations justified the use of peacekeeping forces (the blue helmets) to insure the delivery of aid. The Security Council made this decision using a certain amount of juridical improvisation. Indeed the member states justified themselves less by attributing to the Security Council formal authority in this matter than by referring to the unanimity of its members (permanent or non-permanent) in regard to the interpretation of the law. As is known, the novelty of their approach consisted in asserting that violations of human rights constitute a threat to peace. By so doing, the Security Council could justify armed intervention on the basis of Chapter VII of the United Nations' Charter. Thus, on 5 April 1991, in regard to the vote on resolution 688 dealing with the Kurdish question, Turkey made it clear that it had called for a meeting of the Security Council "because of the grave threats to regional peace and security represented by the tragic events in Iraq."[26] It should be noted that Turkey, although directly affected by the influx of refugees onto its territory, did not call for the Council's action simply because its territorial borders had been crossed by the Kurds; instead Turkey argued that the Council was justified in acting by Iraq's *internal repression*, which *in itself* constituted a threat to peace.[27] This was exactly the Council's argument. In 1993, in the face of massive human suffering in Bosnia, the Council used similar logic to authorize, by resolution 770, the use of *all necessary means* to insure the delivery of humanitarian aid to Bosnia, which implicitly presupposed the use of military might if circumstances required it. Venezuela observed at the time: "This is the first time that the Security Council has made a decision of this kind in order to insure the delivery of humanitarian aid to a country." With resolution 776, it extended this protection to convoys of freed detainees.

The next step was the Council's decision to authorize the use of force in the case of civil wars: here the aim was to organize *operations for the imposition of peace.* After the failure of the UNOSOM I operation in Somalia, a second resolution (number 814), called UNOSOM II, was adopted on 26 March 1993, authorizing the use of force on the basis of Chapter VII of the Charter of the United Nations. The resolution called for the disarming of the Somalian militias. Force was used on several occasions; in particular in response to the attack of 5 June 1993, in which twenty-five soldiers were killed. Air and land operations were carried out. Arms' depots were destroyed between June 12 and 14. Thanks to a second wave of operations, carried out between June 17 and 25, many of the militias' installations and caches of heavy arms were destroyed. On 4 February 1994, the Security Council expanded the mandate of the UNOSOM II forces, calling on them to "protect the essential infrastructure, the principal ports and airports, as well as guarantee that crucial transportation links remain open for the safe delivery of humanitarian aid and reconstruction assistance." The resulting improvement in the security situation permitted humanitarian organizations to work once more under favorable conditions. The most important result of this activity was the elimination of famine.[28] Of course it is true that the withdrawal of the UNOSOM II forces allowed the warlords to reassert themselves: everyone agrees that the operation was a political failure. However, it was a humanitarian success. The members of the Security Council recognized this almost unanimously on 4 November 1994. Its balance sheet was quite different than the one drawn up by the media and opinion makers. Here are a few, randomly chosen, statements made by various delegations: "Although the intervention of non-governmental agencies, humanitarian organizations, and the UNOSOM forces was belated, it succeeded, in spite of extremely difficult conditions, in containing and ultimately reducing, in large measure, this humanitarian disaster" (Kenya). "The humanitarian objective was fundamentally accomplished. Somalia is no longer threatened with famine. Death by starvation no longer threatens an entire people" (New Zealand).

"All information coming out of Somalia is agreed on one point: the humanitarian situation is quite satisfactory" (Djibouti). "The United Nations did not fail in its task in Somalia" (Nigeria). "The humanitarian success of UNOSOM cannot be discounted" (Pakistan). "The worst aspects of Somalia's humanitarian crisis have been overcome" (Argentina).[29] This coincidence of views contrasts sharply with popular opinion on the subject.[30]

Finally, the United Nations' has authorized certain member states to use force when the scope of a civil war goes beyond the military means at the U.N.'s disposal. In such cases, the UN, so to speak, subcontracts the armed intervention to those governments willing to carry it out. The 1991 operation *Provide Comfort* in Kurdistan, which the U.N. simply tolerated, nevertheless put an end to the exodus of the civilian population and made it possible to protect then. The operation *Restore Hope*, carried out in Somalia in 1992 and 1993, drew forces from nineteen different nations before being taken over by the U.N., under UNOSOM II. Operation *Turquoise* in Rwanda in 1994 put an end to a genocidal war. Operation *Support Democracy* in Haiti in 1994 succeeded in overturning a military dictatorship and restoring the legitimately elected government to power.

To date, the Security Council's authorization of armed intervention has only occurred on the territories of states in the midst of civil war. In each case, the international community granted itself the right to limit a State's sovereignty in the name of the defense of fundamental values: the right to deliver humanitarian aid, the defense of human rights, and the re-establishment of democracy. This constitutes undeniable progress. However, at the same time, the Security Council has remained passive or timid in the face of other human rights' disasters: for example, in Chechnya and Burundi ... Sovereignty is still limited selectively; and the great powers, armed with their veto, are not prepared to apply these limitations to their client states. Additionally, the previous operations have been extremely expensive. Not all the bills have been paid. The financial crisis at the United Nation is cause for concern. History will judge its extent.

Notes

1. See M. Bettati, *Le Droit d'ingérence, mutation de l'ordre international*, Paris, 1996.
2. R. Cassin, "Comment protéger les droits de l'homme," delivered on 13 February 1970 and quoted in: M. Agi, *De l'Idée d'universalité comme fondatrice du concept des droits de l'homme d'après la vie et l'oeuvre de René Cassin*, Antibes, 1980, p. 354.
3. Repr. in: *La Pensée et l'action*, Paris, 1972, pp. 63-71.
4. J. Combacau, "Souveraineté et non-ingérence," in: M. Bettati, B. Kouchner et al., *Le Devoir d'ingérence*, Paris, 1987, pp. 230-1.
5. In: *Cahiers de l'Alliance Israélite Universelle*, 120 (1958), p. 97.
6. See Assemblée générale, Documents officiels, troisième session, 9 décembre 1948, première partie.
7. See Article 1 of the Convention for the prevention of genocide, adopted by the General Assembly of the U.N. in Paris on 9 December 1948.
8. R. Cassin (note 2 above), p. 217.
9. The signatories of the letter demanding that the question be put on the agenda of the Third Commission of the General Assembly were: Andorra, Austria, Bolivia, Cape Verdian Islands, Cambodia, Costa Rica, Croatia, Cyprus, Dominican Republic, Equador, Gambia, Greece, Guinea-Bissau, Haiti, Honduras, Italy, Malta, Marshall Islands, Mexico, Micronesia, Monaco, Namibia, Nicaragua, Norway, Panama, Paraguay, Portugal, Romania, Saint-Marin, Salomon Islands, Sweden, Uruguay, Vanuatu, and Venezuela.
10. United Nations, Press Release AG/SHC/149, 16 November 1994, p. 13.
11. Ibid., p. 14.
12. S. P. Huntington, "The Clash of Civilizations?" in: *Foreign Affairs*, Fall 1993, pp. 22-49. Other European authors have written in the same vein, see R.-J. Dupuy, "Les Ambiguitiés de l'universalisme," in: *Mélanges Virally*, Paris, 1991, pp. 273-79; L.C. green, "Universality and Modern International Law," in: I. Taberner and M. J. Pelaez (eds.), *Ciencia Politica comparada y derecho y economia en las relaciones internacionales estudios en homenaje a Ferran Valls*, Vol. XXII, Barcelona, 1993, pp. 6763-91.
13. S. P. Huntington (note 12 above), pp. 40-1. On the overall problem of the universality of human rights see C. M. Cerna, "Universality of Human Rights in Different Socio-Cultural Contexts," in: *Human Rights Quarterly*, Vol. 16, No. 4 (November 1994), pp. 740-53; C. Makhlouf Obermeyer, "A Cross-Cultural Perspective on Reproductive Rights," in: Ibid., Vol. 17, No. 3 (May 1995), pp. 366-82; J. M. Peek, "Buddhism, Human Rights and the Japanese State," in: Ibid., Vol. 17, No. 4 (November 1995), pp. 527-41; H. Bielefeldt, "Muslim Voices in the Human Rights Debate," in: Ibid., pp. 587-617.
14. K. Mahbubani, "The Dangers of Decadence. What the Rest Can Teach the West," in: *Foreign Affairs*, September/October 1993, p. 10; B. Kausikan, "Asia's Different Standard," in: *Foreign Policy*, 92 (1993), pp. 24-31.
15. Quoted in: *Far Eastern Economic Review*, 7 April 1994.
16. J. Bodin, *Les Six Livres de la République* (1583). See also the essay by G. Mairet in: F. Chatelet, O. Duhamel and E. Pisier (eds.), *Dictionnaire des oeuvres politiques*, Paris, 1986.
17. Quoted by A. Truyol Serra, "Souveraineté," in: *Vocabulaire fondamental du droit* (Archives de philosophie du droit), Vol. 35, Paris, 1990, p. 317.

18. H. Grotius, *Le Droit de la guerre et de la paix*, Amsterdam 1729, Vol. I, p. 150.
19. Ibid., p. 178.
20. G. Scelle, *Précis de droit des gens*, Paris, 1932, p. 12.
21. M. Virally, "Panorama du droit international contemporain. Cours général de droit international public, in: *Recueil des Cours de l'Académie de droit international de la Haye*, Vol. V, The Hague, 1983, p. 124; A. Cassese, "La Valeur actuelle des droits de l'homme," in: *Mélanges René-Jean Dupuy. Humanité et droit international*, Paris 1991, pp. 65-75; G. Cohen-Jonathan, "Responsibilité pour atteinte aux droits de l'homme," in: Société française pour le droit international (colloque du Mans), *La Responsabilité dans le système international*, Paris, pp. 101-35; idem, "La Protection internationale des droits de l'homme dans le cadre des organisations régionales," in: *La Documentation française. Documents d'études. Droit International Public*, No. 3.05 (July 1989); idem, "La Protection internationale des droits de l'homme dans le cadre des organisations universelles," in: Ibid., No. 3.06 (April 1990); idem, *La Convention européenne des droits de l'homme*, Paris-Aix-Marseille, 1989; P.-M. Dupuy, "L'Individu et le droit internationale," in: *Archives de philosophie de droit. Droit international*, 32 (1987), pp. 119-33; B. Mangan, "Protecting Human Rights in National Emergencies. Shortcomings in the European System and Proposal for Reform," in: *Human Rights Quarterly*, Vol. 10, No. 3 (1988), pp. 372-94; Th. Meron, *Human Rights in International Strife. Their International Protection*, Cambridge, 1987; B.G. Ramcharan, "Strategies for the International Protection of Human Rights in the 1990s," in: *Human Rights Quarterly*, Vol. 13, No. 2 (May 1991), pp. 155-69; M. Reisman, "Sovereignty and Human Rights in Contemporary International Law," in: *American Journal of International Law*, Vol. 84, No. 3 (July 1990), pp. 866-76.
22. Latin expression meaning "with regard to all." In international law it refers to the absolute opposability of a rule, even with regard to third states.
23. Cours international de justice, *Recueil des Arrêts*, 1970, p. 32.
24. Article 18.
25. Official Documents of the U.N. General Assembly, 45th Session, A/45/587, 27 October 1990, Paragraph 26.
26. Minutes of the U.N. Security Council, 2982nd Session (1991), pp. 3-5.
27. Curiously, no-one was alarmed about the threat to peace posed by the Turkish army when - four years later - it moved across the border to crack down on the PKK in Kurdistan.
28. See the Report by the Secretary General, 17 August 1993 (S/26317), Paragraph 45.
29. Minutes of the U.N. Security Council, 3447th Session (4 November 1994), pp. 2-14.
30. See R. Brauman, *Le Crime humanitaire: Somalie*, Paris, 1993; M. Klen, "L'Enfer somalien," in: *Défense nationale*, February 1993, pp. 135-43; S. Smith, *Somalie. La Guerre perdue de l'humanitaire*, Paris, 1993; J. Stevenson, "Hope Restored in Somalia?" in: *Foreign Policy*, No. 91 (Fall 1993), pp. 138-72.

Interlude
Several Ephemeral Thoughts on Tolerance and Peace

Yehudi Menuhin

The fluctuating dynamism of tolerance must be taken into account in order to understand the nature of peace. Attraction and repulsion, which influence our external and internal worlds in the manner of heavenly bodies, are the forces at work here.

Every living being is equipped with a certain inner ambiance and potential for growth, which is linked to genetic, environmental and educational factors. We are all subject to forces that can increase our vulnerability to sicknesses of mind and emotion. If this were not the case, how could we account for these terrifying and pathetic outbursts of hatred, these longings for murder, self-destruction and madness, these desires to torture and cause suffering to one's self and others for no reason?

It is not only the abuse of privileges, but the abuse of prejudices, that goes largely unpunished. We lack the determination required to reform our attitudes toward tolerance. In fact, we tolerate many intolerable things and perversely pour out our helpless intolerance on society's most vulnerable. And it is often our leaders, skilled at turning the dangerous energies of intolerance on others, who push us to act in this way.

Before we begin to criticize, moralize, and accuse, let us for the moment investigate the intolerable and the limits of tolerance. The intolerant play an important role in this world. They always have. How much better it could be if only they would play a constructive role, maturing and joining with tolerance in order to strengthen it, not annihilate it.

I hail the heavenly rebel. And yet even the heavenly rebel must temper his action with prudence and wisdom, with philosophy, which often expresses itself in symbols and parables alone. Often these rebels must hide, doing their work in the shadows while the dictators are glorified by marching soldiers who sober up in drinking binges, and in so doing remain tolerable to their Masters.

Humans are essentially dreamers, possessed by memory and imagination. More than anything, they are creators and, consequently, destroyers, whose sublime efficacy is revealed above all in the creation in art and life of human beings themselves, followed by their destruction.

Some Spiritual Sources of Tolerance

Paul Ricœur

Tolerance has its arguments, both in morality and in law. It also has its sources, not only in the sense of the origins from which it springs, but also in the sense of that which actuates it and gives it life, that which encourages it and sanctions it – profoundly. Religions take part of these sources, but also take part of this reflexive aspect of ethics that puts into play the final legitimation, the ultimate justification of the norms of our public and private actions. It is with respect to this recourse to the ultimate that religion and ethics intersect without becoming one. Yet it is also in this recourse to the ultimate that one and the other greatly face the danger of temptation. This is particularly the case with religion. It is indeed not enough to simply say that it is the political use of religion that is to blame, and not religion as such, in the long and unfinished history of religious intolerance. We must trace the source of the temptation of intolerance to the very heart of the certainty of religious faith. Any belief, as soon as it defines itself in relation – a relation of any kind, whether of distance or proximity, of alterity or fusion – to an absolute, must be on guard against its own penchant for intolerance. It is not enough, in an opposite sense of the preceding warning, to rely on the critical resources borrowed from sources outside of religion: it is at that same heart of certainty of all religious faith that we must seek the reason for the conviction that it is unjust to look to impose on adherents of other religions, on agnostics and atheists, the truth as it is admitted in good faith by the community of believers of one or another religious confession.

The three articles that follow, each in its own way, contribute to this work of self-criticism of absolute convictions. The first seeks in a model, and simultaneously in a great historical figure, Gandhi, the prophetic invitation to surpass, from the heart of religion itself, from all religions, the urge towards intolerance. The author of the second article looks at the founding texts of one of the world's great monotheistic religions, that is Islam, for the ultimate answer to the tendencies of religion in general. Finally, the third article tries to find, in the convergence of religious teachings at the ethical level, the fundamental motivation of an education of tolerance on a planetary scale.

Mahatma Gandhi
The Prophet of Tolerance

Ramin Jahanbegloo

Mahatma Gandhi was one of those rare human beings who was simultaneously a theoretician and practitioner of tolerance. Gandhi was possessed of an inner conviction that tolerance was not only one of the key words of his own century but of centuries still to come. It is in this sense that his ideas on non-violence and tolerance transcend the context of India itself, even though these ideas were initially conceived in relation to India's independence and future. Nevertheless, in spite of what may seem obvious, it is no mere truism to state that Gandhi would not have been Gandhi had he not been born Indian. We say this in order to underscore that Gandhi's concept of tolerance was rooted in Indian culture.

At the same time, even having developed – at an early stage – an acute awareness of the nature of Indian culture, of its strengths and of its weaknesses, Gandhi also sought support for his ideas of tolerance and non-violence in other cultures.

In all likelihood, it was Leo Tolstoy who exerted the greatest influence on the development of Gandhi's thought. The dialogue between the two men began from Gandhi's side, with a letter dated the first of October 1909, prompted by his reading of Tolstoy's *The Kingdom of God is Within You*. Their correspondence, the primary theme of which was the relationship between non-violence and love, continued until Tolstoy's death in November 1910. "In truth," Tolstoy wrote, "non-resistance is nothing other than the teaching of love, undistorted by false interpretations. The fact that love, i.e. the striving of human souls towards unity and the activity resulting from such striving, is the highest and only law of human life is felt and known by every person in the depth of his soul - as we see it most clearly in children – known and felt by him until he is ensnared by the false teachings of the world. This law has been proclaimed by all the world's sages, Indian, Chinese, Greek and Roman. And I think it has been very clearly expressed by Christ when he says that ' it alone contains the Law and the prophets.'[1] "

Tolstoy's book served both to awaken Gandhi's conscience and provide him with a solid foundation for a reinterpretation of his readings of the Bhagavad-Gita and the Gospels (in particular, the Sermon on the Mount). In 1932 he wrote: "Tolstoy reinforced my faith in something that at the time I only had a vague understanding of ... I worked on the foundations laid down by Tolstoy. Like a good student, I added to what my teacher had left me."[2]

It was thus in this way that the idea of love, as one of the foundations of the religion of Christ and of Tolstoy's philosophy, became the crux of Gandhi's thinking on tolerance. It was an influence that helped Gandhi to more clearly formulate his idea of God-as-Truth. In an interview with Pierre Ceresole, held in Lausanne in January 1932, Gandhi says: "I agree with those who say that God is love. Within me he is love and truth."[3]

Love and truth are the two basic ideas underpinning Gandhi's thinking on tolerance. They are both different from, and complementary to, each other. Truth represents the aim of life. However, love provides the only means by which this truth can be reached and known. This is so because, "he who believes in non-violence and love is filled with hope; and hope gives rise to love, and love gives rise to courage and faith."[4]

Thus, for Gandhi, the experience of truth is revealed in acts of love and tolerance. These acts make no claim to absolute truth. Rather, from this point of view, truth is revealed to each of us in a different way. Truth cannot therefore be approached without a preliminary act of tolerance in regard to the other's truth. "The golden rule," Gandhi writes, "is mutual tolerance, because we never all have the same ideas and we will never see the Truth except in fragments and from different points of view."[5]

In other words, if the key to the spiritual life of all human beings is the search for the Truth, then each of us is free to choose his or her own way. What does it matter if we take different and separate paths, since all of them converge on the same point? The direct and logical consequence of this reasoning is to view all religions as flowing from a single and unique source: they are therefore equivalent. "I believe," Gandhi writes, "that there is but one religion in the world, a single one, but that it is a powerful tree with many branches ... And just as all the branches derive their sap from a single source, so do all the world's religions find their essence in a single stream, which is its source. Naturally, if there is but one religion, there is only one God; and God, who is one and complete, can not have many branches. He remains indivisible and indefinable; consequently, it can literally be said that He has as many names as there are persons on earth. It is unimportant what we name Him, He is one and the same, and there is no second."[6]

Gandhi asks us to respect the faith of others just as we do our own, because without such a spirit of openness there can be no search for the Truth. Moreover, as beings who are still at the stage of searching, we have not yet found the Truth in all its perfection and must therefore be conscious of the imperfections of our own faith. We must consequently respect the faith of others without being weak or indifferent to our own. Gandhi's tolerant attitude toward Christianity, Judaism, and Islam did not in any way affect his own loyalty to the doctrines of Hinduism. In an article dated 20 October, 1927, published in his newspaper *Young India*, Gandhi writes: " From my own experience I believe that Hinduism is the most tolerant of all religions ... Not being an exclusive religion, it offers to its believers not only the possibility of respecting other religions, but also of assimilating and admiring what is good about other faiths. Although non-violence is common to all religions, it finds its fullest expression and application in Hinduism."[7]

All the religions of the world are true, but they are also simultaneously imperfect, since perfection is an attribute exclusive to God. Yet Humanity, Gandhi tells us, can perfect its faith by cultivating tolerance for other faiths as part of its own religious practice. "Tolerance provides us with a power of spiritual penetration that is as far from fanaticism as is the North from the South Pole."[8] Here Gandhi makes use of the traditional Indian doctrine of tolerance, as expressed in its great spiritual texts, as for instance the Rig-Veda: " It is called Indra, Mitra, Varna, and also Gandhiarutman ... The real is one, even if it is known by different names."[9]

The Bhagavad-Gita is also quite clear on this point: "Even those who worship other gods worship me in their love for them ..."[10]

Gandhi's idea of tolerance thus aligns itself with a long tradition of Indian religious pluralism, beginning with Ashoka and continuing into the twentieth century with an important affirmation during the reign of the mogul emperor Akbar (1556-1605). It is therefore not a purely speculative tolerance but one that finds expression in secular experience. Gandhi himself lived this pluralist experience through the Jainist education he received in childhood. However, he came face to face with another problem, through his experiences in South Africa, that oriented him more and more towards the idea of tolerance as the only solution to uniting Hindus and Muslims. In an article dated the 26 August 1905 and published in *Indian Opinion*, Gandhi already mentions his desire for union: "It is a fact that greater tolerance between Muslims and Hindus is needed. Sometimes one is inclined to believe that there is a greater distance between these two communities than between East and West."[11]

In any event, Gandhi never had any illusions about the difficult nature of this problem. As a practicing Hindu he made a point of being seen as often as possible with Muslims; he even went so far as to ask other Hindus to learn Urdu in order to improve communication with India's Muslims. The central thrust of Gandhi's culture of tolerance thus found expression in his practice of non-violence, carried out in the midst of the murderous struggle between Hindus and Muslims.

Aware of the daunting nature of his task, Gandhi nevertheless practiced his technique of non-violence to the limit of his personal strength, engaging in open-ended fasts to put an end to the hostilities raging between the two communities. "My experiences in South Africa," he wrote, "convinced me that the question of unity between Hindus and Muslims would be the one to put my *ahisma* (principle of non-violence) most strongly to the test, and that this problem would also provide the greatest possible application of my experiences with *ahisma*."[12]

On 30 June, 1948, having just ended a period of fasting whose aim was to obtain better treatment of Muslims by Hindus, Gandhi was assassinated by a young Hindu fanatic who believed that the

Mahatma's discourse was dangerous to India's future. Before dying Gandhi had time to look at his assassin and to invoke the name of Ram, thereby introducing his assassin to the idea of tolerance. In this final act, the Mahatma expressed both his own truth and our own hope for a better tomorrow.

Notes

1. Quoted in: M. Semenoff, *Tolstoï et Gandhi*, Paris, 1958, pp. 42-3.
2. Quoted in: J. Herbert, *Ce que Gandhi a vraiment dit*, Marabout University, 1974, p. 73.
3. Quoted in: *Gandhi* (Collection Sup Philosophe), Paris, 1967, p. 24.
4. Ibid., p. 87.
5. Quoted in: J. Herbert (note 2 above), pp. 80-81.
6. Ibid., p. 51.
7. M. Gandhi, *Collected Works*, Vol. XXXV, Navijivan Trust, 1994, pp. 166-67.
8. Quoted in: J. Herbert (note 2 above), p. 52.
9. Quoted in: R. Balasubramanian, *Tolerance in Indian Culture*, Indian Council of Philosophical Research, 1992, p. 17.
10. Ibid., p. 18.
11. M. Gandhi (note 7 above).
12. Quoted in: J. Herbert (note 2 above), p. 114.

On Islamic Tolerance

Abdelwahab Bouhdiba

Why does one hear so much about tolerance today, when as little as a few decades ago it was considered an obsolete virtue, anachronistic and outstripped by the progress of our civilization? When a virtue is lacking we remember it most! Must we conclude from the emphasis placed on tolerance these last few years that we have entered an era of generalized mutual incomprehension? The conquests of the intellect; local, national and international juridical practices; education open to global issues; the intermixing of humanity that has never before "moved" so much under the combined effect of emigration; tourism and the developments in transportation and vast information exchanges served by efficient techniques that make communication one of the greatest benefits of our culture; all this could have led mankind into a surplus of exchanges on all levels, and better mutual appreciation leading to more tolerance.

Intolerance or the Dialectics of Contempt

And yet a kind of evil spirit has done its best to distort interpersonal and international relationships. Modernity, in no longer putting into contact people, communities and cultures but rather individuals and masses, has perhaps contributed – without anyone paying enough attention despite the many warning signs – to fashioning an unexpected human "landscape" that is arrogant and rude, leading us back to the worst moments of our history. The era of mechanized masses has developed a sort of universal contempt for the other: precocious children kill babies, the language of the bomb takes over the planet, State terrorism and just plain terrorism abandon themselves to an infernal one up-manship. In the end intolerance, coming to the fore of inter-human relationships on all levels, would appear to be the widespread cancer of our times. The mystery of the other, the taste for difference, the kindly and gracious attention to the things that make my brother my peer, that is, both "same" and "other," pale before a terribly negative vision. We have leapt right into the era of frantic reductivism. This appears in the basic abstractionism, on many levels, of our current life on this planet, whether we are speaking of great intellectual and philosophical "demands," great economic and commercial strategies of economic world powers and multinational *firms*, or the chaotic reactions that all this produces. We are steeped in monism: the monism of "unique" thought, televisual standardization of customs and taste, with all this crowned by the pseudo-new world order. And since contempt is essentially contemptible, contempt answers contempt in kind, and intolerance finds an un-hoped for function taking shape in many a gospel, many a political program or simple world vision ... This is a suicidal behavior that must be analyzed and if not brought to term, than at least curtailed.

In Praise of Difference

The problem of tolerance, of course, presents itself in its original terms, with due consideration being given to the nature of our world and questions of context. But its founding principles are themselves permanent, universal and indefeasible. More specifically, the Islamic culture to which I belong is one of the cultures that suffers the most from the rise in violence and intolerance even though essentially it bears a great message whose explanation, development and practice benefit us all. Islam was and still is a great school of tolerance, and if we are convinced that it will remain so for a long time, we are just as convinced of the need for a prolonged effort to avoid destructive deviations and mad excesses. As a religion, it takes its place among other beliefs. As a culture, it emphasizes the value of difference. As a civilization, it integrates the other, all others, as such.[1] I know that in France in particular, from Voltaire to Claude Lévi-Strauss at least, and among other important writers, there has been a long tradition that has propagated the false and pernicious idea of Islam as the epicenter of fanaticism and intolerance.[2] In fact, in our effort to promote the spirit of tolerance, the principles written at the heart of the message of Islam today serve, as they did yesterday, as a precious tool.

One cannot broach the subject of Islam without returning to its sources. This recovery of origins is all the more necessary since the inexistence of a church or canonical institution invested with the mission of having the last word on what is or is not Islamic leaves the believer perpetually face to face with the founding texts: the Koran and the *sunna*, the words and deeds of the messenger of Islam. This face-to-face situation is double- edged: it can authenticate my choices and attitudes through a permanent return to the sources, but it also leaves the door open to meddlers who assume the right to interpret things unilaterally and to legislate, without appeal, in my stead. Only through a salutary return to the sacred texts will we be able to put an end to all the fallacious interpretations coming from within as much as from without.

In short, a major declaration runs through the whole Koran: the diversity of the world, and men and the essential affirmation of this diversity is not a chance or accident, but is part of God's design. It cannot therefore be reduced or even minimized. On the contrary, it must be received as a sign of moral, intellectual and cultural plenty. "Men, We created you as males and females, We made you into peoples and tribes in view of your mutual understanding. The most worthy of you in the eyes of God is he who acts with the most piety" (Koran IL 13). The hierarchy among men is based neither on gender, race, language, religion or wealth. Only piety creates a hierarchy among men in the eyes of God. Furthermore, the Koran insists: "Among the signs in the creation of the heavens and the earth is your differentiation into men of different colors and languages" (Koran XXX 22). The more the other is different from me, the more he bears witness to the divine desire to create a world based on differences. An entire philosophy of difference has been unanimously developed by Muslim specialists throughout the ages, countries and cultures embracing Islam. Based on this vision that not only accepts diversity, but also guarantees its legitimacy in the essential, founding and governing choice made by God himself, openness and tolerance are imposed on every Muslim. To be Muslim is to accept all the manifestations of difference, to feel a great joy in them and embrace them with awe. The Koran is an encomium of diversity, and Muslim theology is first of all a theology of difference. The unfolding of life, the blossoming of the individual, the affirmation of the richness of the world come from a single diversifying vein. "Travel," orders the Koran, "go around the world!" (XVI 36), (XXIX 20, XXX 43), "Explore the byways" (LXVII 15). The pluralism of landscapes, nature and human societies is a striking illustration of a pluralism that is generalized and consistent with itself. The resulting divergences are not a flaw in the diamond, and still less a defect in workmanship. They must be regarded within the framework of a concept of difference that Islamic cultures – in both successive and diverse ways – themselves strove to develop in a continuous manner. To be open to the other is a pressing duty. Muslim prayer is aimed at discovering a field of new exchanges every minute. There is no solipsism in Islam. The worst calamity is to be reduced to a prolonged moral, intellectual and social isolation. The Prophet said that a lone traveler is like a devil. Straightaway, then, and for important reasons, openness to the other is the normal condition of the Muslim, and it is in this sense that Islamic fraternity encompasses, it goes without saying in passing, the totality of the human race. Islamic education is an education in the other and in difference. One must assume this difference in going beyond oneself. The movement that projects me toward the other is in fact a movement that brings me closer to God and projects me into His creation. In this sense, the standardization of man is not only a contradiction in terms, but like a sin against creation. Specificity is a trait linked to an inalienable character of the personality whatever the level, as much for individuals as for communities. Irreducible to one another, we all bear witness to the universal, which creates in each of us an autonomy bearing a freedom that shapes our daily lives in an unique and exemplary fashion. By extension, accepting oneself as a source of creativity and freedom implies accepting the other with the same prerogatives. Taking responsibility for oneself involves a double movement: going beyond myself and opening myself to the other. The quest for self and the quest for the other flow from the same source and are part of the same movement.

Reciprocal Amenities

The Arab word for tolerance *(tasâmuh)*, like all the derivations of the sixth semantic form *(tafâ ala)*, means both reciprocity and self-control. *Tasâmuh* means reciprocal amenity. Tolerance, in this case, is the duty to overcome one's own faith and convictions, to go beyond the object of one's own belief, in order to place oneself as if in parentheses, welcoming the other. Furthermore it is a *sine qua non* condition to make him accept me. "Be tolerant, and people will be tolerant of you," recommends Mohammed, for an essential feature of tolerance is being reciprocal and universal. Much more than this, in Islam, tolerance is raised to the status of a divine virtue. For God Himself tolerates my failings and my faults. God makes a "strict rule of clemency," says the Koran (VI 12). He accepts my errors and sins. He absolves them, for He is all pardon and mercy. Tolerance between men is but the human projection of the same attitude that God adopts in His relationships with His servants.

Mohammed never ceased, in this pedagogy of mutual tolerance, insisting on the reciprocity of consciousnesses that creates another reciprocity on the next level, with regard to God Himself. "Be as tolerant toward My servants as God may be toward them."[3] One might say that tolerance is an absolute virtue cut from the same cloth and of the same essence, whether on the level of the Supreme Being or that of daily realities. It is tolerance that allows man, in situating himself in a position of reciprocity with respect to his peers, to strive toward ontological dignity. My spirit of tolerance makes me worthy of God's mercy. At the same time it reminds me of my humble origins. "All of you come from Adam and Adam himself came from clay": such is the last message Mohammed delivered on his Farewell pilgrimage just before his death.[4] The spirit of tolerance, without at all leading me to renounce my own faith, implies a little more modesty, a little more humility. I have the right to be proud of myself, my culture and my world view. But what saves me and authenticates this personality is my awareness that these are merely sources of pride among so many others, which are valid for me as well as for them, and that in the last analysis all men have issued from the same race and originated in the same element.

Freedom as Basis for Tolerance

Islamic tolerance does not stop halfway. Consistent with itself, it is taken all the way. Religious in essence as in practice, it is by nature open to other religions. The unity of faith calls for going beyond one's own religion in order to accept the other with his own specificities. Since the famous works of Louis Massignon, the West is better acquainted with the fundamental unity of Abrahamic faith; Judaism and Christianity are authentic religions *(hanîf)*, whose meanings were simply altered during the course of history. Later the tradition added Buddhism and Hinduism by analogy. While Islam is proclaimed the true religion, it is so not through rupture, but through continuity with all the other manifestations of faith that preceded it. The perception of original diversity mentioned above implies the plurality of religions and beliefs, good or bad, including disbelief. "If your God had so desired, every last one of the earth's inhabitants would have faith. Is it therefore your task to force faith upon another?" (Koran X 55). The call of Mohammed is but a reminder of eternal faith that excludes all forms of coercion. "You are here only to remember. You are not a bearer of oppression" (Koran LXXXVIII 21/22). Hence the sole technique of diffusion of Islam is persuasion: "Call others to the path of your God, with wisdom and fine speech. Discuss with others according to the best paths" (Koran XVI 125). The founding texts of Islam are steeped with this will to not do violence to the consciences of others. Truth is self-evident – faith being its own foundation – and it is fallacious and contrary to the divine order to seek to impose one's own truths on another. "Say: truth comes from God, let he who so desires believe and he who so desires disbelieve" (Koran XVIII 29). Or again, "Whosoever heads toward the right path does so only for himself; he who wanders off does so against his own interests alone. And I am not your tutor" (Koran X 108). One cannot better highlight the autonomous nature of a faith that does not suffer any intervention from outside the person, believer or not, not even on the part of the Messenger of God, *a fortiori* from no other man whatsoever. Hence the great Koranic principle: "No constraints in matters of religion. The true path is very different from delusion" (Koran II 2). Freedom of consciousness is therefore found right within the Koranic program. From it tolerance issues from the start, and intolerance is designated as a cardinal sin. The maxim *lâ ikrâha fildîni* (no constraints in matters of religion) has been very salutary over the centuries. How many lives were spared when in the middle of wars, conflicts and pogroms in which the Muslim societies, like so many others, were the theaters, did one man, emerging from the crowd, armed with these four words, intervene to remind people of the Koranic message and reverse the course of events? Mehrez Ibn Khalaf[5] saved the Jews in Tunis in the tenth century, and the Emir Abdelkader the Christians in Damascus in the twelfth century. So many others were the active witnesses of this constant and unique Islamic tolerance, which reserves the right to believe or not to the individual consciousness and assures every man the right to live free and secure within Muslim society, whose most pressing duty is "to protect his conscience, life, honor and goods" according to the famous principle that the jurists inscribed at the head of the true Islamic *châri'a*.

This amenity of the appropriate behavior with regard to the other is not limited to the religious sphere. The principle of tolerance is spread by the Koran through the ensemble of our inter-subjective relationships and is raised to the status of universal principle in our interpersonal relationships. "Deflect a bad deed with a better one, and he who opposed you in mutual enmity will become like a close ally" (Koran XII 34). Here it is as if a wager were placed on human nature being inherently good, and hostility but a passing accident. "It is possible that God create an affection between you and those with whom you are hostile. God is all capability, all pardon, and all mercy" (Koran IX 8/9). In the same verse – and in the same context – the Koran sets the rules/limits to maintain with the enemy. "God does not forbid you to observe, with regard to those who are not fighting you because of your faith and have not driven you from your own homes, the normal rules of piety and equity with regard to your peers. God forbids you only to make pacts with those who fight you because of your faith, have expelled you from your own homes or who have decided to do so" (Koran IX 8/9). In fact there is much more: the nature of the Islamic faith itself is based on this wager on man, even one's adversary, and from this coextensive hope for humanity as a whole. Only they who have no faith can despair of a peer since "they despair of the afterlife or the dwellers of the tomb" *(ibid)*. In these conditions, tolerance is a veritable hymn to creation. It issues from the awe of the believing consciousness before the diversity of the divine work that is an infinite and open profusion. There is no need to reduce this diversity in order to feel oneself more secure. On the contrary, allowing oneself to be carried along by its exploration (mental, intellectual, physical ...) produces a joy and a priceless peace. This peace with oneself is the basis for peace with others and with the world. Such polycentrism flows from the transcendent unity of God, manifested in the diversity of His work. Tolerance is based on this mutual "pardon" which will never have any meaning if the believer does not first apprehend himself as a person capable of surpassing and "transcending" himself.

The Thresholds of Tolerance

Free conviction is the basis of the freedom of conviction of others. I could not deny my peer's conviction without ruining my own. My freedom is nurtured by his freedom, and his freedom is nurtured by mine. In matters of faith, my conviction justifies itself to the exact extent that freedom of conscience is an unconditional universal. The *tasâmuh*, reciprocal inter-amenity, can only be fully and positively played out within the context of this reciprocal ethics of conviction. It is the common denominator of all faith, which is only as essentially good as the exact extent to which it does not close itself in upon itself and does not mask egotistical and closed passions. Faith must be tolerant, or it ceases to be faith.

Does this mutual character of tolerance imply limits? Is my pardon unconditional? Many, in Islam and elsewhere, have raised the question of the limits of tolerance. Can one accept everything in the name of tolerance? Doesn't a tolerance that accepts everything, and thus anything, including its opposite, intolerance, destroy itself? Only the thresholds of tolerance can allow tolerance to play its role.

Concretely, moreover, the harshness of history projects me into the aleatory and risky sphere of the measuring of ethics and the responsibilities of city life. And, in fact, while it is important forcefully to reaffirm the profound principles of Islam, it is just as important to see how they have "functioned" in daily life. The Koranic vision of ethical pluralism and the diversity of the ways leading to truth is one of the strong points of Arab philosophy. The *Traité décisif* (decisive treaty) of Averroès on the relationships between reason and faith, as well as the Appendix *(dhamîma)*, present a version that has not aged at all. Truth is one, but it can be reached by multiple paths, of which Revelation and Reason are the most important. The monism of truth, by reason of its universality, joins with the pluralism of methods and access routes to truth that are but the result of the diversity of human cultures. It is on the level of this diversity that the scope of our responsibilities unfolds, based on our abilities to distinguish the true from the false, good from evil, the licit from the illicit. On this level, the idea of norms relates to another analysis of "tolerance," conceived not only as a recognition of a principle of freedom granted to the other to believe or disbelieve in what he thinks necessary to follow by choice, but as a "limit" to that which is acceptable in the historical game of the relationships governing people and communities. Hence tolerance takes on a practical aspect and designates the "threshold" of what is acceptable by all, inside a social system as well as outside it. In this way tolerance takes on the guise of a consensus. From this perspective, the concept of *had* was and still is central in Islamic law *(fiq)*, and it designates the point at which the action of an historical subject that exceeds or violates a certain norm leads to rupture, provokes exclusion and thereby becomes liable to punitive sanction. Everything, in fact, has a limit, except the clemency of God, which sets no limit on its own tolerance, but assigns one to human behavior. Let us note once and for all that we are no longer dealing with an issue of faith, but rather a very earthbound one, concerning the "commerce" of men, the *mu'âmalât*, that is, the social consequences of our acts. It is in this sense, and this sense alone, that we can speak of more or less tolerant Muslim societies, that is, those ready to accept a "deviant" "charge" in their midst, which they accommodate or, contrariwise, considerably subjugate if their cohesion, for example, finds itself threatened. The *fiq*, from this point of view, has functioned like a gigantic machine for saying what is licit *(halâl)* and what is illicit *(harâm)*, as a result of the concrete conditions of our acts. In Europe, ever since Pascal's *Provinciales* (Provincials), casuistry has had very bad press. In Islam, it is a very banal method of analysis of all the possible cases that makes it possible to determine, in a variable fashion, according to the authors, but also according to the rites, trends, moments and anthropological and sociological foundations of a group, what it is possible to allow as far as deviant behavior is concerned, on a daily basis. It is a veritable dialectic of the dualism *yusr/'usr* (easy/difficult) that regulates the game of tolerance and rigor and which is left up to the reasoned appreciation of the jurist. A twofold tendency has emerged and marked the history of mores in Islam: the first seeks to set the standard very high, and to allow a minimum of infractions; the second, more lax, minimizes the "immoral" character of our behavior and puts the maximum number of consciences at peace with themselves. The majority of so-called "orthodox" tendencies belong to the first, known as "the golden mean" *(wasat)*, but some belong to the second: Hambalite or Wahhabite moral rigor have played a very important role. In Islam and within the same basic community, either one closes one's eyes to all shortcomings or peccadilloes, or one opens them wide on any infraction, as minor as it may be. It would be fascinating to follow this culpabilizing and deculpabilizing dialectic in detail. But at the same time we would leave the domain of Doctrine for the more unstable one of habits and customs that are on a sociological plane rather than an ethical and even less a theological one. The definition as well as the assessment of deviance derive from the system of social prohibition destined to maintain social equilibrium and preserve collective cohesion.

Rigor and Tolerance

On this level of analysis, we should first of all note that the coexistence of contradictory opinions at the heart of one same collectivity is itself the sign of great tolerance, and within an Islamic community there are always many and diverging responses that are equally authoritative with regard to the same questions. This pluralism has proliferated all the more in Islamic lands, since they have never known a legitimized authority entitled to define what is orthodox and what is not in a unilateral and definitive way. The divergence of opinions is indeed considered to be an authentic sign of the clemency of God *(Alikhtiâf rahma)*. Within a single and same reading of Islamic ethics, there is always room to proceed with judicious modifications of the law to adjust it to any given situation, especially regarding penal matters. The *châri'a* is above all an ensemble of intentions *(maqâssid)* that are universal. But they are modified according to the situation. They aim above all to summon authorized people to equilibrium *(l'tidâl)*, harmony *(istiqâma)* and respect for juridical norms. But this effort, *ijtihad*, or better still, this struggle of self with self, is always an "invention" in the strongest sense of the word, that is, a radical will to understand concrete diversity through a summons, coming from within, which must take into account not only the nature of an action and its context, but also the profound intentionalities of the moral subject. Mohammed said that only intention creates the value of our acts *(innamâ al-amâlu bil-niyati)* and he adds that "to each man comes only that which he had the intention to do" *(li-kulli imri-in mâwa)*.

Islamic Tolerance and Objective Conditions

These fundamental conditions of tolerance are not mere abstractions. They were formulated in very real societies and subsequently brought up to date. Hence in order to understand what has taken place and is currently taking place, we should place the Islamic religious perspective within a reciprocity of outlook with the social framework and practical "needs" of the interested communities. Since Islam has embraced hundreds of cultures and its sway spread over more than fourteen centuries, one can find the most varied responses in this gigantic ensemble, ranging – with the help of surviving customs – from the most rigid closing of the system to the most unexpected laxity. One same Muslim society can walk a veritable tightrope, according to the circumstances, can be in turn (or at the same time) open and closed. In general, when Muslim peoples are on the defensive, when their very survival is threatened, a closing takes place; but when the threats lessen or disappear, openness reigns. Herein lies a precious anthropological grid that makes it possible to "read" Islamic social issues and the interpretation of all its nuances without necessarily bringing into discussion the foundation woven by the Koranic principles. It is also necessary to consider what Islamic tolerance was in reality, based on the facts. Undeniably – and this was noted by many historians from within as well as from without – the spirit of tolerance largely prevailed. And it is with regard to what we call the protection of minorities today that this appears most clearly. Of course there have always been barriers between Muslims and non-Muslims. But they were more or less permeable depending on the contingencies. What could be more normal? However, it was almost always juridical and social barriers that defined the communities, without the disparagement of any group, and which allowed them to coexist. We know today the extent to which these relationships of belonging play an essential role in the formation of a consciousness of self within any grouping. The collective identity is forged – we know all too well, and it is just as true for minority groups as it is for the majority – in its way of emerging from within each global society. The identifying feeling of belonging to a clan, a community or class, and the specificities that come into play, both within and without, are but the counterweight of the diversifications that operate within the whole. In Islam, this differentiation implies a respect for the other. We know just as well, however, that beyond the principles there is a margin of appreciation, valorization and devalorization which is revealed as much on the inside as on the outside, underscoring or masking such specificity. In any society, there are forces at work, both centrifugal and centripetal forces, structuring it, reinforcing its cohesion, underscoring or gluing together the dividing lines and nuances, even accentuating them. Any human grouping is always haunted by the passionate pursuit of founding values and distinctive signs that form the essence of its manner of being present in history. Need we further stress this dialectic between consciousnesses that define themselves by opposing each other and in opposing each other define themselves? And this is true on both sides of the "barriers," so that the "question" of "minorities" is just as much, if not more so, that of the "majority." Such a situation is completely within the order of things and plays itself out "objectively." But it is of utmost importance whether the perception of the other community be made in terms of recognition and respect, or, on the contrary, in terms of apprehension, fear and in the end oppression. We have already analyzed the meaning of the Islamic response, based on the spirit of tolerance and a humanistic concept of inter-individual and inter-community relationships. The status of "protection" *(dhimma)*, so misinterpreted, we must not forget, by Western rationality in the many twistings and violations of which it was the object during the course of history, keeps track of the interests of all and in particular the necessary peaceful coexistence based on the freedom of conscience. *Dhimma* means, *stricto sensu*, that the Muslim state is "responsible" for the security of minority groups integrated into the global society. Let us also remember that the relationships between minorities and majorities are of a political, and not a religious, order: Muslims can very well find themselves in the minority without that in the least changing the meaning of their faith or their beliefs. Once they become the majority, nothing changes in their obligations and duties with regard to other communities that live within them, which implies new duties and responsibilities. *Dhimma* is the "responsibility of the ensemble of those who have power," who must maintain coexistence and social cohesion and make the obligations and responsibilities of everyone respected, while taking into account their belonging to respective communities. Without going into detail, let us note that the status of *dhimma* does not give any particular group – minority or majority – the right to oppress other groups. The model was formerly given by the constitution of Medina, in the first year of Islam, which is the ultimate reference and a constant reminder of the obligations incumbent upon Muslims. Until his last breath Mohammad maintained this requirement, which his Farewell Sermon reiterated as a last reminder.

As a whole, such protective rules have been very efficacious in spite of the excesses that all the Oulemas have condemned and against which they struggled, not without success. Let us cite one of our best specialists, Claude Cahen:

> Inside the Muslim States, the situation of non-Muslims is (...) decent. Let us be neither idyllic or anachronistic. The *dhimmis* receive discriminatory treatment with regard to the *fisc*, inter-professional justice. There were (...) distinctions in their clothing (...); there was often a sort of aristocratic disdain on the part of the Muslims. Nevertheless, considering and comparing them with the other societies at the time, it does not appear that life was difficult for the non-Muslim faiths: those who lived on the borders and could have emigrated did not do so (...). Christian culture became established (...), Jewish culture expanded and the Muslim world was culturally and economically a paradise for the tenth and eleventh century Jews (...) *There was never any segregation, never the equivalent of our ghettos. There were at times, but rarely, for reasons related directly to the faith, instances of mob violence, but those in power intervened to maintain order, even at their own expense.*[6]

Intolerance for Reasons of Security and Intolerance Due to Resentment

Such judgments make the scandal experienced by the Muslim conscience today seem all the more extreme, as it witnesses the rise of dogmatism, fanaticism and terrorism within its own breast. We think we have sufficiently demonstrated how foreign these tendencies are to the letter and spirit of Islam. But it is not enough to show this, nor merely to denounce it. One must try and understand how we got to this point and work for the return of the spirit of tolerance that ennobles man. By demonstrating the "mechanisms" that come into play in our societies, we contribute to the illumination of this path. If we have emphasized the concern for identity that, by placing the accent on actual specificities, comes almost naturally to extreme positions, it was to show that so-called Islamic fundamentalism is first and foremost political. Indeed, it is almost exclusively so! Islam today does not operate within a void any more than classical Islam did, for it is growing in almost pathological conditions: people driven by the struggle for survival or victims of all types of injustices are only too open to overcompensation. When social contradictions, inequalities and exclusions are pushed to the breaking point, when men are denied in their own lands, they become easily open to all doctrines of salvation. This infernal spiral has been going on for a few centuries, almost without interruption. Many have thought for a moment that national liberation, the construction of a modern state, the fight against under-development or the building of a new society would really change the course of history. They have had to sing a different tune. New rules of the game have appeared in local and world relationships, which are far from favorable to them. The dictatorship often associated with that of a sole party, generalized extortion raised to the level of administrative management, back-room Socialism held up as a universal panacea, the ambiguity of countries secured by experts in the politics of "double standards," and the unconditioned and unconditional support of the interests of only the dominant groups here and there, all this has lead the Muslim peoples from defeat to defeat, to the ruin of their moral forces. Is one surprised that so many peoples are waiting, and that today almost all are on the defensive? Are they not seeking identifying references? What could be more natural for them, at this point, to seek themselves in Islamic culture? This culture has a great need to be renewed in the sense of the openness that once appeared essential to us, but which does not always come with a wave of the hand. Things are more serious still: the intolerance and fanaticism that have developed dangerously around us these last years do not merely bear witness to a desire for an identifying withdrawal into the self. When it is mixed with a search for a scapegoat, who will answer for our defeats and humiliations? Our statesmen, our intellectuals, the West, have all in turn been designated as those to strike out against and deny! Intolerance, here, is no longer on the order of an identity-securing mechanism, but pure and simple resentment. Intolerance is but the cement of bad conscience walled up in its own certitudes, but basically unsure of itself. It is the grimace of fanaticism lurking in the darkness of ignorance and moral barrenness. Thanks to a detestable historical, social and economic climate reigning among Islamic peoples, this resentment is so deep that it succeeds in touching some of the most venerable institutions. Hence it is all the more urgent to do homage to our great sages, who knew so well how to assume the heritage of Islam in adapting it to modernity. Sheikh Shaltut, Tahar Ben Achour, Abdelaziz Kamel and so many others all revealed the true tolerant face of Islam.

To resolve a question so serious as that of Islamic tolerance, I would like to say that we must go straight to its core: freedom. Divine transcendence gives it its ontological foundation. The sense of human experience gives it its anthropological dimension. The responsibility of historical agents gives it its concrete content. Finally, tolerance proves itself and is embraced in concrete frameworks in spite of their contingencies, but also by reason of the great promises inherent to life. The sense of struggle between tolerance and fanaticism indeed takes place, both yesterday and today, in the full recognition of freedom in all its complexity, authenticity, but also in the cruel ambiguity of its insertion in the course of history. And if today the struggle for tolerance is once again an issue, it is in fact because modernity rises a bit everywhere like a challenge to freedom. It is here, at the heart of public freedoms, that the true debate takes place and where the truly decisive struggles will unfold.

Notes

1. The literature on this is extensive in Arabic, English, and French. Here it is sufficient to refer to the relevant chapters in UNESCO's *Individu et société en islam*, Paris, 1994.
2. Voltaire's *Mahomet ou le fanatisme* is written in the same vein as his *Traité sur la tolérance* (1762). He focuses on the fanaticism of all religions and all ideologies. The lack of information at the time, the desire to be effective and escape censorship, led Voltaire to "blacken" Mohammed. But surprisingly Voltaire's real struggle against intolerance is the same as that led by the real Mohammed. The thoughts of Claude Lévi-Strauss at the end of *Tristes Tropiques* (p. 429 in the first edition of 1955), however, are surprising coming from a great anthropologist.
3. Suyûti, "Al-jàm'i al-saghir," in: *Recueil des dits de Mahomet*, p. 123.
4. See R. Blachère, "L'Allocution d'Adieu de Mahomet," in: *Analecta*, 1975, p. 140: "Oh people! Your Lord is unique and so is your forefather. You all descend from Adam, and Adam was born from the earth; the noblest of you in the eyes of Allah is the most pious. ... The only superiority of one arab over another is through piety."
5. See A. Chennoufi, "La Tolérance comme valeur à travers l'histoire tunisienne," in: *Al-Hayat Al-Thaqafiya*, No. 76 (June 1996), pp. 22ff. See also the definitive and very learned study by H.H. Abdelwahab, "L'Apport ethnique des étrangers en Tunisie," in: *Cahiers de Tunisie*, No. 69/70, pp. 158ff.
6. C. Cahen, *Orient et Occident au temps des croisades*, Paris, 1992, pp. 18-9.

Global Ethics and Education in Tolerance

Hans Küng

The Crisis of Education

A theologian would be ill-advised if he tried to teach pedagogy to the pedagogues. And indeed it is not my aim to proclaim some way of teaching – even less so after a period of pedagogical experimentation that produced one new model after the other. Rather I would like to buttress the efforts of pedagogues and educators from the viewpoint of ethics at a time when many people talk about an educational crisis. But in so doing I would also like to confine by remarks in two ways:

Against Lamentation and Moralizing

I do not wish to join in the lamentations of cultural pessimists of various shades who argue that present-day youth is as rotten as never before. It is a complaint that has been repeated many times since the days of Plato. Nor do I wish to join in the public moralizing of prominent churchmen who – themselves living in celibacy – do not grow tired of dealing with questions of sexual morality and sex education. Let us not torment ourselves with this kind of morality! Nor will there be any cheap shots at schools or politicians who are being blamed for the crisis.

At the same time there is to be no playing down of the ethical problematic, as if the call for a new ethos that can be heard so frequently these days were to be turned into a new "ethics wave." Rather this call must be seen as a perfectly understandable response to the ever more obvious crisis of the "modernist project." This project had at first rightly promoted the emancipation of the individual before it flip-flopped into individualistic arbitrariness and unrestrained choice that cause individual unhappiness and social ills. The enormous progress that has been made in the field of science, technology, and the economy, but has in many cases also reached its limits today, sadly did not bring us, as had been expected, a commensurate moral advance of humanity.

Against Regulations and Codification

While I do not wish to join in on the lamentations and moralizing, neither would I like to plead for incessant *regulations* and *codifications*. Legal norms and laws, to be sure, are necessary, but they do not make a personal ethical position dispensable. As if a legal system could survive without an ethical foundation! As if a social and political organization could create ethical ties on its own! Neil Postman may have exaggerated when he argued in his book *The End of Education*[1] ("end" in the sense of "terminal point" as well as "goal") that school and education were devoid of any purpose today, i.e., that both lacked ideals and a vision and had succumbed to the false prophets – of science, of technology, of economic utility and of multiculturalism. He may have overdrawn the picture, but by asking after the *raison d'être* of our schools, he nevertheless raises a very pressing question. True, "we can let trains go on time; but why all the trouble if they do not go where we want them to?"[2]

The problem is, of course, exacerbated if the hypothesis of various social scientists is correct that the young generation of our postmodern age is subjected to a process of "*tribalization*." The roughly fifteen million people who belong to the cohort of the 13-25 year-olds in Germany – so the argument continues – are increasingly fragmenting into innumerable "tribes," "groups," "sub-groups," "cliques," and finally "loners." Depending on what "tribe" one is dealing with, tens of thousands would go during the same summer to the Convention of the Evangelical Church in Hamburg or to a "Ravers" love parade in Berlin or Zürich; they would attend the "chaos days" in Hanover or a soccer match or wherever else they might travel.[3] If these groups and sub-groups have all developed their own norms of behavior, their own dress codes, their own sign and speech codes, if, in other words and according to this hypothesis, youth in our postmodern age is no longer bound together by the sense of community and belonging of the one and only youth movement, what then is it that still holds the younger generation and, indeed, society as a whole together, once this generation will finally operate the levers of power?

To be sure, according to a recent study by the *Deutsches Jugendinstitut* in Munich, German youth has again become more achievement orientated; but, faced with the scramble for jobs and the rough climate on the labor market, it also remains without a sense of direction. In these circumstances it may be helpful that programs and periods that allow young people to prepare for a career are on offer. Certainly it is understandable that calls are particularly emphatic to provide orientation, forward perspectives, and ethical foundations in society and among pedagogues today. Educators who are dealing with children and adolescents day in day out are often horrified to discover how many of their charges have lost those foundations that were once self-evident, i.e., norms, rules, yardsticks, and ideals. Allow me to illustrate this by reference to a problem that preoccupies all of us very much, i.e., youth and violence.

Youth and Violence

Youth and violence go together ever since the street battles of the rockers in the 1950s and the student rebellion of the 1960s. However, through the mass media, we have entered a new phase of social history that cannot be relativized by reference to the robber knights of the late Middle Ages who were also violent or the barely more moral entrepreneurs of Manchester capitalism in the nineteenth century. Rather it is a specific symptom of our postmodern age that the representation of violence in the media has, since the 1970s and 1980s and even more so in recent years, assumed alarming proportions. I am thinking here of the broadcasting, on a massive scale, of violence and cruelty with a realism that was previously unimaginable. It is a portrayal of violence that also reaches young people in the films of predominantly "private" television and on videos-tapes that can easily be copied; moreover, there is also a kind of television news-reporting that is to some extent voyeuristic. These representations of violence that do not mention pity or humanitarian feelings or love of one's neighbor must be added to all the other temptations of youth, be they old or new (drugs).

The Media Reinforce the Predisposition towards Violence

Of course, this temptation must not be exaggerated, as if the more or less coincidental or occasional viewing of a violent film or video immediately results in permanent damage. However, we should also not belittle the impact, as if – in line with a now discredited "theory of catharsis" – readiness to use violence would be reduced through an addictive consumption of violent videos and through habituation; as if the viewing of torture, rape, sado-masochistic scenes, or manslaughter had ever made a single person more pacific. According to recent research[4], the opposite is true: the predisposition to use violence and to act aggressively is released and stimulated by violent images, even to the point of committing a crime.

It is easy to see the causal link between violent scenes in films and videos and the readiness of young people in terms of a *reinforcement of this predisposition*, especially if we consider the following four points, i.e., compensation, identification, imitation, and projection.

As for (1) *compensation*, young people who as children have suffered from low self-esteem, who have fears of appearing weak and powerless, and in particular adolescents who were the helpless victims of adults and their severe punishments, are able to compensate their feelings of weakness with the help of (forbidden!) violent videos by developing fantasies of their own power and the power of their clique.

As for (2) *identification*, particularly youths whose self-esteem has been undermined are able to identify with the actors; but whereas adults would normally identify with the victims, they would identify with the *perpetrators*. Like the actors, they would be "cool" and hard-nosed; they would see themselves as Rambos and Terminators who overcome all enemies and dangers and who remain victorious in the end. Young people are particularly prone to adopt, in barely noticeable ways, patterns of behavior they have seen on TV as part of their own repertoire (see the "Monday syndrome" in school play-grounds).

As for (3) *imitation*, it is known how people become accustomed
to violent images, how they adopt the actor's strategies of justification (in films the ubiquitous notion of emergency defense or
emergency rescue) and thus neutralize their own behavior. Imitation is thus facilitated. Research with prison inmates has demonstrated that they are particularly prone to imitation. They deal
with such trash differently from people with no criminal record.
Inmates watched more attentively, recognized more clearly how
far an action was realizable and, in certain cases, imitated a particular crime step by step.

As for (4) *projection*, people whose self-esteem is disturbed are
highly satisfied if they can project their own darker sides onto
others, i.e., minorities, the infirm, and people rejected by society.
A person can upvalue himself, feeling that – as a white male, a
German, a native – he belongs to an elite group. This is why it is
not only among certain underprivileged strata, but also among
ordinary families of petty bourgeois background (more in provin-
cial towns than in cities) that we find sympathetic attitudes for a
right-wing milieu and for skinheads. These are the strata who –
facing many problems that fail to articulate – fear competition
and social decline.

It Depends on the Individual

The destructive potential of videos that are inhumane, sadistic,
mysogynist, and xenophobic, that glorify violence and espouse it
as the only solution to conflict, is considerable. It has had a major
share in generating the view, held not merely by armed gangs in
Frankfurt or Berlin, but also by many other young people, that
violence is a legitimate means for asserting their interests. This is
why many large citizens' initiatives[5] rightly demand TV programs
which, if not completely free from violence, are nevertheless more
humane; they also want to stop all paid advertising in the context
of programs showing violence or human misery. In other words,
they advocate a responsible treatment of violence by the TV net-
works and the effective implementation of existing legislation.

Another major result of recent research in this field has to be
highlighted: it is *dependent on the individual* who consumes this
trash whether the violence seen will lead to long-term damage and

personality changes. What I am referring to here is not just the individual psychological situation, i.e., whether the videos are consumed alone or in a group, whether they are viewed as an escape or as a means of abandoning oneself to a make-believe world. What I mean is above all the milieu of the family, school, and the wider environment – whether the child experiences rejection and insensitivity within the family or warmth, security, and open trust; whether he or she was able to develop a stable self-esteem; whether a strong ego that is capable of coping with the inner and external threats of puberty is also being promoted through school; and, finally, whether the social milieu is likely to approach with hostility or open curiosity what is foreign, unfamiliar, and new.

However, so I ask myself, how is this to be achieved if children who up to the age of 11 or 12 find it difficult, in any case, to differentiate between fictionalized violence in films and actual violence as reported in the news and who are nowadays surrounded by a jungle without points of orientation?

The Jungle without Points of Orientation

Am I exaggerating? Hardly. After all, we live in an age in which a two-year-old is being slowly and calculatingly tortured to death by two 10-year-olds. It happened in Liverpool. And just in that city? We live in an age in which three 11-12 year-olds terrorized a dozen or so families by demanding money over the telephone and threatening murder and rape if the demands were not fulfilled. They did so using a language so brutal that children were at first not suspected of being the anonymous callers. And where did this happen? In Rottenburg near Tübingen. Evidently even the residential towns of bishops and prelates are no longer "havens of innocence." Those three kids were apparently also responsible for a number of other misdeeds (paint daubings, damage to parked cars) and they belonged to a larger gang of children and adolescents. According to the police, they were unable to recognize their wrong-doing[6] and even in retrospect thought their activities to be "funny." Nor did the large prison in their neighborhood act as a deterrent. As one of the 11 or 12 year-olds put it, nothing could happen to them; after all, it was only from age 14 that one becomes legally responsible.

Is Everything That Is Fun Permissible?

It is not only in the United States and in Britain that both the victims and the perpetrators have grown younger and younger. According to the 1994 crime statistics for Germany, over 100,000 felonies were committed by children between the ages of 8 and 14; over 220,000 were committed by juveniles between the ages of 14 and 21, representing a 20 percent increase on 1993. It should be added, however, that, unlike in the U.S., most of these were not serious crimes of violence, such as rape or armed robbery. These latter crimes increased among juveniles from 83,400 in 1983 to 129,600 in 1992. The figure for adolescent murderers alone was up by more than 100 percent, from 969 in 1984 to 2,202 in 1991.[7] (I am not going to cite that steep rise in suicides and attempted suicides among young people.)

To be sure, in Germany as elsewhere, the rise in crime has manifold political and social causes. There is poverty and the lack of a forward perspective among many youths; there is also the hidden persuasion by relentless advertising; and there are the scandals and the corrupt behavior of all too many people in business, politics, and sports. However, it is also undeniable that in many cases children and adolescents evidently lack an ethical foundation, a basic training of their conscience and a minimal standard of morality, without which the existing legal system, including the police and the penal institutions, are largely powerless. As I heard Federal President Roman Herzog say during a recent panel discussion, no country is able to pay for a legal order unless 97-98 percent of the population were also willing to *abide* by it.

The categorical imperative to act in a humane fashion was considered to be virtually innate in all of us during Kant's time. In an age in which Nietzsche's man "beyond good and evil" is being so explicitly promoted and put into practice, this idea is clearly no longer self-evident. If everything that is fun is permissible (and this is how certain TV talk shows justify every nonsense, malpractice or perversity), why should young people then not also be free to threaten and blackmail their fellow-citizens; why should they not be free to smash up bars, defile cemeteries, mug elderly people, and form gangs that wage bloody wars against each other?

Between Authoritarian and Antiauthoritarian Education

It will not be possible to get a handle on the problem simply by putting more policemen on the streets, by tougher sentencing or by increasing welfare benefits. The actual solution starts with us, with our very personal convictions, our willingness to act responsibly and to assume obligations. That is why *pedagogy* should come even before politics, legislation, and the judiciary when we are looking for a reversal of these trends. We need a carefully considered educational approach in schools and families that is neither authoritarian nor antiauthoritarian; an approach that provides young people with spaces for their free development and yet does not refrain from exerting authority; that is considerate and caring, and yet sets clear limits and is not afraid to impose sanctions.

The child in particular should not only be told what his or her ethical duties are; he or she should also be given living examples of what is humane and inhumane, just and unjust, of what is fair and unfair, honest and dishonest. The child must learn in the family, in school, and in church how people deal with each other in humane ways and how one should aim for a resolution of conflicts without resort to violence. Basic behavioral patterns transmitted by the family are frequently responsible for the young people who cannot cope with life, who are unable to find a genuine identity, because parents who are expressly "youthful" and whose tolerance is virtually unlimited do not provide points of conflict and contrast, enabling adolescents to develop their own personality. If children are barely told in their families and schools about the key commandments of the great world religions, if they never hear "Thou shall not kill," "Thou shall not steal," or "Thou shall not tell lies," we should not be surprised if many of them refuse to recognize any norms and live all that happens as "fun." Educators rightly point out that violence prevention must start early and must be part of a long-term project.

For a long time pedagogues like Hartmut von Hentig would not stop polemicizing against the collective repression, the domestication and silencing of the rising generation; they pleaded almost exclusively for individuality, self-reliance, the capacity to criticize, the preparedness to accept conflict, risk and improvisation. In "adapting to the historical situation" they, too, have meanwhile begun to shift gears. To quote von Hentig: "Following a period of extensive liberties, of the dissolution of social ties and of excess, the rising generation requires a stronger education in self-discipline, community spirit, and sense of duty. We shall have to find a new balance if a particular virtue has become extreme and a non-virtue *(Untugend)*; if a love for order has become a compulsion; if the quest for independence has turned into an anything-goes; a sense of justice into conformism; autonomy into egotism; leisure into carelessness."[8] Von Hentig is absolutely correct if he now wants to deal with the welfare state by encouraging self-responsibility, with the market by stressing social obligation, with the freedom of the press, of research, and of the arts by protecting personality rights, by respecting life, and by establishing notions of decency.

Indeed, having ethical values is never merely a question that is directed at "youth," but concerns present-day society as a whole – a society which in an age of a democratically legitimated pluralism of life-styles and concepts of living must constantly pose anew the question of what, ethically speaking, is holding it together. I have already hinted at this: the crisis of values is not just a problem confronting Europe and America, but also the former Soviet Union and China. It is a global crisis. It is for this reason that the question of our ethos quite literally becomes a question of the ethos of the world as a whole. This in turn raises another fundamental problem wherever human beings are involved, i.e., that of the aggressiveness to be found in all human societies. It is an aggressiveness that poses a major challenge for any kind of education.

Education and Aggressiveness

Biologists, psychologists, and anthropologists tend to agree today that it is simply necessary, for animals and humans alike, including children, to develop a certain measure of aggressiveness in order to survive in a given society. For this reason we may wonder whether aggressiveness is simply our destiny, inscribed in us genetically, so that we should not be surprised if even the religions of the world contribute their share to the *homo homini lupus*; if even they have imbibed a measure of aggressiveness that characterizes the beast inside us.

The Ambivalence of Aggressiveness

There is general agreement today that fundamentally there is truth to *two positions*: Humans are genetically programmed as well as directed by the environment, but in neither case totally so. Why? Because a person who is either completely programmed by his or her genes or conditioned by the environment would no longer be human. He or she would either be an animal or a robot! Positively put (and this is a basic point for all pedagogy), human beings are *free* within the limits of their heredity and their environmental conditioning. But free in what sense? They are free in contradistinction to being dependent on instinct, compulsion, and power; they are free in the sense of having choices, of being self-determined and autonomous; they are also free to both follow a particular instinctive impulse or to resist it.

This means, as far as *aggressiveness* is concerned, that it is inherited and fixed in the genome, just as the theories of Freud and Lorenz had postulated. Accordingly, it is not possible simply to condemn it on religious grounds, to combat it morally, and – so to speak – to legislate it away. In this sense aggressiveness is indeed no more than what Konrad Lorenz -somewhat onesidedly to be sure – called "the so-called evil," the apparent evil that also has its good side. In what way? Without aggressive energies neither animals nor humans would be able to defend their territory and to create distance between themselves. There just is no living-together that is free of tensions. Without aggressive energies no child would be able to stand up to his or her parents' restrictions and overprotectiveness. He or she could not develop and grow within a framework of competition with other children; he or she would be unable to learn how to act and react, how to assert oneself and how to stand up for oneself; in short, the child could not develop self-confidence and become independent and adult. In this sense it is simply vital for him or her to go through a phase of aggressive social exploration as a youthful rebel or rowdy teenager. In this way the child tests and expands his or her space and the adolescent develops an assertiveness that is guided by reason vis-à-vis the resistance encountered in the real world. There is no other way for developing, asserting, and realizing one's personality.

Not All Aggressiveness Should Be Suppressed

All this shows that peace education as it was once conceived is problematical. This is an education that tried to prevent, through sanctions and the imposition of restrictions on a child's activities, a child's aggressiveness, anger, rage, and irritability from bursting forth; an education that attempted to impede the satisfaction of his or her drives, as manifested through play, sports competitions and fisty-cuffs, but also through serious fights. However, such an approach resulted in frustrations that were sooner or later bound to be translated into aggression (or, if internalized, into neurosis). In other words, *an antiauthoritarian peace education purveyed by parents, schools, or the churches that represses aggressiveness of any kind and promotes submissiveness misses the mark.* Aggressiveness may be perfectly valuable; nor does it have to violate another person if it demonstrates individual strength through compelling argument rather than physical abuse.[9]

However, this is merely one side of the coin. Aggressiveness is not completely inherited; it is also *learned*, acquired through conditioning. It is not just controlled by the genome, but it is also tested and shaped within a particular milieu. Aggressiveness – as theories of social learning (Bandura, Walters) assume – is thus also a consequence of, and reinforced by, learning through observation. In the course of his or her socialization that child learns to act and react in earnest. To be sure, the child invariably learns on the basis of inherited learning mechanisms. But this does not mean that he or she cannot (and perhaps even should not) learn something else. Even if humans display biologically determined impulses and drives, they are not, like animals, instinctively fixed in their behavior. For example, in the name of some spiritual or political objective, we are capable of voluntary starvation until death.[10] Similarly, a child is not helpless vis-à-vis impulses that might trigger aggressions. Rather he or she can consciously stop these aggressions and learn to rein them in. Normally, the community and role models help the child to distinguish which situations require aggressiveness and which ones do not, and to know when a particular drive may be satisfied.

No Toleration for any Kind of Aggressiveness

Recent research has shown that by no means are all aggressions rooted in frustration, as the theory of J. Dollard and N. Miller of Yale University had assumed in the 1930s. As if all aggressiveness resulted from the non-satisfaction of a particular drive so that aggressiveness could be prevented by preventing frustration and by satisfying all drives![11] Any monocausal theory of aggression is also rejected today by socio-biology which sees in frustration no more than one cause among others.

This second aspect of aggressiveness has similarly far-reaching consequences for education. An education that argues that the child should just be allowed "to grow" and that proposes to satisfy his or her wishes as far as possible in order to promote the growth of a human being who feels no aggressiveness and is peaceful, does not lead to a reduction of aggressiveness. Rather it results in the long run in a dangerous release of aggressive energies that have allegedly been held back. What may be thought amusing about a little horror in the nursery, can assume threatening proportions, inside or outside the home, when we are dealing with an egomaniac or violent boy in his puberty or an adolescent. It is a phenomenon that elderly people walking in the street increasingly complain about. However, those are the realities: If a child has every wish fulfilled and his or her immediate family displays extreme leniency and avoids all conflict, the result is not going to be non aggressive behavior, but the aggressive claiming of ever new needs.

Hence it is the reverse of this education that is true: only if a child is shown, early on and persistently, intelligible and fair limits, a clarification will be achieved that is ultimately also desired by him or her; the quest for an aggressive social exploration, that in itself is so important, will decline. Slowly the child learns to respond to threats constructively rather than aggressively. The young person then appreciates as a matter of principle how far he or she is allowed to go and that being a pure individualist and egotist is impossible. In other words, an *antiauthoritarian peace education that believes in tolerating all aggressiveness, likewise, misses its mark.* It merely turns a blind eye to the dangerous dynamic of aggressiveness which may have very destructive social consequences in the long run; after all, aggressiveness generates further aggressiveness.

The Ethos of Peace as World Ethos

It is undeniable that the religions of the world have been fulfilling a fundamental role for hundreds and thousands of years:

- they have motivated ethical conduct,
- they have made ethical norms more tangible and have illustrated them,
- they have formed the emotional community so vital for ethical conduct.

As we face the threat of a "clash of civilizations," the world religions are being challenged to secure and promote peace and to help legitimize a common ethos of humanity or a world ethos. Roman Herzog, the President of the Federal Republic of Germany, has expressly identified this desideratum when he spoke before the *Börsenverein des Deutschen Buchhandels* at a ceremony awarding a prize to the well-known ethnologist Annemarie Schimmel in 1995. The topic was also discussed at a subsequent symposium at his official residence in Berlin. He believes that the divergent cultures still command "quite different intellectual resources" with which to avoid a "global culture war." He added: "It is worthwhile to try to find the greatest common denominator." What he called "the search for an ethical minimum that transcends the cultures," is identical with the notion of a world ethos.[12]

A Challenge for Present-day Education

In September 1993 representatives of all religions agreed, for the first time in the history of those religions, on a joint basic declaration at the world parliament in Chicago. They ratified a *"Declaration concerning the World Ethos"* which contains the minimum consensus with respect to common values, immutable standards, and basic moral attitudes.[13] The representatives of all the major world religions, in formulating this "World Ethos," did not wish to create a new global ideology. Nor did they intend to establish a uniform world religion above and beyond existing ones; and they certainly did not mean to justify the dominance of one religion over all others. Rather the meeting wanted to raise into consciousness the fact that, doctrinal differences notwithstanding, there exists already a basic consensus concerning binding values, immutable standards, and personal attitudes. Ethos is thus not to be misunderstood as being a sedative in the face of an urgent need for social reform; rather it is to be seen as a fortification against the disenchantment with parties, politics, and even with the existing constitutional order. It was designed to provide a strong impetus for practical social reforms on the basis of individual responsibility. To quote President Herzog once more: "If we were to succeed in making it (i.e., the Golden Rule) at least to some extent the maxim of practical politics – what a boost it would be for international peace and no less so for individual rights!"[14]

The Chicago Declaration is also of greatest significance for present-day *education* because it combines the principle of *simplicity* with that of *concretization*. This means that the Declaration establishes a common ground with respect to one fundamental demand: "All humans (whether man or woman, white or of color, rich or poor) must be treated humanely." This is the *"Golden Rule"* that for millennia characterized the manifold religious and ethical traditions of mankind and that has stood the test of time. To put it positively: "Do onto others as you would have them do onto you." It is from this basic humane position that we are able to avoid this *sterile and exclusively aggressive attitude* – an attitude that combines narcissism with xenophobia; that ties one's own success to the defeat of another person, one's own power to the powerlessness of the other, and that lacks all sense of partnership and mutual support. This Golden Rule should be the immutable and absolute norm for all spheres of life, for family and community, for ethnic groups, nations, and religions.

This principle can be made tangible with the help of four comprehensive and *age-old imperatives of humanity* that can be found in

most of the religions on this planet. Time and again these principles have been violated, and none of us have exactly been saints.
However, what would have happened to humankind without
these maxims, that are to be found in the Declaration and that tar-
get *especially the young generation*? Here they are:

(1) The obligation to create a *culture of non-violence* and of *respect
for all that is living*, i.e., the age-old commandment that "thou shall
not kill." Accordingly the Declaration reads: "That is why young
people should learn in family and school that violence must not
be the means of dispute with others. Only in this way can a culture of non-violence be created."[15]

(2) The obligation to establish a *culture of solidarity* and a *just economic order*, i.e., the age-old commandment that "Thou shall not
steal." The Declaration puts it thus: "For this reason young people
should learn in family and school that property, however, small, carries obligations with it. Its use should simultaneously serve the general good. Only in this way can a just economic order be built."[16]

(3) The obligation to create a *culture of tolerance* and a *life in
truthfulness*, i.e., the age-old demand: "Thou shall not tell lies."
This means as far as education is concerned: "For this reason
young people should learn in family and school to exercise truthfulness in their thinking, speaking, and actions. All humans have
a right to be given the truth and truthfulness. They have a right to
the necessary information and education in order to be able to
make basic decisions about their lives. However, without a basic
ethical orientation they will hardly be able to distinguish between
what is important and what is unimportant. Given today's daily
flood of information, ethical standards provide help if facts are
being distorted, interests are not disclosed, trends followed, and
opinions turned into dogma."[17]

(4) The obligation to create a *culture of equality* and a *partnership
between men and women*, i.e., the age-old maxim: "Thou shall not
engage in adultery." Again here is the Declaration: "For this reason young people should learn in family and school that sexuality
is in principle not a negative, destructive, or exploitative force, but
one that creates and shapes. Its function is to build a community
that affirms life and that can flourish only if it is lived with a sense
of responsibility for the happiness of the spouse."[18]

However, some people will ask whether a world ethos might be a bit too idealistic and too abstract. Is there anything that has meaning to present-day youth? Isn't morality dead? I would like to respond to these questions and to make a few necessary counterpoints that are part of the overall picture.

In Favor of a New Basic Consensus Among the Young Generation

It is ancient knowledge that processes designed to initiate changes in consciousness must take a medium- or long-term perspective. For this reason it is of utmost importance that we begin to discuss the Declaration on all levels and unlock it for students and adolescents through a special didactic effort. As far as I am concerned, there is no question that this Declaration should be discussed as part of religious and ethical instruction. It should be made an indispensable part of the curriculum.

The majority of today's youth is not opposed in principle to an ethos. According to a 1995 survey of the German Emnid Institute, some 92 percent of the 14-19 year-olds do not consider morals as something old-fashioned; indeed one third of them even regard uprightness and correctness as important elements of their identity. Some 86 percent thought shop-lifting to be immoral. Some 80 per cent consider feeling responsible for the environment as their most important concern, while 60 per cent regard wealth and 50 per cent faith as secondary goals. It is by no means a hopeless endeavor to work *for a new ethical consensus, especially among the younger generation.*

The first results from schools are already coming in from different places. Let me merely quote here, as tangible evidence, from a high school senior. He is among those who largely reject bourgeois values and norms, but who was introduced by his philosophy teacher to the text of the Declaration in order to help him rethink his aims: "I am a fan of various Death Metal groups that have exerted a deep influence upon me. The provocative and aggressive music fascinates me just as much as the pessimistic, almost nihilistic attitude of the musicians. I also play in a Death Metal band and in my lyrics I primarily express my upset about how evil the world in fact is. This lesson plan influenced me in the sense that I began seriously to question this attitude. I concluded that this attitude of 'It's too late anyway' is a very easy excuse for withdrawing from responsibility. However, this insight did not induce me to quit my band and to be optimistic ever after; after all, the music provided me with many things (sense of community, friends etc.); rather it persuaded me to use the opportunities I have as a musician and to take responsibility for 'bettering the world.' Thus my idea to donate the income from our next concert (in our case about 500-700 deutschmarks) to a development-aid organization met with much approval among the other members of the band. Most probably a 'Brazil Charity Concert' will take place in the next three months. These ideas do not have much to do with the 'world ethos' of which unfortunately I do not know much so far. ... But in the meantime I have grown curious and will get hold of this booklet" (Frank Nöllenberg, age 18).[19]

The World Ethos Foundation tries to make the Chicago Declaration available to schools for use in religious instruction or philosophy lessons, but also to interested groups and workshops. An excellent *draft lesson plan* on the subject with seven different units to be used in religious studies at high schools is available and has triggered a strong response in our Workshop.[20] The World Ethos Foundation has therefore resolved to launch a *competition* and award prizes of 3.000 deutschmarks each to the best six lesson plans. The conditions have been laid down and a small panel of religious studies teachers (Protestant, Catholic and non church-affiliated) will judge the entries.

A Long-Term Change of Consciousness

There are thus many ways in which a discourse can be set in motion that must go well beyond the realm of pedagogy. We must address not only teachers and students, but also doctors, lawyers, business people, journalists, and politicians. The World Ethos Foundation can also see to it that the Declaration is published in Eastern Europe where it could not appear without a subsidy. There will be no lack of other initiatives; both the InterAction Council of former state ministers and minister presidents and UNESCO (even if there are perennial financial problems) are interested in spreading the idea of a World Ethos. Nor do we wish to neglect future research about the religious situation of our time, about world peace, religious peace, and the dialogue between the churches. On the contrary! However, it should also be possible to facilitate an *haute vulgarisation* of these ideas through a TV documentary series, for which concrete plans have already been laid.

Another more distant hope of these manifold efforts to promote "inter-cultural and inter-religious research, education, and encounters" (thus the sub-title of the World Ethos Foundation) could be the following – if I may be so daring to think aloud about something that I will hardly live to see: the fulfillment of a goal that was first raised in the great debate on human rights in the 1789 French National Assembly and that has now been adopted by the InterAction Council, i.e., to put next to the plaque enumerating the basic human rights *(les droits de l'homme)* another one listing basic human obligations *(les devoirs de l'homme)*.

World Ethos is everything else but a beautiful idealistic dream. It is a vision, but one that we need if the world order of nations, cultures, and religions is to have an ethical foundation. The World Ethos project has taken root in an astonishingly short time and is proliferating. This demonstrates that the *change in consciousness in matters of ethos* that we are aiming for is well underway. In the past decades we have seen a change of consciousness (that was also ethically inspired) in the fields of economy and ecology, peace and disarmament, relations between men and women, and few people still hold views in these matters of 20 or 30 years ago. In the same manner – and this would be consistent – the coming decades will see a change in consciousness in respect of ethical values more generally.[21]

Notes

1. N. Postman, *The End of Education*, New York, 1995.
2. Ibid., p. 86.
3. See *Der Spiegel*, 33/1995.
4. On the behavior of pupils in Baden-Württemberg and Saxony, see R.H. Weiß, *Gewaltmedienkonsum. Video-Gewalt 1992* and *Sächsische Jugendstudie 1992*. Both field studies may be obtained from the *Oberschulamt* in Stuttgart. See also M. Scheunengrab, *Filmkonsum und Delinquenz*, Regensburg, 1994.
5. For example, the "Initiative Gewaltverzicht im Fernsehen" that was started by the Detmold psychologist K.A. Richter who collected 250,000 signatures. See *Focus*, 26/1994.
6. See *Schwäbisches Tagblatt*, 12 October 1995.
7. Statements by U.S. Attorney General Janet Reno, cited in: *International Herald Tribune*, 9/10 September 1995.
8. See H. von Hentig in: *Die Zeit*, September 1995.
9. Intimidating or injuring another person should therefore not *a priori* be included in a definition of aggressiveness. As E. von Gebsattel (in: *Lexikon der Pädagogik*, Vol. I, Freiburg, 1952, p. 40) correctly observes: "By studying animals that hunt, or are in heat, or are being pursued and defend themselves or their brood, it becomes clear that there is no primordial desire among animals that aims primarily at damaging or destroying an other animal's habitat. All aggressive actions by animals – even where their destructive effect is evident – represent no more than drives of self-preservation or procreation."
10. I am following here the illuminating analysis of Gabriele Haug-Schnabel in her unpublished study *Das neue Verhältnis biologischer Grundlagen von aggressiven Verhaltensweisen* (1994).
11. See L. Berkowitz (ed.), *Roots of Aggression. A Re-examination of the Frustration-Aggression Hypothesis*, New York, 1969.
12. See the Federal President's speech on this occasion.
13. See H. Küng and K.-J. Kuschel (eds.), *Erklärung zum Weltethos. Die Deklaration des Parlamentes der Weltreligionen*, Munich, 1993.
14. Federal President Herzog's speech (note 12 above).
15. *Erklärung* (note 13 above), p. 9.
16. Ibid., p. 10.
17. Ibid., p. 12.
18. Ibid., p. 13.
19. Quoted in: J. Lähnemann (ed.), *"Das Projekt Weltethos" in der Erziehung. Referate und Ergebnisse des Nürnberger Forums 1994*, Hamburg, 1995, p. 392. This volume contains rich material on the various aspects of the question of World Ethos and Education.
20. See P. Wagner, *Die Erklärung zum Weltethos. Vorschlag für die Behandlung im Religionsunterricht in Klasse 10 (Gymnasium)* and W. Lange, *Plädoyer für einen ethischen Minimalkonsens an Gesamtschulen*. Both are repr. in: *Rundbrief des Verbandes der katholischen Religionslehrerinnen und Religionslehrer an Gesamtschulen in Nordrhein-Westfalen e.V.*, 10 (October 1995).
21. A modified and amplified version of this article will appear in my book *Weltethos für Weltpolitik und Weltwirtschaft*, Munich, 1997, a continuation of my *Global Responsibility. In Search of a New World Ethic* (1991).

Interlude
To an Expanding World of Mind-Closure

Wole Soyinka

It was at a gathering of Nobel Laureates in Paris, in February 1987, a meeting that was organized by Elie Wiesel under the patronage of President Mitterand, that I first felt obliged to alert the world to the rising aggression of religious intolerance and its territorial ambitions. The triumph of intellectual skepticism over the closed, utopian text called Marxism had created a vacuum, it seemed obvious to me, leaving the way open for its occupation by other utopian texts, of which the most aggressive candidate would prove to be religious fundamentalism. A few months later, the *fatwa* against Salman Rushdie was pronounced, leaving both the "mainstream" religious, and the secular world stunned, and unprepared.

It is unfortunate that, thanks to Western paranoia, especially within its media, the word "fundamentalism" is no sooner uttered than it is equated with an apocalyptic vision of Moslem (that is, barbaric) hordes sweeping down on western civilization and reducing the values of occidental society to prehistoric rubble. Such an attitude ignores the fact that fundamentalism is a feature of, indeed is part of the history of most religions, and that it violates the adherents of such religions even more brutally than outright unbelievers. Having limited a universal phenomenon to specific religious geographies therefore, the Western world finds itself restrained by a fear of sounding xenophobic in reacting to a clearly global disorder. Those of us who are on the direct firing line of fundamentalism in several aspects of social and political life cannot afford however to be restrained by the escapisms of guilt or – to utilize that brain damaged phrase – political correctness. We dare not indulge in the usual palliatives and ploys of appeasement that attempt to cover a virulent phenomenon in evasive language.

Much has happened to confirm the tide of these atavistic offen-
sives in several arenas of conflict – including those that are little
known and poorly publicized. But it is not simply religion that is
at issue here, there is also identity and "otherness" – which, as in
the case of Rwanda, has led to an unprecedented debasement of
humanity in contemporary history. But it all begins with dogmatism in ideas, even intuitions, that then extend to secular life,
tendencies that result in the submergence of rationality within
emotiveness, the expropriation of the individual will by self-right-
eous but hyperactive and power-driven entities, often, ironically, a
minority. It is also a fact of life however that such minorities are
mostly to be found within that emotive world of superstition
known as religion, which has learnt to prey upon the spiritual
yearnings of much of humanity in order to render it captive to its
territorial ambitions.

And yet, the world is not without examples that can instruct
us, examples that should rebuke the arrogance of such impulses
and strengthen the will of the rest to resist their encroachments on
that secular authority that is the common property, common
denominator, and right of all of humanity. Let us therefore never
weary of calling attention to the fact that religions do exist, as on
the African continent, that can boast of never having launched a
war, any form of jihad or crusade, for the furtherance of their
beliefs. (Can anyone knowledgeable of the *orisa* of the Yoruba conceive – to remind ourselves of a quite recent outrage in India – of
the followers of *Obatala* hurling themselves against, and tearing
down a centuries old mosque because of a vision that it stands on
the spot of that deity's emanation in some unwitnessed, antedilu-
vian age?) Despite such pacifism however, these beliefs have
proved themselves bedrocks of endurance and survival – and of
tolerance – transforming communities as far away from that continent as the Caribbean and the Americas. To both victims and
agents of mind closure therefore, be it of the secular or the religious kind, we continue to preach:

> Go to the *orisa*, and be wise. The religion of the *orisa* does not permit, in
> tenets, liturgy, catechism or practice, that pernicious dictum: *I believe, therefore,
> I am*. Nowhere in it will you find the sheerest skein of reasoning in that direc-
> tion to human self-apprehension. Obviously, therefore, you will not find its

corollary: *You do not, therefore you are not.* Orunmila does not permit it. Obatala cannot conceive of it. Ogun will take up arms against it. Not one *odu* of *Ifa* so much as suggests it. This is not weakness in the character of this religion however, it is not even tolerance; it is simply – understanding. Wisdom. An intuitive grasp of the complexity of the human mind and a true sense of the infinite potential of the universe.

Obstacles and Limits to Tolerance

Paul Ricœur

We have presented tolerance, right from the foreword upon which the present study opens, as the difficult course of a crested road between intolerance and the intolerable. Intolerance constitutes the obstacle never surmounted, the intolerable, the limit opposed to the abuses of a tolerance that has slid to indifference.

The three articles reunited in this last section echo those which have been placed under the title: to think tolerance. As has once been said, to think, it concerning a difficult virtue, is to think twice against: against that which makes obstacle, against that which disarms and denatures. The first of these three articles shows, in the dissonance between the respect owed to human rights and the respect asked by all cultures, the ultimate source of intolerance, which makes of it at the same time the first intolerable. It is principally no longer the imperialism of great cultural monologues that makes for a problem today, but pluralism itself behind its multiple faces. The perils of difference succeed then to those of identity. The non-allowance of prohibiting must in its turn henceforth find its limits. Posed in these terms the problem has an epistemological dimension, to the extent that the criteria of validity applied to beliefs are put into question; but it includes also a moral and legal dimension, to the extent that the question of limits touches upon the right to expression; finally a spiritual problem, to the extent that the balance between obstacle and limit rests on a practical wisdom capable of inspiring the education of tolerance.

The second article takes the difficulty to its radical degree, since the ultimate request within which tolerance is summed up consists in recommending to tolerate that which we don't like, that which we morally disapprove. It is in this that tolerance proves to be a virtue. It is as virtue that it encounters its limit with the question: "how far tolerate ?" If it concerned myself alone, I would say:

Paul Ricœur

"all the way !" It concerning license in public space, one has to say: up to the point in which intolerable wrongs in the eyes of enlightened consciousnesses would denounce tolerance as a passivity in the face of the wrong committed, and consequently in the face of the wrong suffered by the most vulnerable.

It is to this function of alarm and alert of the intolerable, it is said in the third article, that the indignation sparked by the intolerable addresses itself, when the asceticism of tolerance, exceeding in a sense its goal, turns against itself in the figure of indifference.

On Tolerance and the Limits of Toleration

Ioanna Kuçuradi

The Problem

Two main but discrepant tendencies characterize the intellectual climate of our world at the turn of the century. We promote, on the one hand, "respect for human rights," i.e. for certain *universal norms,* but on the other hand, equally promote "respect to all cultures,"which are differentiated among themselves by their different world-views and their *parochial norms.* Not rarely do we see that the demands that such parochial norms bring are contradictory to those of human rights.

We are not sufficiently aware of this discrepancy. Still our simultaneous promotion of these two discrepant tendencies has already produced its own facts, among which we see the revival of racisms, nationalisms, fundamentalisms and other similar intolerables.

How to tackle the problems created by these intolerables without giving damage to the so-called fundamental freedoms? This is the dilemma that humanity faces just at this moment, and especially in the so-called developed countries.

At the beginning of our century pragmatism, to face the problems created by the conflicting "truths" of the time, had suggested "pluralism" as an antidote to dogmatism – the corridor of William James. Instead of tackling the problem epistemologically, it tried to solve it by cutting the Gordian knot, i.e. by making out of fact an ideal and by introducing a new "theory of truth."[1]

This pragmatic ideal has become one of the mottoes of our time: the "pluralistic universe" has become now "pluralistic society" or "multicultural society." And now, in view of facing the "conflicts of cultures," and especially those within "multicultural societies," we promote tolerance.

Still, in the turmoil created by the spread of postmodernism, which claimed the equal value of all world-views, norms or cultures in a world in which the "right to freedom of thought, consciousness, expression, etc." is taken for granted and in which unscrutinized pluralism turned out to be a *laisser faire, laisser passer* in practice, i.e. in a world in which "anything goes"; when the increase of racist-nationalist-fundamentalist conflicts has led to an impasse in public life, the question of the limits of tolerance is brought onto the agenda of the intellectual world community.

Thus now, at the turn of the century, we feel, as a humanity, the need to reformulate tolerance "between intolerance and the intolerable," in other words, we feel the need to determine the limits of tolerance.

In our endeavor to do this, there is another recent intellectual development in the approach to human rights that has also to be taken into consideration: the well-minded, very pragmatic "cultural approach" to, or the quest for a "cultural legitimacy" of, human rights, which has led to the application of the "theory of overlapping consensus" to human rights.[2] This approach seems to be a compromise between the two, if unconditionally promoted, hardly compatible tendencies, which characterize the intellectual climate of our days. Probably it escapes attention that what distinguishes one given cultural group from another is its own specific, i.e. different, world-view and norms of evaluation and behavior, which secure the existence of that group *against* other cultural groups; while human rights are demands concerning how human beings have to treat and be treated by other human beings, whatever their specific characteristics – cultural ones included – might be. It escapes attention that cultural norms and human rights – though not all of those demands which *are now* called human rights – are deduced from epistemologically and axiologically different premises and by different kinds of reasoning.

We have to rethink tolerance in connection with all these intellectual and other developments,[3] which have led to the present situation of the world, and reformulate tolerance in connection with the intolerables of our days, still without losing sight of its historical origin, i.e. the historical conditions, in which the idea of tolerance was brought to the fore, in view of facing them. This is what I shall partly try to do in this paper.

What is Tolerance?

If we take a look at the various contexts in which the verb "to tolerate" and the terms "tolerance" and "tolerant" are used in certain European languages on the one hand, and on the other, at the historical conditions existing at the time when the idea of tolerance was brought to the fore, i.e. the religious-sectarian conflicts of the time, as well as all the conditions of the present world, i.e. the cultural-ideological conflicts of our time; we see that it is possible to deal with the question of tolerance at least from two different perspectives: from the view point of the "subject" of tolerance, i.e. to deal with tolerance as a *personal attitude,* and from the view-point of the "object" of tolerance, i.e. to deal with tolerance (toleration) as a *demand concerning the arrangement and administration of public affairs,* or, as a principle concerning an *in abstracto* non-determinable area of *different* views and practices related to the same issues, still an area delineated by the limits where the intolerables start.

Tolerance as a Personal Attitude

As a personal attitude tolerance is closely related to a given conception of being human, which may underlie the way a person looks at others: his looking at other persons – each of whom is unique, and consequently "different"- as *human* beings, whatever their differences, personal characteristics or conditions might be.

What mainly marks the tolerant person is that in concrete situations he *does not do damage* though he is in a position to do so *to the rights* of another person, who is "different", i.e. who possesses a view, opinion, or norm radically different from that which the tolerant person possesses *on the same issue,* and/or who takes an attitude, acts in a given situation or behaves in general, in a way radically different from that which he approves.

The following points have to be emphasized. What the tolerant person "tolerates" is *not* the radically different views, opinions,

165

norms or attitudes, ways of behavior, practices, and given actions of the others, but *the existence of these others*. What, on the contrary, the intolerant person does not or cannot tolerate, is *the existence of views, opinions, norms* which are "different" from those that *he* strongly believes to be "true," or of *the ways of behavior and practices* radically different from those *he* strongly believes to be "good," no matter who possesses or shows them. The tolerant person does not identify the other person with his ideas and practices, which he strongly disproves of, while the intolerant person does so.

What determines the actions of the intolerant person to those who possess radically different views or opinions and behave or act in ways he strongly disapproves of – if it is not his personal interests – is his concern to "defend" what he takes for granted to be "true" or "good." To eliminate the "erroneous" ideas and "bad" practices, he eliminates those who possess or show them, i.e. he causes damage to their rights, if he is in a position to do so. If he is not, as we often see, the intolerant person has recourse to violence: to eliminate the ideas he annihilates – or threatens to annihilate those who, he thinks, personify them.

What, on the other hand, determines the actions of the tolerant person is his looking at others, be they themselves tolerant or intolerant, as *human* beings who, for one reason or another, possess different ideas, opinions or norms from those he approves, but which however are not guises of personal interests.

Thus it appears that what the tolerant person "respects" is not "differences," but that which is *identical* in all human beings. Hence he consciously rejects doing damage to their rights, i.e. he "respects" their rights. This seems to be the reason why bigots can easily exploit tolerant persons, as we sometimes observe in public life.

At this point we can also see why tolerance, as a personal attitude, does not imply that the tolerant person *should not oppose*, or fight against, the views, opinions, norms, practices he disapproves of; or, to use the fashionable expression, that he should "respect" others different views and cultures. Why, for instance, should one "respect" polygamy or blood feud?

In the light of these considerations it appears that "respecting others' different views" is not tolerance, as is usually assumed. Tolerance, as a personal attitude, is respecting *the rights* of those who possess radically different views on a given issue and act in a different way from that which one approves, i.e. it causes no damage to their rights, though it could.

Understanding by "tolerance" a "respect for others' different views," and nevertheless rejecting to tolerate the outcome of some of them, betrays a lack of sufficient philosophical *knowledge* on world-views and norms – a lack which leads many people to conclude from the difficulty of evaluating epistemologically and axiologically given views, norms etc., the impossibility of such an evaluation. In practice such a "respect" amounts to choosing, in the name of "objectivity," to remain indifferent to *any* view, opinion, norm, way of behavior or practice and to let "anything go." It amounts to closing one's eyes to the intolerables.

Tolerance as a Principle of Public Affairs

These considerations, put forward by bringing into focus the subject of tolerance, i.e. the tolerant person, lead us to the core of our inquiry: the philosophical problems we are faced with, when we bring into focus the object of tolerance, or, the question of the tolerable and the intolerable.

This question, raised in connection with the arrangement and administration of public affairs, amounts in fact to three questions of different order. The first is the question of what *can* be tolerated though strange or unusual, i.e. the question of the *permissible*; the second is the question of what *should not* be tolerated and consequently what must be prohibited; and the third is the question of what, though not approved by the majority or a powerful minority in a given place at a given time, *should* be tolerated in public life. The first two questions concern the boundary between the tolerable and the intolerable, or the problem of the limits of tolerance; the third question, in relation to the first one, concerns the boundary between the permissible and the non-prohibitable.

It is not possible to formulate positively, in the technical sense of the term, the tolerable, but only negatively, in connection with the intolerable; because to determine whether something may or may not be permitted, it must be evaluated cognitively in connection with the existing conditions, independently from whoever approves or disapproves of it.

167

It is possible, on the contrary, to positively formulate the intol-erable, i.e. to put forward the common characteristics of the intol-erables, because what has to be done in this case is not to put forward what should not be tolerated, but what *should not be toler-able for the human being.*

Intolerables are facts that result, directly or indirectly from human decisions or actions, or are the fruit of indifference and inertia. Be they conditions, situations, practices, customs, acts etc., they *are* intolerable, because in one way or another hinder the actualization of the potentialities that constitute the specificity of the human being, or they cause damage to what we call human dignity. Still they are: at the moment we are confronted with them, it is never possible to prevent or hinder them.

To "fight" against them, that is, to change them or ensure that they not be perpetuated, it is necessary to dig out the views and norms underling them, and to evaluate those views and norms philosophically, and then subsequently find and carry out what in the given conditions has to be done – in legislation and education – to make them ineffective.

Thus the question at hand can be re-formulated as follows: what are the specific views and norms underlying intolerable facts – be they different or not from the views and norms approved at a given moment by the majority or a powerful minority in a country or in the world as a whole?

This is the question of the epistemically justifiable criteria for selecting norms for legislation on national and international lev-els, and for the administration of public and world affairs, i.e. the criteria for deciding what in general and in given conditions should be tolerable, intolerable or non-prohibitable.

In the present state of affairs, this question of criteria is a crucial one, not only because groups possessing different cultures – dif-ferent and often incompatible views and norms on the same issues – are living intermingled in the same space, and because liberal pluralism, justified by postmodernism, and our unscrutinized conception of "freedoms" has already led to the dilemma I men-tioned at the beginning of this paper; but also because now, after the collapse of the "Second World," the tendency to "minimize the State"and promote international civil cooperation is gaining more and more ground, still without paying special enough attention to the question: "cooperation for and in view of what?" – as is the case today with the unconditional promotion of a "free market" on national and international levels, which seems pregnant with further intolerables.[4]

Viewed philosophically, the core of the question concerns determining the ground to stand on in approving and tolerating or opposing and rejecting a *given* view or norm. It concerns the problem of the *right* evaluation of views and norms. This is the evaluation in order *to know* their epistemological and axiological specificities, and *not* the evaluation from the viewpoint of any different view or norm touching on the same issue.

By emphasizing this point, I wish to call attention to the following: the *difference* of an idea, view, norm, or practice, way of behavior, etc., with respect to the prevailing ones at a given place and time, does not automatically necessitate its becoming an object of tolerance: it is enough that it is an object of philosophical evaluation. What determines whether it may, or may not, or even should at least, be an object of toleration, is not its being "different," but its epistemological and axiological quality. It is not excluded that such an evaluation might even show that a given norm or practice which is radically different from the prevailing one on the same issue, may be not only tolerated should be promoted as well.

If we know the epistemological and axiological specificities of norms, i.e. what distinguishes them from knowledge, and their kinds, we may become able to evaluate single norms and see *the limits of tolerance* to be drawn in legislation, as well as distinguish between what may be and what should be tolerated in public life.

In the light of these considerations, it appears that it is only possible to conceptualize tolerance, as a principle of public affairs, in relation to intolerance, still in relation to two different objects of intolerance, those which *are not* tolerated in public life, those which are not though may be tolerated; and those which are not though they should be.

This means that it is not possible to develop *positive* criteria to use as touch-stones for selecting those ideas, norms, practices which may be tolerated in general. Even the fact that certain prac-

169

tices and ways of behavior may be tolerated in real given conditions does not necessitate that they be tolerated in different conditions as well. But it is possible, by looking at the intolerables and finding out what makes them "intolerable," to formulate certain *positive* criteria to use for distinguishing the views, ideas, norms, practices, etc. – be they different from the prevailing ones, or, be they the most prevailing ones, which should not be objects of toleration, i.e. whose propaganda, teaching, or exercising should be prohibited in public life.[5] In other words, this means that we have first to formulate the criteria of the intolerables, so as to distinguish intolerance -can be shown with respect to anything which differs from what is accepted as "true" or "good" – from the intolerable: *that which should not be tolerable* for the human being.

Regarding views, it is knowledge that draws the limits of the intolerable. This means that if there is a clash between a *view* and *knowledge* on a given issue, this view should not be allowed to become a determinant in public affairs. This criterion is especially important when it is put in connection with our promotion of "democracy," because, while the truth or falsity of a piece of knowledge is not a question of "democratic" decision, its becoming or not becoming a determinant in public affairs mostly is, as it is the case with *all kinds* of views.

Regarding norms, customs, practices, the limits of the intolerable start where cultural-religious and other norms and practices of empirical origin[6] cause direct or indirect damage to *basic human rights*. When such a norm or practice clashes with a clearly conceived human right and prevents it, directly or indirectly, from determining the arrangement and administration of public affairs, it may not be an object of toleration: in other words, it should not be allowed to determine the course of pubic affairs.

Thus knowledge and human rights constitute not only the criteria of the tolerable and the intolerable, but are also the criteria of what *should be tolerable*, without consideration of whomever likes it or not: these are the implications and consequences of knowledge and human rights in given concrete conditions.

Thus, the tolerable – that which may be object of toleration – has to be distinguished from what should be tolerable, because they have different implications for legislation.

Keeping this distinction in mind, we may understand tolerance, as a principle of public affairs, as a double imperative: what may be tolerable *in given conditions,* no matter how different from what prevails, *must not* be prohibited; and what should be tolerable *may not* be prohibited, no matter who approves or disapproves of it.

The issue of tolerance as a principle of public affairs is closely related today with the so-called cultural rights and with the question of group rights in general.

In the present state of affairs, tolerance may be formulated as the demand that the transmission of collective views and the collective exercise of practices, that are different from the prevailing ones in a given place and *do not clash, directly or indirectly, with knowledge and human rights,* should be permitted; as well as the demand that the implications and consequences of knowledge and of human rights *at least* should not be prohibited in public life.

Some Implications and Difficulties to be Faced

If we look at the issue of tolerance from the two perspectives mentioned above, we can also see that the problem of the limits of tolerance concerns tolerance only as a principle of public affairs, but not as a personal attitude. Tolerance as a personal attitude has *no* limits.

It has no limits, because its object is not the radically different views, norms or practices of other persons, consequently it is an attitude taken independently from the epistemological and axiological quality of those views and norms, and because there is no limit to respecting others' rights, which have, nevertheless, to be carefully distinguished from others' interests.

This understanding of tolerance which consists in respecting, or not causing damage to, the rights of those who think or behave in a way radically different from that which we approve, secures the possibility of its sincere exercise in life; while the widespread understanding of "respecting the different views, beliefs, behaviors and practices of others," unless equated with indifference, makes such an exercise impossible.

This understanding makes possible its exercise by those who possess divergent world-views and cultural-religious-ideological norms, because it does not expect from them an attitude in and of itself impossible: "respecting" something held as "false" or "bad." It also makes possible its exercise, because it does not exclude intolerance – especially while exercising public functions – against views and norms underlying the intolerables.

As a principle of public affairs, tolerance is related to questions concerning the object of toleration and consequently to problems of legislation. Here I shall confine myself to pointing out only a few of the theoretical difficulties relevant to the problem of the limits of toleration, and in fact only those related to norms.

A bundle of difficulties faced in this respect consists of epistemological problems. Put very briefly, it concerns the concept of "truth" and is due, so far as I can see, to the lack of ontological differentiation among the objects of knowledge. This latter prevents, among others, from differentiating epistemologically between universal and parochial norms and leads to understanding by "universality" not an epistemological specificity of a kind of norms, but "worldwide validity." It escapes the attention that it is possible, by following the due procedure, to enforce, i.e. make valid, any norm.

Another bundle of difficulties consists of axiological problems. These problems stem from the lack of distinction between "value" – the value of something – and "values," but also between "values" and "value judgments," i.e. claims about that which is "good" or "bad" etc.

This makes it impossible to differentiate among epistemologically different activities, all carried out *in the name* of evaluation and leads, in the face of varying and often discrepant judgements on a given object of evaluation, to the skeptical assumption of the impossibility of carrying out evaluation as a cognitive activity – i.e. as an activity whose outcome is verifiable and falsifiable, but only "rationally" justifiable (in the sense of the German *begründen*) or unjustifiable.

As a chain result, norms and other kinds of *claims* become objects of "rational" or "scientific" justifications, which do not take into account their epistemological specificities. It escapes the attention that many opposite or contradictory justifications are both made "rationally" or "scientifically," i.e. not "metaphysically," as we see today for example in bio-medical ethics.

These are only a few of the theoretical problems we are faced with when we deal with questions of norms – problems which nevertheless have consequences for national and international legislation and which at this moment, on the one hand, lead to the enforcement of norms which exclude each other,[7] and on the other hand, prevent the enforcement of certain other norms, e.g. the introduction of obligatory AIDS tests. In other words, these problems make us tolerate intolerables and not tolerate positive or negative implications of human rights.

This understanding of tolerance makes me think that "education for tolerance" cannot be separated from philosophical education – an education for all, aiming at helping those who undergo it, become conscious of their human identity through a training in philosophical ethics and the philosophical teaching of human rights.

Notes

1. See also I. Kuçuradi, "Introduction to the Seminar," in: I. Kuçuradi and R.S. Cohen (eds.), *The Concept of Knowledge. The Ankara Seminar*, Dordrecht, 1995, pp. IX-XV.
2. T. Lindholm, "Prospect for Research on the Cultural Legitimacy of Human Rights," in: in: A.A. An-Na'im (ed.), *Human Rights in Cross-Cultural Perspectives*, Philadelphia, 1992, pp. 387-426; J. Rawls, "Lecture IV. The Idea of Overlapping Consensus," in: Idem, *Political Liberalism*, New York, 1993, pp. 133-72.
3. For these other developments see I. Kuçuradi, "Les droits de l'homme et la décennie du développement culturel," in: *Birlesmis Milletler Türk Dernegi 1988 Yilligi*, Ankara, 1990, pp. 25-33, and "Cultural Morals and Global Morality in the Light of Ethics," in: *WASCO '88. The World Community in Post-Industrial Society 4*, Seoul, 1989, pp. 41-47.
4. See also I. Kuçuradi, "Economic Disparities and the Fashionable Linking of Human Rights, Democracy and Free Market," in: *Violence and Human Coexistence*, Vol. V, Montreal, 1995, pp. 330-36.
5. I am well aware that I am saying something here that seems at variance with a widespread understanding of notions of "freedom of thought" and that this is something dangerous *so long as* this understanding prevails. But are we obliged to take this understanding for granted?
6. On the specificity of such norms see I. Kuçuradi, "Normlarin Bilimsel Temellendirilebilirligi (The Scientific Justifiability of Norms)," in: *Çagin Olaylari Arasinda (Among the Events of Our Time)*, Ankara, 1980, pp. 182-89.
7. On this point see I. Kuçuradi, "Human Rights Instruments Questioned in the Light of the Idea of Human Rights," in: I. Kuçuradi (ed.), *The Idea and the Documents of Human Rights*, Ankara, 1995, pp. 75-92, in which articles 18 and 19 of the International Covenant on Civil and Political Rights are given as examples.

How Far Can Tolerance Go ?

Monique Canto-Sperber

How define tolerance?[1] Tolerance consists in abstaining from intervening in the actions and opinions of other persons when these opinions or actions appear disagreeable, frankly unpleasant or morally reprehensible to us. But each will feel that there exists a real difference between that which is disagreeable or unpleasant and that which is morally repugnant. To respect this intuition, I would propose to distinguish between *a narrow sense* of tolerance – I tolerate that which appears displeasing or disagreeable to me, but I do not tolerate that which I judge to be morally wrong – and *a broad sense* in which I tolerate even that which I disapprove of morally. If we adopt the narrow sense, we have at our disposal a first answer to the question of knowing how far to tolerate: I tolerate that which relates to displeasure or to annoyance, but not that which I believe to be wrong.

Let us consider at present the broad acceptance of the term tolerance, for it is often in radical formulations that we discover that which is conceptually interesting. In this broad sense, tolerance presents itself as an ideal that goes contrary to what each does spontaneously (when one finds something immoral, he refuses do to it, or looks to prevent such a thing from happening). But what sense would there be to speak of a virtue of tolerance if all we did was tolerate what we like or what we can at the very outset endure? It is precisely because it recommends to tolerate what we don't like, that is what we really don't like, that tolerance is a virtue.

In pursuing the analysis of this broad sense of tolerance, we will arrive then at a difficulty. If tolerance is a virtue or a moral ideal, it is in this that it would be morally right to accept a thing that we judge to be morally reprehensible. This is not simply about saying: "I don't know if it is right or wrong, I rather have a tendency to think that it is wrong but because I cannot have any certitude in the matter, I tolerate it." That which makes the difficulty is that the decision to tolerate does not depend on a skeptical position, but on a form of certitude: I know that it is wrong, but if tolerance is such an absolute virtue, it implies that it is morally right to accept also that which is wrong.

Let us admit that this is here a defensible thesis. Let us admit that there is an intrinsic moral value to accepting opinions, or even acts, that we judge to be wrong. The consequence of such an admission is that to the question "how far tolerate?", one has to answer "all the way." If we tolerate in this sense, we tolerate everything, and the more that we tolerate that which is morally wrong, the more virtue there will be to tolerating it.

This is obviously an absurdity. But why is this broad sense of tolerance hardly acceptable? I will try to answer this question by studying tolerance from a philosophical point of view. It goes without say that the critique of the concept of tolerance that I shall outline does not in any way call into question the practical certitude that tolerance remains the first value to be respected in the public sphere.

A tolerance without limits is hardly admissible, and this for several reasons. Firstly, because there exists a narrow link between moral evaluations and the determination to act. When I have strong reasons for thinking that an action is morally wrong, I have a tendency to try to prevent it from happening. There is something psychologically unbelievable in imagining that despite sure moral evaluations, we could systematically force ourselves into abstention.

Secondly, when we consider from up close the formulation that seemed to us so difficult to admit, namely that it would always be right to accept that which we believe to be morally wrong, it quickly appears that such a formulation becomes absurd as soon as the wrong in question exceeds a certain degree. Up to a certain point, it is a good thing to tolerate a bad one. But once this threshold has been crossed, it is not a good thing to tolerate a bad one, it is a bad one, one almost as serious as the fact of committing it. If that which we judge to be morally wrong is not too serious, we can admit that it is morally right to tolerate it, because there are intrinsic advantages, or a value (at least, in liberal cultures) in the fact of not intervening in the actions or opinions of others. But to persist in maintaining that that which is morally wrong, as dreadful as it may be, does not lead to the consequences that it can *only be a bad thing* to accept such a wrong, is to make of passivity the ultimate moral good. Moreover, what is negative about the fact of intervening in what others say or do, and thereby restraining their liberty, seems often to be a minor wrong compared with most of the wrongs that we judge to be intolerable. The difficulty attached to the possibility of a very broad tolerance is therefore fertile when it is about tolerating the wrongs of a relative seriousness (even if these provoke a reaction that goes beyond displeasure or annoyance), on the other hand, the formulation loses all its meaning as soon as it is about more important wrongs. In this case, it is not a good thing to tolerate them, it is a bad one. And this prompts a searching for the wrongs that are never right to tolerate, because such a search would permit a better understanding of the limits of tolerance.

The common explanation advanced to justify that tolerance is a good thing, but to a certain point only, consists in remarking that we cannot tolerate a certain number of things that call into question tolerance itself. Tolerance is a reflexive virtue. As Voltaire said: "that they begin by not being fanatics to merit tolerance." It is precisely because tolerance is a good thing that it is necessary, in order to preserve it, to oppose the plotting of those who want to destroy it. The actions, declarations or behaviors that risk in the short or long term to menace the existence of tolerance are intolerable. This is a first criterion for defining the limits of tolerance.

Another criterion often invoked to determine that which is intolerable has to do with the threat to the liberty, interests, rights of other persons. But as soon as we introduce this criterion into the discussion, we cannot help but have other elements also interfere. How define indeed that which brings harm to others? Furthermore, thoughts, discourses, publications, actions will not have the same type of harm on others. Finally, discourses, depending on whether pronounced in private or in public, can do more or less harm to others.

But the most characteristic question remains the one of knowing the subject or the entity that can, in the most characteristic way, evince tolerance. For depending on the case the definition of the limits of tolerance is made very differently . Let us consider first the tolerance that is practiced by an individual. The resolution to tolerate or not to tolerate has a considerable moral importance for a private person. This type of decision or attitude is the result of long personal formation, of what the lived experiences have taught, and without a doubt of the capacity to identify with the situations of others. The will to be tolerant, taken in this sense, contributes to defining the moral orientation of the person with respect to the world. Beyond personal life, such an attitude of tolerance has real value in a private sphere such as the family where a more or less large tolerance towards the peculiarities of character or behavior of others, especially in parent-child relations, can greatly contribute to the quality, and even the maintenance, of the life led within the family. We can say the same thing of work relations, of associations, etc.

But the exigency of tolerance has obviously a completely different impact when we situate ourselves in the public sphere, when the fact of not tolerating has as effect a prohibition emanating from public power *(puissance)*, in short when the exercise of tolerance no longer comes from private persons but from the State. The stakes are different when the capacity of prohibiting is at stake, of employing public force to maintain this prohibition and legal order to sanction those that would violate it. Henceforth, one must attempt to answer to the question of the limits of tolerance of the State.

In the public sphere, three reasons seem to justify the necessity of limiting tolerance. These have to do with, the first, the existence of actions and behaviors that call into question the exercise of tolerance, the second, the actions and writings that bring harm to the interests of others, the third finally, the acts that compromise common social existence. Conversely, we can remark that there exists in the public sphere a number of domains for which the question of the limits of tolerance should not be asked, because these domains are not those where the State can intervene. As Spinoza says in the twentieth and last chapter of the *Theologico-Political Treatise* ("Where it is shown that in a free State each has a right to think what he wants and to say what he thinks"), "the goal is to act by a common decree, but not to judge and to reason in common."[2] The aim of the State is then the acting in common or the cooperation, but, under no circumstances, the fact of establishing the truth, even less of imposing it by forcing consciousnesses to abandon their wrong beliefs and to adopt the right ones.

All of the great writings in favor of tolerance were composed, from the end of the seventeenth century to the end of the eighteenth century, in favor of religious tolerance, or, more precisely, against religious persecution.[3] All advance the following argument. As wrong as we deem the private opinions of persons, and in particular their religious opinions, to the extent that these opinions belong only to consciousness, no repression can be efficient or justified and tolerance is the only attitude possible. It is Locke who, in *A Letter Concerning Toleration*, presents the most convincing argument for establishing the inefficiency of any persecution. It proceeds as such:

- Public power *(puissance)* can only constrain voluntary behaviors.
- Yet beliefs are not voluntary (in particular religious belief).
- So, public power *(puissance)* does not have the means to attaining consciousnesses; it is neither will, nor menace nor constraint that permit to change religious belief (or at the price of an incessant persecution or surveillance than no one can wish for, even those who condemn most harshly the opinions in question). Religious consciousness is precisely what resists, as Voltaire very well underlines when he mocks the *compelle intrare* ("you will force them to enter"). Generally-speaking, what the battle in favor of tolerance sets out to prove is neither the virtues of pluralism neither the force of tolerance as moral virtue, but the irrationality of religious persecutions.

The certitude that there can be no limit to tolerance in matters of private opinion and that the liberty of consciousness has to be total is inherited from this battle. It also applies to the world today, especially with respect to all of the opinions of which we have the certitude that they are morally reprehensible. But we cannot let the matter rest at this. As the classical authors have equally remarked, the liberty of opinion is worth nothing if it is not associated with the liberty to speak, to seek to persuade and to publicize. Spinoza perfectly analyzed this. Every human has a natural right, he says, "to make free usage of his reason and to judge of all things," "no one can prescribe what has to be admitted as true or rejected as false"; yet "humans cannot help but confide their objectives in others, even when silence is required." To the entire liberty of expressing opinion and judging, one has to necessarily associate "that of speaking, as long as we don't go beyond simple speech or teaching, and that we defend our opinion with reason alone, not by ruse, anger or hatred."

John Stuart Mill will say the same thing, in the Introduction of his work *On Liberty* (1859).[4] He defines three fundamental forms of liberty: the liberty of thought, that of expressing one's thought, and that of living as one sees fit. The first liberty is practiced in "the intimate domain of consciousness that necessitates the liberty of consciousness in the broader sense: liberty to think and to feel, absolute liberty of opinions and of feelings on all subjects, practical or speculative, scientific, moral or theological." As for the liberty to express and to publicize one's opinions, it is almost as important, and practically indissociable from the first. Finally, the third form of liberty has to do with everything that favors the autonomy of individuals and the development of their potentialities, it is the liberty to "lead one's life as one sees fit, to act as one pleases and to risk all of the consequences that would result from it, even if our kind find our behavior to be insane, perverse or wrong." But it goes without say , and this is as important a thesis for Mill as the affirmation of the intrinsic value of liberty, that the exercise of each of these three liberties must not in any case harm others. This restriction weighs very heavily on the last form of liberty (we can certainly lead the life we want to lead and all types of life are tolerated, but at the express condition that it doesn't harm others, which considerably limits the types of life in question). It does not weigh in this way on the first form of liberty (the liberty of opinion, which belongs only to the individual). On the other hand, it is very difficult to know to what extent the liberty to express one's thought and publicize it can be exercised without harming others. It is here however, with respect to what we generally call the liberty of expression, that it would be most useful to dispose of a criterion which would tell us how far to tolerate. Indeed, the decisive role of this form of liberty holds to the fact that it is closely associated to the liberty of consciousness (it is even the possibility of rendering effective the liberty of opinion), but that it belongs also to "this part of individual conduct that concerns others" and in this respect must in a certain way be limited.

There is here a true difficulty. First because it is not easy to decide, in matters of expression and publication, if a harm is done to another, especially concerning a moral harm. Let us take the case of slander, of this particular case of slander which consists in telling lies about an individual or a community. In principle, these lies should not be tolerated. If the harmed persons are not in a state to defend themselves, their representatives can do it in their place. But this principle cannot be applied in an absolute fashion, for then we would be forced to prohibit a considerable number of publications. Yet if tolerance is a good thing, there is always a price to prohibiting, prohibiting even that which in a certain way would merit it. This price is attached to every attack, even when justified, on individual liberty. If, in principle, nothing of which harms others should be accepted, it remains that it is better to tolerate certain harms if so doing should prevent a multiplication of attacks on individual liberty. A principle of level-headedness *(pondération)* seems therefore to be necessary. Yet, among the publications that lie, there are some that declare false things and others that threaten the moral person. To say of an individual that he is obsessive or that he has an impossible character is a very disagreeable thing for the individual in question and certainly wounds his sensibility, but to say that this individual has lied, stolen or deceived represents a much more serious attack. It seems to me that the harms are not of the same nature and that the first can be endured, while the second should not be tolerated. An additional distinction can therefore be advanced: tolerance can be exercised towards that which harms the morality of others. But the definition of this "practical" limit of tolerance has not been defined from the examination of the concept of tolerance, but from the analysis of that which can truly harm others. This is a first reason to think that the concept of tolerance does not permit, by itself, to define the limits of its application.

Another element can also render particularly difficult the assessment of the harm done to others. We can subjectively feel as the cause of an extreme harm an act or a discourse that other persons consider as insignificant. The feeling of being harmed and the profound conviction that one shouldn't tolerate that which is its cause cannot suffice to justify that we not tolerate it. Let us take the case of blasphemy. A person brought up in such or such a religion can feel abominably harmed by a blasphemy and in himself feel the strong obligation of prohibiting that which is its cause. But other persons, without religion, would find such an obligation absurd and refuse to admit that there is objective harm. In this case either does it seem that the analysis of the concept of tolerance can serve to define a criterion permitting to know where tolerance must stop.

To the extent that the conceptual elucidation of tolerance is of poor help in defining the limits of the application of the virtue of tolerance, a solution can be to closely relate the understanding of this concept to a group of substantial moral truths. No reasonable doubt is possible about the truth of certain moral values, on the fact that genocide, slavery, rape, racism are wrongs. The practice of tolerance has to stop in front of such wrongs and nothing proceeding from them must be tolerated. But does the certitude that these are moral truths suffice to found or to justify the limits of tolerance? I don't think so. For the reason that Spinoza had already highlighted: the State must not legislate on that which is good or bad, the State cannot have a vocation of prescribing the good moral values nor of prohibiting that which opposes them. It is not entitled to preventing persons from thinking what they want and to a certain extent from seeking to publicize it. That what they think be untruths in morality is not pertinent here. There is not, it seems to me, a reason to limit tolerance in their respect.

For it seems impossible to define a limit to tolerance from the exigency of respecting truth. As certain as we are to being in truth regarding the moral certitudes I have been evoking, one has merely to look at the history of the four last centuries to notice the dangers there are to founding a right to intolerance on truth. Bossuet said in a sentence that has remained well-known: "I have the right to persecute you because I am right and you are wrong." Three centuries later, Herbert Marcuse, in a work published in

1966, *Critique of Pure Tolerance*,[5] maintained that the content of the notion of tolerance had to be changed. The so-called democratic societies rest on a form of domination so subtle that the majority accepts it and even demands, under this old value of liberal tolerance, its own alienation. True tolerance, politically necessary today, according to Marcuse, must therefore be exercised by the revolutionary Left, and manifest itself by a form of preventive intolerance vis-à-vis the Right, governments in place and institutions. Given that the values defended by the reactionary Right are false and wrong, just as well take a step ahead and say that they are intolerable even before they have been expressed.

But to say that true tolerance is an intolerance that is a product of truth is conceptually absurd. The intolerance that is founded on truth can be as intolerant as the intolerance founded on error, and I do not see what conceptual or ideological conjuring trick could transform it into tolerance. Intolerance can sometimes be absolutely necessary (especially if we deem it the only way to legitimizing truth), but one has to then assume calling it intolerance, instead of calling it new tolerance. Generally-speaking, there is no systematic link between tolerance and truth. A common justification of tolerance, of voltairian type (explicit in the article "Tolerance" and in the *Treatise on Tolerance*), is to underline that, given that we don't know where the truth is, there is no reason to persecute. Tolerance is therefore associated to skepticism, and dogmatism is to intolerance. Yet nothing permits to establish this link. Locke was in no way skeptical in the matter of religion, he nonetheless recommends religious tolerance. In addition, there are very numerous examples of skeptics who advocated, for reasons of civil peace and order, intolerance.

The only criterion of limitation of tolerance retained up to this point has to do with the wrong done to another, in particular with moral wrong. If publications applaud racism or rape, we certainly have an excellent reason not to tolerate them, but what reason? Not a reason that relates to their moral falsity, but to the fact that, being always expressed in such and such circumstance, with respect to such and such a person or group, these publications cannot fail to bring harm to these persons or groups. This probably makes little difference in practice, but a considerable difference in the modes of justification of prevention. Tolerance does not seem itself to be able to furnish the principle that provides this delicate work of limits. It does not permit, for example, to assess the range of wrongs done to others, to put them in balance with the necessity of preserving the liberty of expression of the individual, and to proceed to this form of level-headedness so necessary between the safeguard of individual liberty and the prevention of certain wrongs.

If we take tolerance in the narrow sense, in the sense in which we tolerate that which we find displeasing or that which we don't so much like whereas we do not tolerate the rest, tolerance becomes a pretty poor exigency. But if we take it in the broad sense, as a moral ideal, we have seen that it was untenable and especially undetermined. Tolerance therefore gives us only very few indications of what could be its intrinsic limits. There are certainly limits, but they come from elsewhere.

Hence the suspicion that tolerance can no longer remain in the position of principle. It is rather an attitude of spirit in the application of a principle, but it can't itself define what must be its object (what must necessarily be the object of tolerance or what must not be on any account its object). Tolerance must remain an ideal, an exigency, but without being able to truly permit determining the conditions of its application.

To attempt to answer to the question "How far tolerate?", I will propose then to have two principles intervene, that are, it seems to me, more amenable to helping us define the limits of tolerance, in a world in which the diversity of opinions is very great, in which the capacity of diffusion of false as of true is considerable, in which the means put in service of certain ideas, and especially of certain extremist ideas, are very accessible means (firearms, extremely rapid communications) and ones that can cause appalling ravages, but in a world also in which the force of conformities is very large.

Against this power *(puissance)* of conformity, it is necessary to preserve individual liberty, even if a liberty of error, even when concerning morality. Rosa Luxembourg refused that the defense of truth be rolled up in the defense of liberty, for the right to error is an essential aspect of this liberty. To define the limits of tolerance, we need a principle that respects individual liberty and founds it on the intrinsic value accorded to the diversity of opinions, but also of ways of living and of experiences of life, namely *a principle of pluralism*. But we also need a principle that prevents certain of these ways of living from becoming hegemonic and from jeopardizing the expression of others, namely *a principle of neutrality*.

I will begin with this last principle, which is today the object of numerous debates within political philosophy. We designate by "neutrality" the neutrality of the State with respect to the different opinions and conceptions of good chosen by individuals. The State must itself abstain from subscribing to a certain conception of good and from imposing it. Such a conception of neutrality has a political reach and it serves to justify the action of the State. This neutrality is exercised with respect to individuals, with respect to the concrete manner in which they interact, and not with respect to certain ideas that these individuals can defend. Finally, this neutrality does not necessary lead to the retreat of the State. Society is conceived rather as a neutral arena, it being understood that, if one aspect of this neutrality is to make sure that no group be favored, the other aspect is to prevent any particular group from persecuting another and from harming it.

This principle of neutrality can help us, it seems to me, to define the limits of tolerance. First, because the defense of neutrality has as a condition that this neutrality have a value – it is the only claimed value –, which already rules out any form of totalitarian State, where the State is not neutral, which rules out as well any form of religious State. Then, this neutrality as principle is necessarily attached to the defense of certain exigencies of impartiality, equality of treatment, universality that form a background of consensus which the State can refer to in order to demonstrate neutrality and eventually then prevent certain things to the extent that they compromise the maintenance of these exigencies. This form of minimal consensus is the condition of the exercise of neutrality, more than it is its object. Finally, this attitude of neutrality has a necessary link to truth, not to moral or religious truth, but to the truth of ordinary belief, that of empirical experience, historical facts, analytic statements.

Let us take the case of the education of children. Parents exercise a considerable power over their children. We justify such a power by emphasizing that they seek their good and meet their needs. If this power went as far as to transmitting false beliefs, the State would worry about it. Why tolerate that parents transmit a religion, moral values, a whole system of evaluations that is their own, but not tolerate that they teach them false mathematics or false historical truths? The notion of neutrality permits to sketch out an answer to this question. It expresses itself as non-intervention in matters of religion and morality, precisely because we have the idea that, on the condition of staying within certain limits, religious and moral convictions are all the same and that the child, once adult, will in all cases know of other values and convictions which he will then have the liberty of adopting (the State can then take positive dispositions so that it is the case). But it would express itself as intervention in the case in which false epistemic and historical beliefs would be transmitted precisely because of this common background of impartial learnings and knowledges without which neutrality is stripped of meaning, or in the case in which the transmission of moral beliefs would contribute to making a complete delinquent of the future citizen the child would become.

To briefly present the principle of pluralism, one must distinguish between the fact of pluralism, that John Rawls, for example, speaks of in *Political Liberalism* (1993),[6] and a much stronger thesis by which there are, for reasons that are essential and linked to the nature of morality itself, several ways, heterogeneous and incompatible, to pursue good. Pluralism tends to recognize that the numerous and varied ways of life pursued by individuals are perhaps all doted of real value, but cannot be pursued all together in a same society.

There are two possible interpretations to this pluralist principle. An optimistic interpretation is that defended by John Stuart Mill. Mill considers that, pluralism being true as principle, one has to apply it with the greatest tolerance possible. For to let be expressed opinions we believe to be false is to provide the means to ameliorating the reasons we have of believing this or the other thing as true (for this one needs a *market-place of ideas*, a *forum*). We have the hope that rational discussion will permit to enlarge the consensus, but always with the idea that this intrinsic diversity is a means of constant amelioration and perfectioning. Most importantly, we consider this diversity as a good thing, even if the elements which compose it are not all good. The philosopher Joseph Raz goes as far as to consider that these displeasing moral opinions are not wrongs, but restrictions without which the relating virtues could not be realized.[7] We would thus have a possibility of infinite justification of the negative traits of existence, which would lead to say that in the absence of such negative traits, good would not be there either. The common trait of the optimistic interpretations of pluralism is to thus consider that if we take pluralism seriously, we cannot put any limit on tolerance except procedural and cautionary limits that are related to the conciliation of rights, liberties and interests.

The other interpretation of pluralism is more pessimistic, and it is the one to which I would subscribe. It brings to the forefront the "tragic" aspect of the thesis according to which ways of life and values cannot be pursued all together, and therefore there needs to be, more essentially, a limit to tolerance with which we apply the principle of pluralism. A radical incompatibility can exist between certain modes of life or certain moral values – incompatibility which we cannot remedy by saying that these are true moral values while those are not (as Isaiah Berlin shows in *Four Essays on Liberty*).[8] There is therefore conflict and competition. The limits of tolerance hold to this competitive and conflictual diversity of different conceptions of good, and they must equally be founded on the idea of neutrality and of harm done to others. The "search for a common ethical space" not done with the keen consciousness of this unreconcilable morality would reveal itself vain. The greater the repugnance we feel in front of opinions deemed morally aberrant and pernicious, the fiercer the desire to make them disappear, one must not forget that it is not the only wrong of our contemporary societies. There is also, among many other wrongs, the power *(puissance)* of conformities and stereotypes, namely that of moralization.

Notes

1. An earlier version of this article was published under the title "Les Limites de la tolérance," in: R.-P. Droit (ed.), *Jusqu'où tolérer?*, Paris, 1996, pp. 131-45.
2. See Spinoza, *Oeuvres II*, Paris, 1965.
3. See, for example, P. Bayle, *Pensées diverses sur la comète*, Paris, 1984.
4. New edition: Harmondsworth, 1964.
5. New York, 1966.
6. New York, 1993. See also C. Larmore, *Modernité et morale*, Paris, 1993, to indicate the tendency of individuals in present-day societies to diverge on moral questions.
7. J. Raz, *The Morality of Freedom*, Oxford, 1986. See also S. Mendus, *Toleration and the Limits of Liberalism*, London, 1989.
8. Oxford, 1969.

The Erosion of Tolerance and the Resistance of the Intolerable

Paul Ricœur

Tolerance is the fruit of an asceticism in the exercise of power. It is a virtue. An individual virtue, and a collective virtue. It would in fact be a mistake to believe that it only takes on meaning with a form of power, that of the State. Intolerance has its first impulse in the power that each of us has of imposing our beliefs, our convictions, our manner of leading our lives on others, from the moment that each believes only these to be valid, only these to be legitimate. For each of us, to act is to exercise a power over ... This initial asymmetry of action makes it such that every act has an agent and a receiver, a passive agent. But if intolerance is armed with a power over ..., it is justified in the eyes of the one exercising it by the alleged legitimacy of the belief, of the conviction. This presumption of legitimacy results from the *disapproval* of opposed or simply different beliefs, convictions, ways of life. Two elements are therefore necessary to intolerance: the disapproval of the opposed beliefs and convictions of others, and the power of preventing them from leading their life as they see fit. It is here that lies the double reason for the propensity towards intolerance in the human heart. We could think that intolerance only rages when, on the one hand, the power to prevent sits in the hands of the public force, using the secular arm, and when, on the other hand, the disapproval takes the form of a public condemnation by a State partisan professing a particular vision of good. In this respect the religious wars of Europe would constitute the lasting paradigm of intolerance, the Church – or the Churches – offering the *unction* of truth to the States and the State furnishing the *sanction* of the secular arm to a given Church. In accordance with this ancient paradigm, the residual religious fanaticisms of old Europe would today find

themselves relayed by the fundamentalist fanaticisms coming principally from Islam. It is also against this version of intolerance that
the discourse of tolerance constituted itself in the Western world in
the seventeenth and eighteenth centuries. But if the power of the
State, joint until a recent past to ecclesiastical power, is alone in
giving a public dimension to reprobation and an historical efficiency to the power of prevention that individual will lacks, public
force ultimately only operates through the individual passions that
serve as relays in the direction of the most intimate dispositions of
the human heart. Even the tyrant needs a sophist to extort the
belief by persuasion, flattery or intimidation. It is in the last
instance within the individual, even driven by fear, that the destiny
of intolerance plays itself out. To reduce the discontinuity between
the individual and the institution, it is legitimate to underline the
role of what Michael Walzer calls in *Spheres of Justice* "shared
understandings": it is true that we can always find intermediary
communities of allegiance, conviction and power between the individual level and the state level. It is even at this privileged intermediary level that the education of passions which we will discuss
later on can be exercised .... In the same way, to return to the period
of Enlightenment, it is as much to the individuals called out of the
voluntary state of minority (Kant) to the States invited to lift the
censorship and also to the enlightened part of the public that the
Encyclopedists' plea in favor of tolerance addresses itself. From
this moment it is in a double – or even triple – sense that tolerance
is a virtue. The ultimate reason is that power is a general anthropological structure which lets itself be discerned at all levels in which
one's power *(puissance)* to act is susceptible to affecting the other's
power *(puissance)* to act and to diminishing it (Spinoza).

Tolerance, as announced at the start, is the fruit of an asceticism of
power. It consists indeed in a renunciation, the renunciation, on
behalf of who may have the power, of imposing on others his manner of believing, of acting, in short of leading his life as he sees fit. To
renounce is always difficult and costly. This renunciation consists of
an asceticism of which the stages can be punctuated as follows:

1 – I endure against my will that which I disapprove, but that
   which I don't have the power *(puissance)* to prevent;

2 – I disapprove of your manner of living, but I make an effort to understand it without though adhering to it;

3 – I disapprove of your manner of living, but I respect in it your liberty to live as you please and I recognize your right to manifest it publicly;

4 – I neither approve nor disapprove of the reasons for which you live differently than I do: but perhaps these reasons express a relation to good that escapes me because of the finitude of human understanding;

5 – I approve of all ways of life, as long as they do not manifestly harm third parties; in short I leave be all types of life because they are expressions of human plurality and diversity. *Vive la différence!*

A few remarks on the phases and transitions of this asceticism.

It is not indeed about a simple, but a double asceticism: admittedly a visible asceticism of the power to prevent; but – an affectively and intellectually more concealed and more costly asceticism – that of the conviction as directed towards others under the figure of approval and of disapproval.

The renunciation of power, but not yet of disapproval, begins at the very first threshold. It is the minimal sense that dictionaries inform. Thus the *Robert* states under title n° 1: "Tolerance: fact of tolerating something, of not prohibiting or requiring whilst one could. The liberty that results from this abstention." It is justly from such an abstention that things began to move in the seventeenth and eighteenth centuries on the occasion of the religious wars in Europe: the peace of Westphalie, in Germany, partially broke down the monopoly of ecclesiastical power when enacting: *cujus regio, ejus religio*; the Edit de Nantes, in France, brings about a split, alas provisional, in the sacrosanct principle: one faith, one law, one king; for a time, two Christian confessions find a place, according to certain draconian restrictive conditions, within one same public space. But it is certainly against their will, and under the sign of a mutual disapproval, that the two confessions and their members endure one another without being able to prevent each other from existing. A third party arbitrator forced them to cohabitate.

The mutation of disapproval begins with the second stage. It consists in an internal schism – or even in a rift – between the adhesion to one's own conviction and the effort of imagination and sympathy by which we try hard to understand a manner of thinking, acting and living, finally a conception of good other than our very own. This schism has as its seat the individual, this same one that the philosophers of the Enlightenment invite to think of in and of himself. It is a generally isolated individual who, in advance of the majority current of the society of his time, sweeps up little militant communities as the ecumenical attempts have testified to, in the midst of the religious wars, following an Erasmus, a Mélanchton, a Leibniz. More generally, we can attribute to a situation of permanent confrontation, at the heart of the Western world, the destiny of a rifted belief between the critical tradition coming from Greece and the tradition of faith inherited from Judaism and from Christianism. It is on this destiny that the institutional conquest of tolerance detaches itself: the secular State will one day be able to abstain from recognizing and subsidizing any cult, because civil society will have been worked in the confrontation between criticism and conviction.

The decisive step is only however taken at the third stage; it is the product of an attempt to surmount the intimate rift that breaks down belief. This step is not yet taken, at least explicitly, even at the time of the Enlightenment: the religious beliefs criticized by the Encyclopedists are held as superstitions attributed to ignorance, to stupidity, to hypocrisy and relegated to the irrational part of the human soul. In fact, a true pluralism of beliefs and of ways of leading life – finally: visions of good – is very difficult to assume in a non-skeptical way, that is, without the loss of some deep-rootedness in a conviction. It is from here that we will pick up again later on, with the help of the intolerable. But first let us dig further and derive the benefit of this new step. It is taken in favor of the disjunction between truth and justice. It is not in the name of truth as it appears to me – the medieval's apparent good – that one accepts (and not just simply endures) the other, but in the name of his equal right to mine to live his life as he sees fit. Here is a veritable asceticism of power, to the extent that, as it has been said above, one's power is power over the other. On this initial asymmetry between acting and being acted upon, at the heart of human interaction, comes about one's propensity to submit the will of the other to one's own. The recognition of an equal right to exert one's power of existing and acting amounts to a surpassing of the asymmetry by reciprocity. It is the spiritual movement that Hegel describes in the *Phenomenology of Spirit* under the title of the "Dialectic of Master and Slave." The initial inequality of these two emblematic figures is dialectically surmounted by that which the philosopher designates "recognition." This is no less about the equal power of thinking placed under the new figure of the stoic, proceeding from the exchange of positions between Epictetus the slave and Marcus Aurelius the emperor. Further on we will point out the pitfalls of this symbolic equalization that the contemporary destiny of tolerance has not failed to repeat. But the inestimable acquisition owed to this equalization must first be noted. Of the equal right of the other to mine to express his power *(puissance)* to act derives the entire list of fundamental liberties. It starts with the liberty of opinion, the concrete expression of thinking for oneself; it continues with the liberty of expression and the other public liberties (association, education, publication, demonstration etc.); it culminates in the liberty to actively participate in the constitution of political power. In democratic societies tolerance is effective to the extent that public liberties are themselves protected and promoted by a State that itself professes no particular conception of good. But tolerance does not cease to be a virtue for all that, to the extent that it rests on the forever reiterated vow of each citizen to hold as equal to his own the right of others to accede to fundamental liberties. In this respect, tolerance is no less a virtue of non-state institutions, such as associations, societies of thought, religious institutions. It is even to these that is particularly entrusted the most difficult to exercise asceticisms of power. And this of course because of the past: but the Gordian knot between the unction conferred to political power by the leading authorities of the dominant confession and the sanction conferred by the secular arm to the demonstrations of ecclesiastical power is today, generally-speaking, cut in the West. But there is a more fundamental reason to expect more from religious confessions than any other association of thought; this reason is due to the natural propensity of an institution of salvation to impose on everything it holds, from the bottom of its conviction, like their supreme good. Where there is supreme – in religion and in politics – there is subjugation in the air. For a religious community, whichever one, it is by a permanent work on oneself, from each of its members as well as from its authorities, that can be set down, willingly and kindheartedly, a limit, not of truth, but of justice, to the public expression of the conviction shared by the ecclesiastical community. It is even by this intimate asceticism of his conviction that the religious man can contribute to the progress of tolerance on all of the other fronts where his convictions are in competition.

If the third stage doesn't go past, at the level of truth, a polemical version of tolerance, the fourth stage orients it towards cooperation, in the mode of what we can call conflictual consensus. It seems to me that, with this new stage, we cross a critical threshold where tolerance, all the while appearing to attain its culminating point, has perhaps already swung over towards something else which we will say later. And we will see further on how the intolerable can act as a recourse figure against the slippage that begins with this stage and consumes itself with the next. Where is situated the critical threshold in question?

I neither approve nor disapprove: this is a subtle mutation no longer of the propensity to constrain, but of the legitimizing motivation ordinarily professed upon the said propensity. In other words, the displacement no longer affects the power but the conviction itself and its demanding of truth. What is indeed a conviction without a "holding-as-true," at least at the time professed, whether it be within the internal forum or in the public space ? It is nonetheless about a schism of the presumption of truth. We can understand, if not the necessity, at least the plausibility of this new step, if we consider the unbearable character of the anterior schism between truth and justice (in the same way that the passage of the second to third stage was motivated by the concern of getting past the schism between conviction and comprehensive sympathy). And what if, saying to myself, my conviction was not equal to the Truth (with a capital T)? After all, I don't have the truth; I only hope (and I remind myself here of my master Gabriel Marcel) to be in truth. All human understanding (I would add in my heart) is limited, and so also that within which ineluctably expresses my conviction. Is this not itself the destiny *par excellence* of a conviction which touches the Absolute by some side ? "I am who I am," says the God of Exodus, escaping thus the capture of literary genres in which his relation to men let itself be inscribed: stories, legislations, prophesies, hymns, words of wisdom, etc. And if I add that it is in a circular relation that a religious community recognizes itself as founded in Writings of which it has in exchange delimited the code and transmitted through the centuries the major historical interpretations, must I not conclude that this founding word in regards to my community is both supreme (in the sense that it is subordinated to nothing at all that is superior in its own meaning space) and inexhaustible, in the sense that a gap deepens between the origin of its donation and the history of its reception and its transmission. If it is indeed as such, must I not have to admit that there is also *some* truth other than for me ? If I am capable of this step, I will have converted tolerance from the passive to the active, from the enduring to the accepting. I will have simply let the other be.

We will have noticed that I have written this entire paragraph in the first person, in a different manner from the preceding paragraphs, where the I still let itself be converted (and even had to be converted) into whomever or into each of us. The asceticism now proposed is only practicable by the individual, in the kierkegaardien sense, that is anti-hegelian. It is the rare asceticism of a few sages of planetary religions. An entire culture would only have access to it thanks to a radiance from person to person, from small communities to small communities. And this, in a radically anti-sectarian climate.

This is when I turn back over the road that has been taken. Can a well ordered society, to borrow from John Rawls's expression, massively, or even by a majority, propose itself to surpass the third stage where truth and justice remain separated? Is not wisdom about joining the public virtues of stage three with the private virtues of stage four, at the risk of seeing the highest wisdom take refuge in an incommunicable elitism? And let an abyss dig itself between wisdom and citizenship?

The same scruple finds reinforcement in the spectacle that gives, at the level of collective consciousness, the contemporary destiny of tolerance. If the sages of stage four mustn't move away from the citizens of stage three, it is because the curve of tolerance has already swayed itself beyond its summit within society that some call post-modern, so of Western society posterior to the Enlightenment. Everything is happening, in fact, as if tolerance describes a vast historical curve first ascending, then today descending, starting from the level of intolerance then culminating somewhere between stage three where justice and truth remain juxtaposed, and stage four, where the idea of truth explodes to put itself in conformity with what justice has already premonitioned, and as if tolerance pursues its course beyond its culminating point. But to go where?

I've outlined, under the title of stage five, the profile of a profession, implicit or explicit, of indifference. This stage, the one we have attained today, is the one in which we approve of everything, because everything is the same, because everything is equal. It is of such a mutation that Antoine Garapon refers to here: for him, the model of tolerance arising from the resolution of religious wars has exhausted its resources, because today there are no longer professions of faith to reconcile and first to constrain to cohabit. In the absence of common reference points, the two common residual concerns, that of public security in the face of new forms of danger, and that of public health in the face of threats made to the body, project to the forefront the arbitration of the judiciary institution with its accepted procedures and the protection of the medical institution. Arbitration and protection: the new figures of tolerance. But it is no longer about accomplishment, but substitution. In the same way, the attacks of post-modernist writers against the rationality of the Enlightenment and against "modernism" come to comfort, most involuntarily, the break down from the inside of the patient structure that, as we underlined it in commenting the third stage, has brought to its pinnacle the profession of Human Rights, become today ideologically obsolete. Admittedly, everyone is fighting for Human Rights; but the work of asceticism, as much of conviction as of power, as much at the level of the individual as that of the institutions, has ceased to be pertinent; it has become unreadable, nonsensical. It therefore becomes troubling to ask oneself what secret connivance, and this one much involuntary as well, can exist between the ultimate asceticism of stage four and the fall into indifference in stage five? A troubling relation like everything that renders secretly complicit the authentic and the inauthentic. Indeed nothing resembles more the sentence: "There is also truth other than for me," than the sentence: "Differences are indifferent." Did not Hegel anticipate this descent that transmutes the same into its other when he made the figure of the skeptic follow that of the Stoic. If the slave and the emperor are similar insofar as they "think," then everything that distinguishes them, that is all the historical differences, are insignificant, in-different. How then stay on the crest? How prevent the admission of truth of the other from feeding the arguments of indifference, that is if it argues? How restitute to tolerance the historical flesh that the evocation of some far away common fundamental seems to have evaporated ?

It is here that unexpectedly arises the question of the intolerable as the ultimate refuge from a thought and a wanted tolerance.

The intolerable is what we would not want to tolerate, even though we could or even we should. In this sense, the intolerable is the polar opposite of intolerance, this behavior of reprobation and of prevention that tolerance wanted to surmount. The intolerable is only problematic against the background of an acquired or a being acquired tolerance. That which renders it problematic is claiming to place a limit on tolerance. It is in fact on the same line of disapproval as tolerance. But while this latter abstains itself, the intolerable enjoins to suspend abstention. This is why it is only wholly pertinent in a culture educated by and for tolerance. It is for this precise reason that we can expect a reawakening effect from it in a culture without precise reference points in which tolerance has already swerved into indifference.

But to justify this expectation upon which we will return to finish, one has to have answered a number of prior questions: at what do we recognize the intolerable? What is typically intolerable? In the name of what do we denounce the intolerable?

One has to start with the first question because, as we shall see this instant, one risks getting lost in the dispersion with the answer of the second . The intolerable is recognized at the passion that detects it, that is to say indignation, an eminently reactive passion. It is in this capacity that it breaks with the dominant apathy of a society ready to accept everything as equally insignificant. Indignation is foremost a scream: It's intolerable! Indignation is a moral anger, an attesting and contesting figure of virtue.

But if indignation lets itself be recognized, by its sweeping reactive character, through the diversity of its manifestations which would call for a subtle phenomenology, it is harder to find it a common object. The occasions to be indignant present themselves in dispersed order: what is there in common between the disgust sparked by the crime of a pedophile, the horror that continue to inspire the stories of deportation and extermination camps , the contempt ignited by vicious attacks of rampaging slander directed against an honest man, the revolt against the manifestations of racism, against the disguised returns of slavery, against the extreme inequalities, against the politics of exclusion? It seems that we are condemned to proceeding inductively: but with what seat in sight? The figures of evil, if indeed about wrongs, that indignation denounces, without being capable of designating the good of which they are the reverse side, are not these figures by nature dispersed? If good is ultimately one, is not evil principally legion? Let us try nonetheless.

It is easy to discern a certain number of "indignant" behaviors: those that *harm* the exercise of tolerance itself. Tolerance, as it is said here, is a reflexive virtue in wait of reciprocity. This is equivalent to saying that the first intolerable is intolerance itself. Surprising statement which seems to bring everybody back to the starting point. This is not however truly the case. Intolerance, whether it be religious like at the long period of religious wars in Europe, or today in diverse parts of the world, or whether it be political and cultural, like with dictatorships where a directing class attributes to itself the policing of standards, intolerance has *become* intolerable only compared to a state of culture in which the third stage described above finds itself affected by a significant number of political regimes sustained by enlightened public opinions.

But not all of the intolerable lets itself be reduced to the resistance of intolerance to the maintaining of acquisitions and to the ulterior progresses of tolerance in the world or in ourselves. Perhaps one has to concentrate then on one word: *harm.* We will have remarked that it is the only clause in the definition of tolerance at the fifth stage that has not been commented upon: "I approve of all ways of life *as long as they do not manifestly harm third parties.*" To harm is the negative flip side of assistance, help, benevolence, voluntary action, all of which are susceptible to augmenting the power *(puissance)* of existing of the other (to remain within the spinozist vocabulary here privileged). Do no harm, minimal ethic. Prevent harm, minimal politic. Dispersed figures of harm, but parented by all the harms gathered by indignation. The negative of the object "harm," faced with the negative of the feeling "indignation." In this respect, in the same way that Jonas speaks of a heuristic of fear – in a sense finally closer than it appears to our theme of indignation – there would be a heuristic of indignation, last bastion of a common morality in ruins. And if we follow for a moment Jonas's lead, on the road that joins the "principle-responsibility" to this privileged guarantor who would be the fragile, would there not be some sense in saying that the heuristic of indignation alerts moral vigilance to the immense front of the fragile, that is of vulnerability to harms? Harm then: wrong done to the power *(puissance)* of existing of the other, prevention done to his growth. In this instant arises for a second time under our gaze the abject figure of the pedophile assassin. Rejoining him are the tormentors, the enslaving clandestine entrepreneurs, all of the exploiters of a vulnerability that, without coming down to it, concentrates itself in that of childhood. In this movement of expansion from the home of mistreated childhood, the thematic of the fragile intersects, as Jonas had proposed, this other fragile that constitutes the democratic State itself, to the extent that, deprived of transcendental legitimacy, it rests – at least at first approximation – only on the will to live together of the greatest number in the just institutions protective of fundamental liberties. The child and the State: polar opposite figures of the fragile.

If then it were possible to recognize in indignation, an eminently reactive feeling, a positive motivation, it would be the responsibility with regard to the fragile in its multiple forms, deploying itself on the horizon of the planetary environment. This attempt at restituting to indignation the obverse of which it is the reverse brings us to the threshold of the last question asked above:

in the name of what denounce the intolerable? John Rawls, questioning the moral depth upon which his principles of justice are supposed to furnish a rational argument, of the contractual and procedural type, speaks of "carefully weighed convictions" and seeks to establish a sort of "reflective equilibrium" between these and his meaningful argument. It is a "reflective equilibrium" of another kind that I would propose, between the virtuous anger of indignation and a return to the forgotten roots of our culture. If indignation must be able to block the moral indifference in which tolerance is sinking, it is to the extent that it rings like an alarm. It shouldn't be said, in fact, that democracy lies on a void; it expresses rather an over-full, that which overflows from the forgotten roots of our culture. The culture of the West, for its part, results from the conflictual but finally fertile encounter between the greco-roman and the judeo-christian heritages, the successive Renaissances, the Reform, the Enlightenment, the national and socialist movements of the nineteenth century, etc. It would then be a complimentary task, on the side of a plea for tolerance, where the primary accent remains on the abstention of prohibiting and preventing, to draw from the resources of indignation, themselves excited by the intolerable, so as to extract from them the energy of a moral re-founding of democracy. This re-founding could only be multiple and proceed by crossed heritages. If indignation didn't result in such a work on oneself, at the end of which our multiple traditions would recognize themselves as cofounders of a same will to live together, these would risk arming the arm of a righter-of-wrongs who, on the pretext of limiting the abuses of tolerance, would reinvent intolerance behind virtuous guises.

It is particularly when indignation invites repressive behaviors, entering into open conflict with one or another of public liberties, at the forefront of which the liberty of expression places itself, that the restrictions imposed as such risk being perceived as intolerable by the most free of spirits. In this respect, Monique Canto-Sperber, confronted with the same problem as I am in this volume, pleads for the spirit of "level-headedness" *(pondération)*. Level-headedness is indeed in my eyes a major expression of practical wisdom in the tradition of tragic and aristotelian *phronesis* and of the prudence of the scholastics. Level-headedness, as its name indicates, weighs the for and against of an unlimited tolerance which risks letting wrong be done to the most fragile in the name of liberty and risks a return to intolerance under the cover of moral order. A major expression of this level-headedness would be to renounce reconstituting a moral consensus that cannot exist in a pluralist society; wisdom is to be content with fragile compromises, in line with what Rawls calls "consentment by cross-checking," itself corrected by what he names "recognition of reasonable disagreements." A second expression would be to not constrain to a premature or forced conclusion of disputed questions, such as abortion (justly decriminalized, but not yet out of its uncertain status of least harm) or euthanasia and in a general way the problems posed by the relation of private and public morality to life and to death. The important thing in this respect is that the conflict be held as pertinent by all the implicated protagonists. The vehemence of a settled discussion would attest with force to a consciousness awoken from its indifference by the vigor of indignation. But the advice of wisdom remains. One has to also put limits on indignation and its fury. "Nothing too much" proclaimed the wisdom of the Greeks.

Horizons

Desmond Tutu

Why do we learn some lessons more easily than others – indeed with alacrity and enthusiasm? Often these are not of the most attractive sort. It seems so frequently as if there is a sheer perversity in us.

During the awful days of apartheid's repression and injustice, the Government of the day had a particular way of dealing with its opponents and those who dared to criticize their evil policies. They showed scant tolerance of opposing views. Apartheid's critics were most often vilified and pilloried in both the print and electronic media – the latter being, without too much embarrassment on their part, propagated by agencies of the Government, sycophantic echoes of their master's voice, when the objects of their venom were hardly ever accorded the right to rebut whatever had been said about them or even the opportunity of stating their side of the story reasonably fairly. The equally lick-spittle sycophantic print media projected the Government's critics as enemies of the nation, misrepresenting their views and caricaturing them mercilessly. That was one way in which the apartheid Government operated. Goebbels would have been in his element. This way of operation did have the advantage for its victim that it did not pose much of a physical threat. It was generally really no skin off the victim's nose, apart I suppose for the pain of being depicted as an ogre who most loved to hate and apart from the danger of building up an atmosphere which made it something that could be contemplated that such "enemies" enemies be eliminated, that made assassination possible.

There were other ways in which the apartheid Government were not nearly as innocuous. Its opponents were often detained without trial for arbitrary periods usually without access to a doctor or lawyer of their choice and almost always without contact with their families and loved ones. Many such detainees were subjected to torture and some died mysteriously in detention, e.g.

Steve Biko. Other Government opponents were placed under banning orders which reduced them to a twilight existence when they might not attend a gathering – which was defined as one other person. It meant they could not go on holiday, or to a picnic, or the movies and might not leave the magisterial area to which they had been confined – and all this without due process of law. They were condemned to be prisoners at their own expense.

And now with the revelations being made before the TRC it is coming to light that the apartheid authorities used even hit squads to assassinate those who were identified as *enemies*.

What is the lesson that most of us learned so easily and often so eagerly? We copied a very bad example set us by our apartheid overlords, that someone who disagreed with you was your enemy and the best kind of enemy was the enemy you had shut up or better still whom you had eliminated.

We did not, by and large, say everyone is entitled to their point of view, even a wrong point of view. We did not live by the dictum "I may disagree with you, but I will defend to the death your right to your view point." We refused to give people who might differ from us a fair hearing. We shouted them down; we intimidated them but what is worse, we even killed them if they did not change after physical assault.

And so we saw violence becoming endemic especially in Kwa-Zulu-Natal. People spoke of black on black violence with some glee. Some of us pointed out that most of the violence was being fueled and manipulated by a sinister third force. At the time we were ridiculed and pooh-poohed. We are now being vindicated by the evidence before the Truth and Reconciliation Commission. But that still does not exonerate us. We were willing to be manipulated because we acquiesced in shutting up those who differed to the point of even killing them.

What is so obvious seemed to elude us – that using force, intimidation or whatever to shut up someone who differed from you or who disagreed with you was already to concede that your case was not strong enough to stand on its own to persuade your opponent.

We tried to persuade our people to change and be more tolerant, not to regard opponents as foes but as potential friends and supporters just waiting to be converted.

I have often used a saying my father was very fond of, "Don't raise your voice – improve your argument." But we have learned a bad lesson only too well. It is taking a while to make people realize that each of us is entitled to space – emotional, intellectual, physical space in order to be human. *Diversity is of the Essence.*

We have sought to point out that a rainbow is a rainbow precisely because it has different colors. We are a rainbow nation because of our diversity. We should celebrate our differences, we should affirm them because they make us need one another since it is clear none of us is self-sufficient. We need others in order to be human. Hence our African idiom – a person is a person through other persons – and each person is unique and entitled to that uniqueness, including having a peculiar point of view.

Intolerance can be fatal.

The Declaration of Principles on Tolerance

The Member States of the United Nations Educational, Scientific and Cultural Organization, meeting in Paris at the twenty-eighth session of the General Conference, from 25 October to 16 November 1995,

Preamble

Bearing in mind that the United Nations Charter states "We, the peoples of the United Nations determined to save succeeding generations from the scourge of war, … to reaffirm faith in fundamental human rights, in the dignity and worth of the human person, … and for these ends to practise tolerance and live together in peace with one another as good neighbours,"

Recalling that the Preamble to the Constitution of UNESCO, adopted on 16 November 1945, states that "peace, if it is not to fail, must be founded on the intellectual and moral solidarity of mankind,"

Recalling also that the Universal Declaration of Human Rights affirms that "Everyone has the right to freedom of thought, conscience and religion" (Article 18), "of opinion and expression" (Article 19), and that education "should promote understanding, tolerance and friendship among all nations, racial or religious groups,"

Noting relevant international instruments including:
- the International Covenant on Civil and Political Rights,
- the International Covenant on Economic, Social and Cultural Rights,
- the Convention on the Elimination of All Forms of Racial Discrimination,
- the Convention on the Prevention and Punishment of the Crime of Genocide,
- the Convention on the Rights of the Child,

- the 1951 Convention relating to the Status of Refugees and its 1967 Protocol and regional instruments,
- the Convention on the Elimination of All Forms of Discrimination against Women,
- the Convention against Torture and other Cruel, Inhuman or Degrading Treatment or Punishment,
- the Declaration on the Elimination of All Forms of Intolerance Based on Religion or Belief,
- the Declaration on the Rights of Persons Belonging to National or Ethnic, Religious and Linguistic Minorities,
- the Declaration on Measures to Eliminate International Terrorism,
- the Vienna Declaration and Programme of Action of the World Conference on Human Rights,
- the Copenhagen Declaration and Programme of Action adopted by the World Summit for Social Development,
- the UNESCO Declaration on Race and Racial Prejudice,
- the UNESCO Convention and Recommendation against Discrimination in Education,

Bearing in mind the objectives of the Third Decade to Combat Racism and Racial Discrimination, the World Decade for Human Rights Education, and the International Decade of the World's Indigenous People,

Taking into consideration the recommendations of regional conferences organized in the framework of the United Nations Year for Tolerance in accordance with UNESCO General Conference 27 C/Resolution 5.14, as well as the conclusions and recommendations of other conferences and meetings organized by Member States within the programme of the United Nations Year for Tolerance,

Alarmed by the current rise in acts of intolerance, violence, terrorism, xenophobia, aggressive nationalism, racism, anti-Semitism, exclusion, marginalization and discrimination directed against national, ethnic, religious and linguistic minorities, refugees, migrant workers, immigrants and vulnerable groups within societies, as well as acts of violence and intimidation committed against individuals exercising their freedom of opinion and expression – all of which threaten the consolidation of peace and democracy both nationally and internationally and which are all obstacles to development,

Emphasizing the responsibilities of Member States to develop and encourage respect for human rights and fundamental freedoms for all, without distinction as to race, gender, language, national origin, religion or disability, and to combat intolerance,

Adopt and solemnly proclaim this Declaration of Principles on Tolerance.

Resolving to take all positive measures necessary to promote tolerance in our societies, because tolerance is not only a cherished principle, but also a necessity for peace and for the economic and social advancement of all peoples.

We declare the following:

Article 1
MEANING OF TOLERANCE

1.1 Tolerance is respect, acceptance and appreciation of the rich diversity of our world's cultures, our forms of expression and ways of being human. It is fostered by knowledge, openness, communication and freedom of thought, conscience and belief. Tolerance is harmony in difference. It is not only a moral duty, it is also a political and legal requirement. Tolerance, the virtue that makes peace possible, contributes to the replacement of the culture of war by a culture of peace.

1.2 Tolerance is not concession, condescension or indulgence. Tolerance is, above all, an active attitude prompted by recognition of the universal human rights and fundamental freedoms of others. In no circumstance can it be used to justify infringements of these fundamental values. Tolerance is to be exercised by individuals, groups and States.

1.3 Tolerance is the responsibility that upholds human rights, pluralism (including cultural pluralism), democracy and the rule of law. It involves the rejection of dogmatism and absolutism and affirms the standards set out in international human rights instruments.

1.4 Consistent with respect for human rights, the practice of tolerance does not mean toleration of social injustice or the abandonment or weakening of one's convictions. It means that one is free to adhere to one's own convictions and accepts that others adhere to theirs. It means accepting the fact that human beings, naturally diverse in their appearance, situation, speech, behaviour and values, have the right to live in peace and to be as they are. It also means that one's views are not imposed on others.

Article 2
STATE LEVEL

2.1 Tolerance at the State level requires just and impartial legislation, law enforcement and judicial and administrative process. It also requires that economic and social opportunities be made available to each person without any discrimination. Exclusion and marginalization can lead to frustration, hostility and fanaticism.

2.2 In order to achieve a more tolerant society, States should ratify existing international human rights conventions, and draft new legislation where necessary to ensure equality of treatment and of opportunity for groups and individuals in society.

2.3 It is essential for international harmony that individuals, communities and nations accept and respect the multicultural character of the human family. Without tolerance there can be no peace, and without peace there can be no development or democracy.

2.4 Intolerance may take the form of marginalization of vulnerable groups and their exclusion from social and political participation, as well as violence and discrimination against them. As confirmed in the Declaration on Race and Racial Prejudice, "All individuals and groups have the right to be different" (Article 1.2).

Article 3
SOCIAL DIMENSIONS

3.1 In the modern world, tolerance is more essential than ever before. It is an age marked by the globalization of the economy and by rapidly increasing mobility, communication, integration and interdependence, large scale migrations and displacement of populations, urbanization and changing social patterns. Since every part of the world is characterized by diversity, escalating intolerance and strife potentially menaces every region. It is not confined to any country, but is a global threat.

3.2 Tolerance is necessary between individuals and at the family and community levels. Tolerance promotion and the shaping of attitudes of openness, mutual listening and solidarity should take place in schools and universities and through non formal education, at home and in the workplace. The communication media are in a position to play a constructive role in facilitating free and open dialogue and discussion, disseminating the values of tolerance, and highlighting the dangers of indifference towards the rise in intolerant groups and ideologies.

3.3 As affirmed by the UNESCO Declaration on Race and Racial Prejudice, measures must be taken to ensure equality in dignity and rights for individuals and groups wherever necessary. In this respect, particular attention should be paid to vulnerable groups which are socially or economically disadvantaged so as to afford them the protection of the laws and social measures in force, in particular with regard to housing, employment and health, to respect the authenticity of their culture and values, and to facilitate their social and occupational advancement and integration, especially through education.

3.4 Appropriate scientific studies and networking should be undertaken to co-ordinate the international community's response to this global challenge, including analysis by the social sciences of root causes and effective countermeasures, as well as research and monitoring in support of policy-making and standard setting action by Member States.

Article 4
EDUCATION

4.1 Education is the most effective means of preventing intolerance. The first step in tolerance education is to teach people what their shared rights and freedoms are, so that they may be respected, and to promote the will to protect those of others.

4.2 Education for tolerance should be considered an urgent imperative; that is why it is necessary to promote systematic and rational tolerance teaching methods that will address the cultural, social, economic, political and religious sources of intolerance – major roots of violence and exclusion. Education policies and programmes should contribute to development of understanding, solidarity and tolerance among individuals as well as among ethnic, social, cultural, religious and linguistic groups and nations.

4.3 Education for tolerance should aim at countering influences that lead to fear and exclusion of others, and should help young people to develop capacities for independent judgment, critical thinking and ethical reasoning.

4.4 We pledge to support and implement programmes of social science research and education for tolerance, human rights and non violence. This means devoting special attention to improving teacher training, curricula, the content of textbooks and lessons, and other educational materials including new educational technologies, with a view to educating caring and responsible citizens open to other cultures, able to appreciate the value of freedom, respectful of human dignity and differences, and able to prevent conflicts or resolve them by non-violent means.

Article 5
COMMITMENT TO ACTION

We commit ourselves to promoting tolerance and non violence through programmes and institutions in the fields of education, science, culture and communication.

Article 6
INTERNATIONAL DAY FOR TOLERANCE

In order to generate public awareness, emphasize the dangers of intolerance and react with renewed commitment and action in support of tolerance promotion and education, we solemnly proclaim 16 November the annual International Day for Tolerance.

Notes on the Contributors

Mario Bettati, born in 1936, is professor of International Law at the University of Paris 2 and honorary dean of the Faculté de Droit of Paris-South. He has pursued many teaching and research missions in several countries across Europe, Africa, Asia and America. His publications include: *Le Nouvel ordre économique international* (1985); *Les ONG et le droit international* (1986); *Le Devoir d'ingérence* (1987); *L'ONU et la drogue* (1995, in collaboration); *Droit humanitaire* (1996).

Norberto Bobbio, born in 1909, taught Philosophy of Law at different Italian universities beginning in 1935, then Philosophy of Politics at the School of Political Sciences of the University of Turin. His many works include: *The Future of Democracy* (1987); *Democracy and Dictatorship* (1989); *Liberalism and Democracy* (1990); *The Age of Rights* (1996).

Abdelwahab Bouhdiba is president of the Tunisian Academy of Letters, Sciences and Arts, and professor of Islamic and North-African Sociology at the University of Tunis. He has published about twenty works, among which a certain number have been translated into several languages: *Criminalité et changements sociaux; Á la Recherche des normes perdues; Raisons d'être; L'Imaginaire maghrébin; Quêtes sociologiques; La Sexualité et l'Islam....* A human rights militant, he is also the author of two special United Nations reports on: "Les violations des droits de l'homme dans le Kampuchéa démocratique" and "L'exploitation du travail des enfants."

Monique Canto-Sperber is a philosopher and research director at CNRS. She has published a number of essays, among them: *L'Intrigue philosophique* (1987); *Platon, Ménon* (1991); *Les Paradoxes de la connaissance* (1991); *La Philosophie morale brittanique* (ed., 1994); *Dictionnaire d'éthique et de morale* (ed., 1996). In press: *La Philosophie grecque.*

Antoine Garapon was born in 1952 and is a judge and Doctor of law. He became General Secretary of the Institut des Hautes Études sur la Justice following several years of acting as a judge to children. A member of the editorial committee of the journal *Esprit*, he has published: *L'Âne portant des reliques, essai sur le rituel judiciaire; La Justice des mineurs, évolution d'un modèle* (1995); *Le Gardien des promesses, le juge et la démocratie; La République pénalisée,* (1996, both these titles in collaboration with Denis Salas). He is director of the collection "Le Bien commun" (Editions Michalon).

Vaclav Havel was born in 1936 and is a playright, writer, and politician. Imprisoned and liberated several times (from 1977 to1989) for "subversive activity against the State," he was President of Czechoslovakia from 1989 to 1992, and is currently President of the Czech Republique. Among his works published in English: *The Power of the Powerless* (1985); *The Anatomy of Reticence* (1986); *Politics and Conscience* (1986); *Living in Truth* (1987); *Summer Meditations* (1992); *The Garden Party and Other Plays* (1993).

Jeanne Hersch was born in 1910. She is professor of Philosophy at the University of Geneva and at Hunter College in New York, visiting professor at the University of Colgate, Hamilton (U.S), and head of the Division of Philosophy at UNESCO in Paris between 1966 and 1968. Her works include: *L'Illusion philosophique* (1936); *L'Être et la forme* (1946); *Idéologies et réalités* (1956); *L'Âge de l'homme* (1980); *Le Droit d'être un homme* (1984); *L'Etonnement philosophique* (1993).

Ramin Jahanbegloo is an Iranien philosopher and associate researcher at the French Institute of Research inTeheran. He is the author of many articles on Mahatma Gandhi in French, English and Persian. Upcoming: *Gandhi et l'Occident.*

Ioanna Kuçuradi was born in 1936. She is professor of Philosophy, president of the Department of Philosophy at the University Hacettepe of Ankara, and president of the Human Rights Council in Turkey (1994-1996), as well as a member of several international cultural organizations. She has published many articles in international journals. Among them: *Nietzsche ve Insan* (Nietzsche's Conception of Man), 1966; *Insan ve Degerleri* (Man and Values), 1971; *Etik* (Ethics), 1988; etc.

Hans Küng, born in 1928, is a theologian and university professor (Universities of Münster, Chicago, Tübingen ...). His numerous works translated in English include: *The Church* (1967); *Does God Exist?* (1980); *Christianity and World Religions* (1986); *Global Responsibility. In Search of a New World Ethic* (1991); *Yes to a Global Ethic* (1996).

Yehudi Menuhin was born in New York and made his debut as a violinist at the age of 7 years old. Today he is president and conductor of the Royal Philarmonic Orchestra, after having directed the most well-known orchestras of the world. Attracted to many different forms of musical expression, he has for example played with Ravi Shankar and Stéphane Grappelli. A Doctor *Honoris Causa* in 25 Universities, and an honorary citizen of numerous cities, he founded the Yehudi Menuhin School in England for musically gifted children in 1963; in 1991, he created an International Foundation in Bruxelles that encourages among other things, the MUS-E project: music, source of balance and of tolerance.

Octavio Paz was born in Mexico in 1914. He is the founder and director of several literary reviews (*El Popular, Taller*), was ambassador in India from 1962 to 1968, and professor of Latino-American Studies at the University of Cambridge. In 1984, he received the Peace Prize, and in 1990, the Nobel Prize for literature. He has published numerous works, among them: *Anthology of Mexican Poetry* (1958); *Labyrinth of Solitude* (1967); *The Bow and the Lyre* (1973); *The Collected Poems, 1957-1987* (1987); *Convergences* (1987); *In Search of the Present* (1990).

Paul Ricœur was born in 1913 and studied at Rennes, then at Paris-Sorbonne. He was professor of the History of Philosophy at the University of Strasbourg (1948-1957); professor of General Philosophy at the Sorbonne (1957-1966) and at Nanterre (1966-1981); and professor at the University of Chicago (1970-1988). Among his publications: *Fallible Man* (1965); *Freedom and Nature* (1966); *The Conflict of Interpretation* (1974); *Hermeneutics and*

Human Sciences (1981); *Lectures on Ideology and Utopia* (1986); *Figuring the Sacred* (1995).

Wole Soyinka is a Nigerian writer, born in 1934. He has taught at the universities of Lagos, Ibadan, Ife; professor of Comparative Literature and dean of the Department of Dramatic Arts at Ife. He received the Nobel Prize for literature in 1986. His works include: *The Lion and the Jewel* (1959); *Kongi's Harvest* (1965); *Death and the King's Horsemen* (1975); *A Scourge of Hyacinths* (1992, theater); *Season of Anomy* (1973, novel); *A Shuttle in the Crypt* (1972); *Mandela's Earth and Other Poems* (1988, poetry).

Desmond Tutu was born in South Africa in 1931 and studied at the Bantu High School, the Bantu Normal College, and at King's College (London). He is bishop of Lesotho and Johannesburg, archbishop of Cape Town, chancelor of the University of Western Cape, and president of the Conference of Pan-African Churches. He obtained the Nobel Peace Prize in 1984, as well as the Martin Luther King Prize for Peace in 1986. His works include: *Crying in the Wilderness* (1982); *Hope and Suffering* (1983); *The Rainbow People of God* (1994); *An African Prayer Book* (1996).

Ghislain Waterlot was born in 1964 and holds an agrégé and PhD in Philosophy (1996). His thesis was submitted on "Tolérance et modernité. Généalogie et destin d'un concept." He teaches Philosophy of Education at the IUFM Nord-Pas-De-Calais; pursues research in the field of morality and political-theology; and has published several aricles on tolerance or questions of moral philosophy. The following work is in press: *Voltaire. Le procureur des Lumières.*

Bernard Williams was born in 1929 in England. He has taught at the Universities of California, Oxford, Cambridge, London, etc., and has been a visiting professor in Ghana, Princeton, Harvard, University of California at Berkeley, etc. Recent publications include: *Moral Luck* (1981); *Ethics and the Limits of Philosophy* (1985); *Shame and Necessity* (1993); *How Free Does the Will Need to Be?* (1994), etc.

Acknowledgments

The editorial offices of the journal Diogenes *wish to sincerely thank the persons who have contributed to the achievement of this issue: first, Mrs. Jeanne Hersch and M. Edgar Morin; the Delegations of Brazil, of Turkey, and the national French Commission of the UNESCO for their support in this project; the Unité pour la tolérance, directed by M. Serguei Lazarev, for his interest and his encouragements; and, in the course of the months and for different reasons, M. Emo Lessi, Mrs. Cecile Goli, M. Pierre-Emmanuel Dauzat and Ms. Ana Font Giner.*

A pair of slaps are what taught me tolerance. It came to me from my father who was the most gentle and the most tolerant man in the world.

I was six years old. I was on the balcony of a house overlooking the Isar, in Munich. Men in brown shirts marched while singing behind flags that were branded with swastikas. It was beautiful outside. It was very gay. Hitler was taking power. The people, in the street, were saluting the procession. From up in my balcony, I started to applaud. My father dealt me a blow. It is the only one I ever received. It is the only one he ever gave.

My father hated violence. He hated war. He hated hatred. He was well forced to hate Hitler and national-socialism. I learned at the age of six that intolerance is intolerable and that there was no tolerance for the enemies of tolerance.

Jean d'Ormesson